HIROSHIMA AND THE HISTORIANS

The decision to use atomic bombs on Hiroshima and Nagasaki has been considered the most important – and perhaps most controversial – event in twentieth-century history. It ushered in many of the major developments of our time: the end of World War II, the beginning of the atomic age, the establishment of the American world order, and the start of the Cold War arms race. Kenneth B. Pyle illuminates both the complexities of the event itself and the debates among historians that continue today, as they wrestle with the moral issues of the decision, its necessity, and its alternatives. While producing no final resolution to the controversy, historians have nevertheless advanced and deepened our understanding of this event. This accessible and thought-provoking analysis is a case study in the intricate nature of the historian's craft and a reminder of the value of historians in a free society.

KENNETH B. PYLE is a historian of modern Japan, creator of the *Journal of Japanese Studies*, and emeritus professor at the University of Washington.

HIROSHIMA AND THE HISTORIANS
Debating America's Most Controversial Decision

KENNETH B. PYLE
University of Washington

CAMBRIDGE
UNIVERSITY PRESS

CAMBRIDGE
UNIVERSITY PRESS

Shaftesbury Road, Cambridge CB2 8EA, United Kingdom

One Liberty Plaza, 20th Floor, New York, NY 10006, USA

477 Williamstown Road, Port Melbourne, VIC 3207, Australia

314–321, 3rd Floor, Plot 3, Splendor Forum, Jasola District Centre, New Delhi – 110025, India

103 Penang Road, #05–06/07, Visioncrest Commercial, Singapore 238467

Cambridge University Press is part of Cambridge University Press & Assessment, a department of the University of Cambridge.

We share the University's mission to contribute to society through the pursuit of education, learning and research at the highest international levels of excellence.

www.cambridge.org
Information on this title: www.cambridge.org/9781009477451

DOI: 10.1017/9781009477482

© Kenneth B. Pyle 2024

This publication is in copyright. Subject to statutory exception and to the provisions of relevant collective licensing agreements, no reproduction of any part may take place without the written permission of Cambridge University Press & Assessment.

When citing this work, please include a reference to the DOI 10.1017/9781009477482

First published 2024

A catalogue record for this publication is available from the British Library.

A Cataloging-in-Publication data record for this book is available from the Library of Congress.

ISBN 978-1-009-47745-1 Hardback
ISBN 978-1-009-47744-4 Paperback

Cambridge University Press & Assessment has no responsibility for the persistence or accuracy of URLs for external or third-party internet websites referred to in this publication and does not guarantee that any content on such websites is, or will remain, accurate or appropriate.

For Anne

CONTENTS

List of Figures   page viii

Acknowledgments   x

Note on the Text   xii

Introduction   1

1 The Historian's Craft   18
2 The Hiroshima Decision   37
3 Participants and Their First Draft of History   61
4 The Revisionists   91
5 Historians and Moral Judgments   125
6 Military Historians   155
7 Gauging Japanese Responsibility   183
8 A Wider Perspective   208
9 Controversy as a Way of Life   239

Suggestions for Further Reading   248

Index   257

FIGURES

2.1 General Leslie Groves and Robert Oppenheimer at Alamogordo, NM, view the base of the steel tower on which the first atomic bomb hung was tested on July 16, 1945. The intense heat of the bomb melted the tower. Source: Bettmann/Getty Images *page* 41

3.1 James Conant (center front) with other leading scientists involved in the Manhattan Project (left to right): Ernest O. Lawrence, Arthur H. Compton, Vannevar Bush, Conant, Karl T. Compton, and Alfred L. Loomis at the University of California, Berkeley, in 1940. Source: Gado Images/Alamy 67

3.2 War correspondent John Hersey, author of the bestselling *Hiroshima* (1946), which described the suffering of the bomb's victims. Source: Bettmann/Getty Images 75

3.3 President Truman and Secretary of War Henry Stimson in the Oval Office on August 8, 1945, discussing prospects for Japanese surrender after the atomic bombing of Hiroshima. Source: Bettmann/Getty Images 80

4.1 Churchill, Truman, and Stalin, meeting in Potsdam, Germany, July 1945. Source:

LIST OF FIGURES

Keystone-France/Gamma-Rapho/Getty Images 118
5.1 Atomic bomb survivors in Hiroshima, suffering the effects of radiation. Source: Ann Ronan Pictures/Hulton Archive/Getty Images 135
6.1 Tokyo was repeatedly fire-bombed in 1945 along with sixty other cities. Source: Keystone-France/Gamma-Keystone/Getty Images 179
6.2 Days after the Hiroshima bombing, an Allied correspondent stands in the rubble, looking toward the ruins of the Prefectural Industrial Promotion Hall, now preserved as the centerpiece of the Hiroshima Peace Memorial Park. Source: Los Angeles Examiner/USC Libraries/Corbis/ Getty Images 180
7.1 Emperor Hirohito is the subject of much debate for his wartime role. He is shown here on June 28, 1930. Source: Imagno/Getty Images 193
7.2 General Anami Korechika, war minister, committed suicide following Japanese surrender on August 15, 1945. Source: Bettmann/Getty Images 205
8.1 Roosevelt meeting with Prime Minister Winston Churchill in Casablanca, Morocco, announcing to the press the unconditional surrender policy, January 24, 1943. Source: Bettmann/Getty Images 216

ACKNOWLEDGMENTS

This book grows out of an honors seminar on "Hiroshima and Nagasaki" which I have taught at the University of Washington for over twenty-five years. The seminar has attracted a remarkable group of students and it has been my privilege to engage with them as they have discussed and debated the many difficult and troubling issues raised by this most controversial decision in America's recent history. Sharply different interpretations among historians compelled students to also consider historiography and the nature of the historian's craft.

Many people have helped me with this course. I particularly want to thank Mark Vanderveen, my doctoral student who assisted me for many years with the Hiroshima seminar. Azusa Tanaka, curator of the Japanese Collection for the Tateuchi East Asian Library at the University of Washington, organized and preserved the student research papers written over the many years that I taught the seminar. Martha Walsh, the managing editor of the *Journal of Japanese Studies*, has supported my work on this project for many years. I wish to thank Lucy Rhymer of Cambridge University Press for overseeing the review process and for her choice of two anonymous reviewers who made valuable suggestions to improve the manuscript. My colleague Dan Chirot made excellent contributions to improve the manuscript. Cindy Chirot likewise read it and gave me confidence that the book would be accessible to an informed general audience.

ACKNOWLEDGMENTS

My wife Anne and our children Annie and Will read the manuscript and made useful contributions.

I have written several articles on the historiography of the Hiroshima decision. After reading one of these articles, the late Ezra Vogel encouraged me to continue writing on the subject. I incorporate in this book brief passages from my *Japan in the American Century* (Belknap Press of Harvard University Press, 2018) chapters 2 and 3, and from "The Making of Postwar Japan: A Speculative Essay" in the *Journal of Japanese Studies*, volume 46, number 1 (Winter 2020). I am grateful to these publishers for the opportunity to build on my earlier works in this new book.

My greatest obligation, as it has always been, is to Anne, my companion and best friend for over six decades, for her constant support, inspiration, and love. This book, as with all my work, is dedicated to her.

NOTE ON THE TEXT

Japanese names as they appear in the text are presented in Japanese fashion with family names first, followed by given names.

Introduction

From my student years in Japan, I well remember one day walking out of a class on Japanese literature with my Waseda University professor. We were discussing the relations of our two countries when unexpectedly he asked me, "Would America have dropped an atomic bomb on Germany?" Surprised by the question and not having studied the issue, I could only answer, "I don't know." He was wondering, as many Japanese have, whether racism had played a part in the decision. The question stuck with me.

When I became a university professor myself and began teaching Japanese history, I found that the American decision to use the bomb on Hiroshima and Nagasaki sparked immediate interest with my own students. How was it, the American students wondered, that our country is the only one to have used the bomb on other people? Responding to their interest and my own wish to explore the topic, I created a new course – an honors seminar – to address the American decision to use the atomic bomb. I began the seminar by introducing some different interpretations. And as new interpretations emerged in the more-than twenty-five years that I have taught the course, I focused the seminar not simply on the decision itself but on its historiography as well. Why was it, I posed the question, that historians studying the same event, apparently examining the same facts, came to such different and often conflicting interpretations?

INTRODUCTION

I found that the widely varying ways in which historians have interpreted the decision to use the atomic bomb on Hiroshima and Nagasaki proved a rewarding way to explore the nature and function of the historian's craft. Tracing the anatomy of the debate over the use of the bomb offers a valuable means for understanding the many aspects of the historical profession and the varieties of history. The Hiroshima decision has often been called the most controversial decision any American president has made. Historians have interpreted it in more divergent ways than perhaps any other event in recent American history. The motivation and causes of the decision have provoked continuing controversy. "No single decision ever made by an American president has aroused more discussion and debate," wrote McGeorge Bundy, President John Kennedy's National Security Advisor, in his important study of the first fifty years of policymaking on the bomb.[1]

Because of its controversial nature and its huge historical importance, it has also been "one of the best studied decision-making cases in history."[2] Primary source material, existing archives, have been mined by historians and subjected to a wide range of debate about the issues raised.[3]

---

[1] McGeorge Bundy, *Danger and Survival: Choices about the Bomb in the First Fifty Years* (New York: Vintage, 1990), p.54.

[2] Nina Tannenwald, *The Nuclear Taboo: The United States and the Non-use of Nuclear Weapons since 1945* (Cambridge: Cambridge University Press, 2007), p.74.

[3] For a discussion of the historiography of the decision to use the atomic bomb, see Tsuyoshi Hasegawa, ed., *The End of the Pacific War:*

INTRODUCTION

A mountain of literature has grown as historians and others have obsessively written about it. "A complete bibliography of relevant writings on the bomb," writes one historian, "could easily comprise a book."⁴ Despite the extensive research and debate over the topic, historians have come to so many varying and conflicting interpretations that the British military historian John Keegan concluded that "historians are committed to controversy as a way of life, and [the Hiroshima] controversy may never be settled."⁵

There are many reasons why historians have devoted so much attention to the Hiroshima decision, some immediately obvious and others that require more reflection. First, and most profoundly, the advent of nuclear weapons was an existential event. For the first time in human history, humans had the capacity to let loose weapons that could bring civilization to an end. In discussing its possible use in the war, Secretary of War Henry Stimson, who was given charge of the project to build the atomic bomb, said that it was not simply a new weapon but rather represented "a new relationship of

---

Reappraisals (Stanford: Stanford University Press, 2007); and Michael Kort, *The Columbia Guide to Hiroshima and the Bomb* (New York: Columbia University Press, 2007).

⁴ Sean L. Malloy, *Atomic Tragedy: Henry L. Stimson and the Decision to Use the Bomb against Japan* (Ithaca: Cornell University Press, 2008), p. 193, n24. For an excellent Japanese historiographical review of Japan's decision to surrender, see Akagi Kanji and Takita Ryōsuke, "Shūsenshi kenkyū no genzai: genbaku tōka/Sōren sansen ronsō to sono go," *Hōgaku kenkyū: hōritsu seiji shakai* 89, no. 9 (2016):1–43.

⁵ John Keegan, *The Battle for History: Re-fighting World War II* (New York: Vintage Books, 1996), p. 28.

3

man to the universe."⁶ With the enormous horror of the new weapon came the realization that a great scientific achievement threatened humankind's very survival. Its first use signaled to human beings the tenuousness of their future. For the Indian leader Mahatma Gandhi, recalling the moment he heard of the use of the bomb, "I did not move a muscle. I said to myself, 'Unless the world now adopts nonviolence, it will spell certain suicide for mankind.'"⁷ The French philosopher Albert Camus wrote on August 6, 1945, "Faced with the terrifying perspectives which are opening up to humanity, we can perceive even better that peace is the only battle worth waging. It is no longer a prayer, but an order which must rise up from peoples to their governments – the order to choose finally between hell and reason."⁸

The Hiroshima decision initiated what scholars now call "the nuclear revolution." The advent of nuclear weapons, their proliferation, technological advance into thermonuclear weapons, the strategies for their possible use either in conflict or deterrence, all brought about a rethinking of the geopolitical order.⁹ The eminent scholar of international relations Hans Morgenthau wrote that nuclear weapons had forever changed the nature of foreign policy. Nuclear weapons represented "the only real revolution which has occurred in the structure of

---

⁶ Martin J. Sherwin, *A World Destroyed: The Atomic Bomb and the Grand Alliance* (New York: Vintage Books, 1977), p. 296.
⁷ Kai Bird and Lawrence Lifschultz, eds., *Hiroshima's Shadow* (Stony Creek, CT: The Pamphleteer's Press, 1998), p. 258.
⁸ Bird and Lifschultz (eds.), *Hiroshima's Shadow*, p. 261.
⁹ Michael D. Gordin and G. John Ikenberry, eds., *The Age of Hiroshima* (Princeton: Princeton University Press, 2020), p. 3.

international relations since the beginning of history, because it has radically changed the relationship between violence as a means of foreign policy and the ends of foreign policy."[10] The newly present threat of nuclear holocaust had to weigh heavily on leading diplomats. As Henry Kissinger wrote in the opening lines of his first book: "It is not surprising that an age faced with the threat of thermonuclear extinction should look back nostalgically to periods when diplomacy carried with it less drastic penalties, when wars were limited and catastrophe almost inconceivable."[11]

In addition to the existential implications of the first use of nuclear weapons, historians have focused their attention on the Hiroshima decision because it is a central event in the twentieth century that changed the course of international politics. At the turn of the millennium, in 1999, in a poll taken of prominent journalists and scholars, the decision to use the atomic bomb on Hiroshima and Nagasaki was chosen as the most important event of the twentieth century.[12] This horrific event was at the center of the major developments of our time: the end of World War II, the beginning of the atomic age, the establishment of the American world order, and the Cold War nuclear arms race. Historians have linked the decision to use the bomb with all of these major developments and, therefore, placed it at the center of modern history.

---

[10] Barry Gewen, *The Inevitability of Tragedy: Henry Kissinger and His World* (New York: Norton, 2020), p. 227.
[11] Gewen, *The Inevitability of Tragedy*, p. 392.
[12] Associated Press story carried in the *Seattle Times*, February 24, 1999.

INTRODUCTION

Historical controversy has involved many issues:

1. What motivated decision-makers to use this horrific new weapon?
2. Was it necessary to use the bomb if Japan was already defeated and on the verge of surrender?
3. Were there not viable alternatives such as a demonstration of the bomb or a naval blockade or modification of unconditional surrender policy or waiting for Soviet entry into the war?
4. Did the use of the bomb save lives by averting an invasion?
5. Was the second bomb on Nagasaki necessary?
6. Can the bombs be morally justified?

To these and many other questions historians continue to offer many conflicting interpretations.

Another reason for such intense and ongoing attention by historians arises from the continuing public debate on the topic. Public opinion polls in recent years show that the majority of American and the Japanese people view the decision in opposite ways. In 2015, on the occasion of the seventieth anniversary of the end of World War II, the Pew Research Center carried out a joint opinion poll that found that 79 percent of Japanese said the bombing was "not justified," while 56 percent of Americans considered it "justified."[13] Japanese believe that they were already defeated and on the verge of

---

[13] See Pew Research Center, "70 Years after Hiroshima, Opinions Have Shifted on Use of the Atomic Bomb," July 31, 2015, which showed declining support in both the United States and Japan for America's bombing of Hiroshima and Nagasaki.

surrender, while a majority of Americans still hold that the use of the bomb was necessary to end the war and saved massive American casualties. One of the pillars of Japan's postwar national identity, about which virtually all Japanese (whatever their political persuasion) agree, is the belief that Japan, as the only nation to have suffered an atomic attack, has a unique mission to lead the world in banishing nuclear weapons.

In the many years that I have taught the course on the Hiroshima decision, most of my students have been Americans, but I also have had many students from other countries whose interest and approach to the Hiroshima decision are different. Japanese students have a mix of views, many feeling, as the opinion poll indicated, the bomb was unnecessary because Japan was already defeated. To Chinese and Koreans, however, the decision brought the end of the war and their suffering under Japanese imperialism. As one of my Chinese students wrote in his term paper:

> The main question at the heart of the atomic bomb debate in China and Korea, to the extent one exists, is not "Were the bombs necessary to induce Japan's surrender?" [or] "Should alternatives to the bombs have been explored?" or "Were the bombs militarily justified?" but simply: "Were the atomic bombings morally justified as a retribution for Japan's own atrocities against other Asian peoples?" For them, the overwhelming answer is undisputedly, "Yes."[14]

---

[14] Jesse Du, "In the Crossfire of Nationalism: National Identity and the East Asian Controversy over Hiroshima and Nagasaki," Unpublished essay, 2017.

INTRODUCTION

The Oxford historian Rana Mitter writes that for the Chinese, as for the Americans, World War II was "a good war."[15]

Many, perhaps most, Americans have had a sense of unease about having been the only nation to use the bomb. We find it difficult to square with our belief that we are a nation of exceptional virtue and we find it painful when foreign observers remind us of the decision. In 2003, when President George W. Bush announced the invasion of Iraq, Nelson Mandela angrily questioned American self-righteousness in light of Hiroshima and Nagasaki. "Because they decided to kill innocent people in Japan, who are still suffering from that," Mandela said, "who are they now to pretend that they are policemen of the world?"[16] A leading Israeli scholar of modern Japanese history, Ben-Ami Shillony, in a lecture on the bombing reached the harsh judgment that "Auschwitz and Hiroshima ... represented a new level of atrocity that human beings can perpetrate on each other."[17] Adversaries take pleasure in emphasizing American guilt. Osama Bin Laden, mastermind of the 9/11 terrorist attack, often condemned American use of the bomb as itself a "terrorist act" that victimized "women, children, and elderly people."[18] Russian President Vladimir Putin observed that Stalin was "a tyrant, but I very

---

[15] Rana Mitter, *China's Good War: How World War II Is Shaping a New Nationalism* (Cambridge, MA: Belknap Harvard University Press, 2020).

[16] *New York Times*, February 1, 2003.

[17] Ben-Ami Shillony, "Auschwitz and Hiroshima: What Can the Jews and the Japanese Do for World Peace?" *International House of Japan Bulletin* 27, no. 1 (2007): 2.

[18] John W. Dower, *Cultures of War: Pearl Harbor/Hiroshima/9-11/Iraq* (New York: W. W. Norton, 2010), p. 87.

much doubt that in the spring of 1945, if he had been in possession of an atomic bomb, he would have used it against Germany."[19]

American politics have made the issue a third rail and not permitted politicians to express regret. In 1991, on the fiftieth anniversary of Pearl Harbor, reporters asked President George H. W. Bush if an American statement of regret for Hiroshima might be forthcoming if the Japanese apologized for Pearl Harbor. "Not from this president," he replied. "I was fighting over there. ... Can I empathize with a family whose child was victimized by these attacks? Absolutely. But I can also empathize with my roommate's mother, my roommate having been killed in action."[20] In Japan, Bush's response at once doomed the Diet's own consideration of whether it might make an apology for Pearl Harbor. Four years later, in 1995, on the fiftieth anniversary of the Hiroshima bomb, President Bill Clinton told the American Society of Newspaper Editors that America owed Japan no apology and that President Truman had made the right decision "based on the facts he had before him."[21]

Barack Obama cautiously broached the issue in the first foreign policy speech of his presidency, April 5, 2009, which he devoted to the need to strengthen the Nuclear Nonproliferation Treaty. He observed that America was obligated to take the lead in ridding the world of atomic weapons because

---

[19] Gordin and Ikenberry, eds., *Age of Hiroshima*, p. 74.
[20] Robert Jay Lifton and Greg Mitchell, *Hiroshima in America: A Half Century of Denial* (New York: Avon Books, 1995), p. 222.
[21] *Washington Post*, April 14, 1995.

"as a nuclear power – as the only nuclear power to have used a nuclear weapon – the United States has a moral responsibility to act." He was at once chided in a *Wall Street Journal* editorial for offering "a barely concealed apology for Hiroshima [which] is an insult to the memory of Harry Truman, who saved a million lives by ending World War II without a bloody invasion of Japan."[22] In a historic gesture of reconciliation, in May 2016, Obama became the first sitting US president to visit the Hiroshima Peace Memorial. He told the Japanese press that he did not intend to offer an apology because

> I think it is important to recognize that in the midst of war, leaders make all kinds of decisions. It's a job of historians to ask questions and examine them, but I know as somebody who has now sat in this position for the last seven and a half years, that every leader makes very difficult decisions, particularly during time of war.[23]

Presidential candidate Donald Trump at the time tweeted, "Does President Obama ever discuss the sneak attack on Pearl Harbor when he is in Japan?" and told a campaign rally that Obama's being in Hiroshima is "fine. Just as long as he doesn't apologize."[24]

The Smithsonian Controversy

Most controversies among historians remain within the academy and attract little public notice. The Hiroshima decision is different. A great many Americans are now aware of the

---

[22] *Wall Street Journal*, April 7, 2009. [23] NHK News, May 21, 2016.
[24] *Reuters*, May 28, 2016.

controversy and have an opinion. What drew mass public attention to the historical controversy was an exhibit planned by the Smithsonian's National Air and Space Museum at the time of the fiftieth anniversary of the atomic bombing in 1995. The exhibit was to feature the refurbished *Enola Gay*, the B-29 that dropped the bomb on Hiroshima, with an accompanying text which would interpret the issues that the bombing raised. Planning for the event exploded in a firestorm of criticism that gained immense public attention and left a legacy of public controversy over the American use of the bomb.[25]

The Museum director, Martin Harwit, a Cornell astrophysicist, wanted to interpret rather than simply celebrate the event. Harwit assembled a group of his curators to write the script for the exhibition. His intention was to "tell the whole story, from the American as well as the Japanese side."[26] Harwit and his curators were convinced that "scholarly research would show using atomic bombs against Japan had been a mistake."[27] They drew advice from historians who inclined strongly to revisionist critiques of the use of the bomb, questioning the motives, morality, and casualty estimates of the decision-makers.

The slant of the curators' text was evident in its opening statement: "For most Americans, this war was

---

[25] The most detailed account of the Smithsonian controversy in any language is Fujita Satoshi, *Amerika ni okeru Hiroshima/Nagasaki: Enora/Gei ronsō to rekishi kyōiku* (Tokyo: Sairyusha, 2019).

[26] Gregg Herken, "The Smithsonian's Decision to Exhibit the 'Enola Gay,'" *Public History Weekly*, October 6, 2022.

[27] Robert P. Newman, *The Enola Gay and the Court of History* (Bern: Peter Lang, 2004), p. 98.

fundamentally different than the one waged against Germany and Italy – it was a war of vengeance. For most Japanese it was a war to defend their unique culture against Western imperialism."[28] An advisory board of historians suggested changes in the curators' text, but it was too late. Given a chance to preview the text, veterans groups, with support from the media, were outraged and protested to members of Congress that the narrative was unpatriotic in its neglect of Japan's treacherous attack that began the war, was dismissive of the suffering and sacrifices the GIs had made in the Pacific, and was oblivious to the massive American casualties that an invasion would have cost and that the bomb had prevented. Harwit asked for an internal review by a group of largely military historians who agreed the text was biased, unbalanced, and unacceptable. The script went through repeated modifications but, unlike other controversies surrounding historical commemoration such as the Vietnam Veterans Memorial Wall, a compromise could not be reached. The veterans groups demanded that the text acknowledge that there was no alternative to the use of the bomb and that a million lives had been saved.[29] They took their case to Congress. The Senate passed a resolution condemning the text as offensive. The House demanded the resignation of the director, threatened to cut off funding of the Smithsonian, and announced hearings. Harwit resigned and the exhibition opened with only the forward fuselage of

---

[28] See Philip Nobile, ed., *Judgment at the Smithsonian: The Bombing of Hiroshima and Nagasaki* (New York: Marlowe, 1995), p. 3.

[29] Herken, "The Smithsonian's Decision."

the *Enola Gay* on display and no interpretive text. When I visited the exhibit on the Mall in Washington, I found only a minimal statement explaining the bombing, a short video with recollections of the pilot and crew members of the *Enola Gay*, and the fuselage looming overhead.

Commenting on the controversy, a British observer wrote that "the memory of the atomic bombing of Hiroshima, and of World War II as a whole, holds a very special place in the cultural psyche of America. A notion of World War II as being a 'Good War' prevails in American society. An America without that heroic image is unimaginable."[30] The Stanford historian Barton Bernstein, a member of the advisory board, was dismayed by the critics and wrote that "their insistence on hewing to the 'official' version of the bomb story despoiled the very democratic values that were at stake in World War II" by blocking "free inquiry, dialogue, questioning, and dissent."[31] Those who engage in public history as the Smithsonian curators did are taking a risk when they challenge the deeply held assumptions of national identities. In such circumstances, public history may be like "doing history without a safety net." Harwit later ruefully reflected that "the losers in this drama were the American public."[32] Ironically, however, this controversial exhibition did more than anything else to attract

---

[30] Mattias Eken, "The Exhibit That Bombed: The Enola Gay Controversy and Contested Memory," Network for the British Association for American Studies, December 14, 2020.

[31] Barton J. Bernstein, "Misconceived Patriotism," *Bulletin of the Atomic Scientists* 51, no. 3 (May–June 1995).

[32] Martin Harwit, *An Exhibit Denied: Lobbying the History of the Enola Gay* (New York: Springer-Verlag, 1996) quoted in Herken.

INTRODUCTION

public interest to the nature of the debate over the Hiroshima decision. It was no longer simply an academic debate. It was now a public controversy.

This Book

This book took shape over many years of teaching on the Hiroshima decision. I have given public lectures on "Hiroshima and the Historians" and written several articles by the same title.[33] In this book, I am gathering my thoughts for several purposes. First, it is a study of the anatomy of the debate among historians about an event that was central to major developments in modern history. I have to be highly selective, choosing from the voluminous writings of historians a judicious number of interpretations for scrutiny because they represent the main lines of a controversy unfolding over the last seventy-five years. The ones chosen here are works I used in my teaching.

Let me emphasize that when I refer to "the Hiroshima decision" I am also including Nagasaki. As the historian Martin Sherwin wrote: "[T]he destruction of Hiroshima and

---

[33] I first expressed my views of the historiographical issues in Kenneth B. Pyle, "Hiroshima and the Historians: History as Relative Truth," *Pacific Northwest Quarterly* (Summer 2013): 123-132, reprinted and slightly revised in Kenneth B. Pyle, "Hiroshima and the Historians: History as Relative Truth," *Asia-Pacific Review* 22, no. 2 (November 2015): 14-27. I also gave my views in the 2013 Griffith and Patricia Way Lecture at the University of Washington, available on YouTube.

THIS BOOK

Nagasaki was the result of a *single* decision."[34] From the beginning of deliberations on the use of the bomb it was widely assumed that more than one would be used and that it would be left to the military to determine. The military drew up a target list of cities and when Kyoto was struck from the initial target list of cities, Nagasaki was added. Kokura was to be the second city hit by the bomb, but when the crew on *Bockscar*, the plane carrying the bomb, found it under the clouds, they proceeded on to the next target. Nagasaki might well have been avoided, but weather, human decision, and misfortune befell it.

The book's second purpose is to explain the nature of the historian's craft. Most of the writing on the nature of the historian's craft is of a philosophical and abstract nature. What I do in this book is somewhat unusual. I want to illustrate the nature of the craft by seeing it at work on a concrete and contentious topic. The book demonstrates the many ways in which historians' interpretations are shaped and influenced. I show how and why, despite agreement on basic facts, historians have come to multiple competing interpretations. The Hiroshima controversy teaches us a lot about how historical knowledge progresses. We learn that the clash of ideas is the means by which historians pursue truth. From the debate and contention over more than seventy-five years we have gained a deep understanding of the decision to use the bomb. But this will not be the final word.

The book's third purpose is to show the value of historians in a free society. Authoritarian regimes go to

---

[34] Sherwin, *A World Destroyed*, p. 209. Italics in original.

great lengths to rewrite history to undergird their power, but democratic societies also face challenges to the writing of history. The role of a robust historical profession in a critical examination of the past is fundamental to the health of a democratic society. As the British historian John Tosh explains:

> [T]he essential characteristic of democracy is persuasion by argument. Public issues should be subject to public argument, and that requires a level of knowledge of the facts of the case and the grounds on which those facts can be variously interpreted. Popular debate, in short, is the life-blood of a democratic political culture. This is the context in which the relationship between history and citizenship is strongest.[35]

In the present day, when the foundations of democratic societies are weakened by rampant disinformation and propaganda, historians must preserve their profession as a model of integrity in the pursuit of truth.

My mentor, the American historian Ernest May, who introduced me as a student to the study of historiography, observed that professors write books for other professors. That is the path to promotion, tenure, and attention in the academic world. In a book reflecting on uses of the study of history for policymakers, he and his coauthor wrote: "Of any book written by a professor, the presumption should be that its intended audience is other professors. There are fortunately a number of exceptions, but not enough to warrant

---

[35] John Tosh, *Why History Matters* (New York: Palgrave Macmillan, 2008), p. 138.

a different rule."³⁶ This book is one of those exceptions. It is written for a broad audience. My hope is that this book will be accessible for an informed public and especially for students interested not only in the Hiroshima decision but also in history and historiography.

---

[36] Richard E. Neustadt and Ernest R. May, *Thinking in Time: The Uses of History for Decision-Makers* (New Yok: The Free Press, 1986), p.264.

1
The Historian's Craft

What do historians do? In a free society, historians have an important responsibility. They are custodians of the public memory, trained to carefully and critically reconstruct how things happened in the past. They help us understand ourselves and the world in which we live. The German historian Johann Droysen put it quite simply: "History is the 'Know Thyself' of humanity – the self-consciousness of mankind."[1] Historical knowledge orients us and tells us how we arrived at our present situation – where we came from, how we got here, who we are. To understand who we are, we have to understand who we've been. We learn our identity. It steadies us. It has been said that people who lack knowledge of their own history are like cut flowers, lacking a root system to sustain them. The historian William McNeill suggested that people who are ignorant of their history are akin to an individual with a defective memory. Think of waking up some morning unable to remember who you are! Disoriented and uncertain about your past, you would be unable to make informed choices about the future.[2]

---

[1] Fritz Stern, *The Varieties of History: From Voltaire to the Present* (New York: Meridian Book, 1956) p. 201.

[2] William H. McNeill, "Why Study History?" American Historical Association (1985), Home Page.

Knowledge of the past helps us learn what influences shaped us, what errors or mishaps could have been avoided, what patterns are discernible, and what lessons may be learned for future use. With such understanding we can better prepare for the future. Not that we can predict the future, not that history repeats itself, but rather that it enlarges our perspective, broadens our horizons, and sensitizes us to the ways in which human events unfold. We learn to expect surprises, contingencies, and unexpected consequences.

The integrity of historical knowledge is vital for an informed citizenry and democratic governance. From the time of their founding, Sophia Rosenfeld writes in her *Democracy and Truth*, governments "premised on the idea of self-rule typically depend on the idea that the people should not be deceived, that veracity and authenticity matter as moral qualities for all."[3] An accurate knowledge of the past is critical to the choices that citizens must make in determining public policy. A widely shared collective memory is the foundation of a stable society. "A realistic understanding of the past," the historian Bernard Bailyn stressed, "free of myths, wish-fulfillments, and partisan delusions, is essential for social sanity."[4] This is what I meant when I wrote that history steadies us.

As Joyce Appleby, Lynn Hunt, and Margaret Jacob write, "Historians support the long-term goals of democratic

---

[3] Sophia Rosenfeld, *Democracy and Truth: A Short History* (Philadelphia: University of Pennsylvania Press, 2019), p. 26.
[4] Bernard Bailyn, *Sometimes an Art: Nine Essays on History* (New York: Knopf, 2015), pp. 21–22.

societies when they insistently and honestly reconstruct past experience." They can save us from myths about our identities. Diverse groups may try to maintain their own view of the past whether to serve their self-interest or simply to accommodate their pride. Nation-states build idealized versions of their past to instill civic pride. In the face of such popular and patriotic versions, it is the role of historians to maintain independent scholarly inquiry. "Democracy and history always live in a kind of tension with each other. Nations use history to build a sense of national identity, pitting the demands for stories that build solidarity against open-ended scholarly inquiry that can trample on cherished illusions."[5]

We are all familiar with the importance of a free press in protecting democracy by holding those in power to account. By the same token, the role of a robust historical profession in a critical examination of the past is fundamental to the health of a democratic society. There have long been arguments over how to tell the American story. They are very much with us today. When President George H. W. Bush initiated a plan to establish the first-ever national standards for what schools should teach about the national past it turned into a bitter controversy. More recently, controversy has surrounded the teaching of the history of slavery and race in America.[6] So, too, one of the major issues in telling the American story is how to explain our use of the atomic bomb on Japan.

---

[5] Joyce Appleby, Lynn Hunt, and Margaret Jacob, *Telling the Truth about History* (New York: W. W. Norton, 1994), p. 289.

[6] See, for example, Jake Silverstein, "The 1619 Project and the Long Battle over U.S. History," *New York Times*, November 9, 2021.

As we will discuss in the succeeding chapters, historical study of Hiroshima has been a challenge to Americans' self-image as a virtuous nation. In the Introduction, we discussed how the Smithsonian Institution's exhibition became embroiled in controversy. Veterans groups and their supporters in Congress argued for a patriotic interpretation of the Hiroshima decision. They saw the proper role of the Smithsonian as memorializing the nation's victories and not questioning its past. In the end, the text was discarded and the exhibition was curtailed. But shielding Americans from engaging the difficult issues is not beneficial to a democracy.

Attempts to control the writing of history pose a recurrent threat to democratic societies. We live in an age of rampant disinformation, which challenges people's ability to distinguish fact from falsehood. "Blatant lying about history," writes Lynn Hunt, "has become more common owing to the influence of social media." Whether it is about the Holocaust or the birthplace of Barack Obama, "the world-wide web has enabled historical lies to flourish."[7] Historians may differ in their interpretation of evidence about the past, but to the best of their ability they must stick to what is found to be factually accurate. As a community of scholars united by common purposes and values, historians are enjoined to practice their craft with integrity so as to preserve their reputation for trustworthiness. "It is their single most precious asset."[8] When

---

[7] Lynn Hunt, *History: Why It Matters* (Medford, MA: Polity Press, 2018), p. 4.

[8] American Historical Association, *Statement on Standards of Professional Conduct* (updated 2019).

a democracy loses its collective trust in common knowledge it undermines cooperation and weakens the institutions upon which democratic politics depends. The philosopher Hannah Arendt wrote in *The Origins of Totalitarianism*, "The ideal subject of totalitarian rule is not the convinced Nazi or the convinced Communist, but people for whom the distinction between fact and fiction (i.e., the reality of experience) and the distinction between true and false (i.e., the standards of thought) no longer exist."[9] Losing the ability to tell truth from untruth, the civic life of a democracy loses its equilibrium, its respect for the norms and values that make it work. The study of history contributes to the civic virtue that is the foundation of democracy. "Democracy," the historian Timothy Snyder writes, "requires individual responsibility, which is impossible without critical history. It thrives in a spirit of self-awareness and self-correction. Authoritarianism, on the other hand, is infantilizing. We should not have to feel any negative emotions; difficult subjects should be kept from us." Authoritarian governments guide the public memory by asserting a mandatory view of the past. History is made to serve the national interest. War on history becomes a war on democracy.[10]

There is no greater testimony to the value of historians' work in a free society than to compare it with what happens in totalitarian regimes where critical historical inquiry ceases. Those regimes go to great lengths to manipulate history and

---

[9] Quoted in Jonathan Rauch, *The Constitution of Knowledge: A Defense of Truth* (Washington, DC: Brookings Press, 2021), p. 164.

[10] Timothy Snyder, "The War on History Is a War on Democracy," *New York Times*, June 29, 2021.

restrict the work of historians. The pursuit of truth through the writing of history cannot be permitted. Authoritarian societies impose a master narrative of the past that meets the needs of the state. Pressed into the service of the state, history becomes a means of indoctrination and securing the legitimacy of the rulers. George Orwell saw this more clearly than anyone. Readers of his novel *1984* will remember the wretched protagonist Winston Smith who kept the records according to the ruling party line in the Ministry of Truth. The Commissar instructs Smith what his responsibility must be. "We the Party, control all records, and we control all memories. Then we control the past, do we not?" Warming to his point, the Commissar quotes the Party slogan: "Who controls the past controls the future; who controls the present controls the past."[11] Without memory of the past, the people will believe whatever the Party may tell them.

Writing his novel in 1949 and living in the shadow of Hitler and Stalin, Orwell feared the time when history would again be willfully manipulated in still more extreme ways. Authoritarian regimes would rewrite history to obliterate from memory public figures, heroes, and events that challenge government policies. In our own time, we are witnessing the Chinese Communist Party revise history to erase from memory events such as the Tiananmen uprising and the cruelties of the Mao era and thereby to establish with the new technology control over the future. For the Chinese leadership, the journalist Ian Johnson writes, "the first priority is controlling the

---

[11] C. Vann Woodward, *American Attitudes toward History* (Oxford: Clarendon Press, 1955), p. 10.

past.... To make sure that history really appears to be on its side, the party spends an inordinate amount of time writing and rewriting it and preventing others from wielding their pens.'"[12] This authoritarian control of the past is becoming the nightmare that Orwell feared.

The Historian's Craft

How are historians in a free society trained to meet their responsibilities as custodians of the collective memory? Writing history is considered a craft. Like other crafts, it has skills that have been developed and passed on from master to apprentice. The idea comes directly from medieval German guilds "where admittance required that one had trained under a master craftsman and had also produced an original piece of work, hence the word 'masterpiece.'"[13] As an academic discipline, these skills can be taught by guild-like training in graduate school study. In professional training, one learns certain techniques – the quasi-scientific aspects of how to analyze documents, treat sources critically, weigh evidence, document sources, and develop narrative skills.[14] Above all, training in the guild is focused on historiography, critical study of the secondary literature, and learning what is already known and what are the existing issues and interpretations.

---

[12] Ian Johnson, "A Most Adaptable Party," *New York Review of Books*, July 2021.

[13] Richard Cohen, *Making History: The Storytellers Who Shaped the Past* (London: Weidenfeld and Nicolson, 2022), p. 253.

[14] Bernard Bailyn, *On the Teaching and Writing of History* (Hanover, NH: University Press of New England, 1991), pp. 48–50.

As the body of knowledge has grown, training requires specialization in one of the many subfields of history, such as social history or cultural history. Also, historians' training demands knowledge of ancillary disciplines such as economics or the acquisition of necessary foreign language capability. One also learns from observing the skills of highly regarded historians. Gifted craftsmen acquire, or may be born with, the art of representing the past in ways that bring it to life. In the hands of a master craftsman, history becomes an art. It becomes akin to literature.

Professionalization of the Craft

Prior to the nineteenth century, for two thousand years, writing history was the work of amateurs, people who had another occupation but decided to write about happenings that attracted their interest.[15] Thucydides, who had been a military leader, decided to write about the Peloponnesian War in which he had participated. For centuries, history writing was an avocation or a handmaiden of literature, theology, or philosophy. Only in the industrial era as universities became more developed centers of learning did history begin to have a systematic methodology and autonomous purpose. In the German universities of the nineteenth century, the study of history was professionalized under the influence of Leopold von Ranke, who said that his intention was to structure the past "as it actually was" or "as it essentially

---

[15] Theodore S. Hamerow, "The Professionalization of Historical Learning," *Reviews in American History* 14, no. 3 (September 1986): 319–333.

was" (*wie es eigentlich gewesen*). History became an academic discipline and training for the craft began to be developed. It was to do this by the scientific ideal of relying on the archives, the written records, and eyewitness accounts from the period being studied. History was to be less storytelling and instead must be a rigorous science written by professionally trained historians. Their goal was an objective and impartial rendering of the past.

The first American professional historians embraced the scientific ideal, what one called a "noble dream" that their profession could fulfill a mission of achieving objective truth. Objectivity became "the founding myth of the [American] historical profession."[16] For the founders of the American Historical Association (AHA) in 1884, history was a science that demanded rigorous pursuit of facts, scrupulous research, long hours spent in archives, critical appraisal of the sources, uncovering the facts that the original documents had to reveal. Historians would be objective and detached in relation to their materials. They would explain precisely what happened, free from their personal biases. History would be on "a footing comparable to that of the natural sciences."[17] Their "scientific history tended toward a rigid factualism."[18] The historian, one said at the time, must "collect facts, view

---

[16] Peter Novick, *That Noble Dream: The "Objectivity Question" and the American Historical Profession* (Cambridge: Cambridge University Press, 1988), p. 268.

[17] Richard Hofstadter, *The Progressive Historians: Turner, Beard, Parrington* (New York: Knopf, 1968), pp. 304–305.

[18] John Higham, *History: Professional Scholarship in America* (New York: Harper Torchbooks, 1973), p. 99.

them objectively, and arrange them as the facts themselves demanded."[19] The reward of such scientific rigors, they believed, would eventually be a definitive understanding of what actually happened in the past. How stunned they would be if they could foresee the inexhaustible controversy over the Hiroshima decision and the endless interpretations historians continue to offer of the facts.

Can the Past Be Known?

In time, the hope of the first professional historians of achieving objective truth in their writing faced growing doubts. Was it really possible for historians to "extinguish the self," as Ranke wished, and write an objective account of past events?[20] The word "history" has two meanings. It refers to what happened in the past, but it also refers to what historians write about the past. They are not the same. And that is the problem. Historians can never fully recapture the past. It is too complex. Historians will each see it in a different way, depending upon their own personal makeup. Their version of the past will be an interpretation, one that is partial, provisional, and incomplete.

In the wake of World War I, historians had growing doubts about history as a "science." Controversies over their competing and conflicting interpretations of the war and other past events strained the belief that historians could attain objective truth. There were too many disagreements. By the 1930s the confidence that historians could be impartial

---

[19] Novick, *That Noble Dream*, pp. 38–39.
[20] Stern, *Varieties of History*, p. 25.

and detached in construction of the past was widely challenged. In his presidential address to the AHA in 1931, Charles Beard mocked the "noble dream" that it was possible to be objective in reconstructing the past. "Every student of history knows that his colleagues have been influenced in their selection and ordering of materials by their biases, prejudices, beliefs, affections, general upbringing, and experience."[21] Beard's contemporary Carl Becker used the memorable phrase "everyman his own historian" to subsume his thesis that history is "an imaginative creation, a personal possession which each one of us, Mr. Everyman, fashions out of his individual experience, adapts to his practical or emotional needs, and adorns as well as may be to suit his aesthetic tastes."[22] The past is continually revised. "Every generation, our own included, will, must inevitably, understand the past and anticipate the future in the light of its own restricted experience, must inevitably play on the dead whatever tricks it finds necessary for its own peace of mind."[23] Beard and Becker took obvious pleasure in dispelling the noble dream. Historians may agree on basic facts about the past, but the meaning of the facts begins when historians interpret them. Facts don't speak for themselves. Facts are inert until something is made of them. From Beard and Becker's time on, the hope that historians could be so detached as to achieve objective reality in their reconstruction of the past faded.

---

[21] Novick, *That Noble Dream*, p. 254.
[22] Carl Becker, "Everyman His Own Historian," *American Historical Review* 37, no. 2 (January 1932): 228.
[23] Becker, "Everyman His Own Historian," p. 235.

Conscientious historians can strive – the conscientious historian *must* strive – to describe and interpret as faithfully as possible the actuality of what happened, but one inevitably falls short. Try as they must for a disinterested and dispassionate approach to their subject, their judgments will still be influenced by their own times. The problems they choose to study, the evidence they select to emphasize, and the perspective they have are to some degree relative to their own time.

Doubts about the possibility of achieving objective truth continued to mount beyond what Beard, Becker, and other critics had argued. In the post–World War II period a new set of theoretical doubts about the nature of historical knowledge arrived as the school of "postmodernism." Originally formulated by French philosophers Jacques Derrida and Michael Foucault, postmodernism as found in the work of Hayden White and other historians became the most controversial and extreme critique of the possibility of objectivity. "One must face the fact," wrote White, "that, when it comes to the historical record, there are no grounds to be found in the record itself of preferring one way of construing its meaning rather than another."[24] Historians are not uncovering the past, they are inventing it. There is no such thing as objective truth. One perspective is as good as another. By such reckoning, history is storytelling. History is akin to literature, historians to novelists. Each is telling a story as he

---

[24] See John Tosh, *The Pursuit of History: Aims, Methods and New Directions in the Study of History* (New York: Routledge, 7th ed., 2022), p. 174.

or she sees it. All interpretations are equally valid. There cannot be any such thing as historical truth. All versions of the past are subjective, the product of one individual's mind.

A further reason for doubt about the goal of objectivity emerges from the neurosciences, cognitive psychology, and clinical medicine.[25] Research on the complex ways the brain stores memory suggests that the evidence of eyewitness accounts must always be treated with caution by historians. Conflicting testimonies of the same event by eyewitnesses in judicial courts are common and suggestive of this caution that historians must adopt along with legal experts. Such testimonies are reminiscent of "the *Rashomon* effect."[26] Akira Kurosawa's 1950 film *Rashomon*, one of the most famous films ever made, illustrates the problem of conflicting testimonies. Set near Kyoto at the end of the Heian period (794–1185), it is about a bandit who proudly confesses to killing a samurai after a sexual encounter with his wife. A woodcutter claims to have witnessed it all. The film consists of a recounting of this crime by four characters in the film, the bandit, the spirit of the samurai (speaking through a medium), his wife, and the woodcutter. But each recounts

---

[25] James M. Banner, Jr., *The Ever-Changing Past: Why All History Is Revisionist History* (New Haven: Yale University Press, 2021), pp. 255–261.

[26] "The Rashomon effect is a combination of a difference of perspective and equally plausible accounts, with the absence of evidence to elevate one above others, with the inability to disqualify a particular version of the truth, all surrounded by the social pressure for closure on the question." Robert Anderson, "What Is the Rashomon Effect?" in Blair Davis, Robert Anderson, and Jan Wells, eds., *Rashomon Effects: Kurosawa, Rashomon and Their Legacies* (New York: Routledge, 2016), p. 71.

a different version of events. Each of the versions is plausible but none can be reconciled with the others. Even the witness's account is subject to doubt. There is no evidence to elevate one account over the others. The mystery is never solved, and the movie leaves the viewers to ponder for themselves the persuasiveness of the different versions and the veracity of the storytellers. "Thus," as a Japanese encyclopedia concluded, "truth is revealed as relative and reality itself is questioned."[27]

In addition to postmodernism, other new approaches to the study of history emerged in the postwar period. History writing had once focused largely on past politics, but a growing number of historians turned their attention to groups in society estranged from power and influence, individuals and groups previously neglected and oftentimes voiceless. By far the most impactful of the new developments was women's history, first formulated during the 1970s, which challenged the masculinist assumptions of academic knowledge. It soon moved on to incorporate men in its scope. "Those who worried that women's studies scholarship focused too narrowly and separately on women," the American historian Joan Scott wrote, "used the term 'gender' to introduce a relational notion into our analytic vocabulary."[28] As its implications have been pursued, for example in power relations, gender history has had an impact on historical writing comparable to the Marxist history's attention to "class." (The birth of women's studies in the

---

[27] *Japan: An Illustrated Encyclopedia* (Tokyo: Kodansha, 1993), vol. 2, p. 1247.

[28] Joan W. Scott, "Gender: A Useful Category of Historical Analysis," *American Historical Review* 91, no. 5 (December 1986): 1054.

THE HISTORIAN'S CRAFT

1970s was a reflection of the professional makeup of the time. When I was appointed assistant professor of history at the University of Washington in 1965 there was only one woman tenured in the department. Today, women make up the majority of tenured appointments in the department, and the chair is a woman.) In his tracing of the development of the American historical profession, Peter Novick concluded that by the 1980s there were now so many different approaches, and so many subfields, that the profession was losing its coherence.

More new approaches continue to emerge. The Indian historian Dipesh Chakrabarty, writing in 2000, complained that historical scholarship has not outgrown the age of Western imperialism. Professional scholarship has been dominated by "Eurocentric" tendencies reflecting Western academics failing to take seriously the traditions of historical writing outside of Europe as worthy of their attention. As Lynn Hunt wrote, "neither history nor the concern for historical truth is Western."[29] Japanese, in fact, had argued in the 1890s that study of the history of the East (tōyōshi) was of equal importance as Western history (seiyōshi).[30] Chakrabarty contended that Western academics remained ignorant of non-Western historical writing.

What then are we to conclude? If there are so many doubts about the ability of historians to discover the reality of the past, to write objective accounts of what happened, what

---

[29] Hunt, *History*, p. 46.
[30] Stefan Tanaka, *Japan's Orient: Rendering Pasts into History* (Berkeley, CA: University of California Press, 1993), pp. 47–49. See also Kenneth B. Pyle, *The New Generation in Meiji Japan: Problems of Cultural Identity* (Stanford: Stanford University Press, 1969).

value is history? If Beard and Becker succeeded in dispelling the noble dream of history as a science, if postmodernists can legitimately claim that history is no more than a form of literature and storytelling, if neuroscientists cast doubt on the reliability of memory, if historians can find no agreement on their approaches, should we then question the value of the historical profession? By no means!

The British historian Richard Evans liked E. H. Carr's observation that "It does not follow that because a mountain appears to take on a different shape from different angles of vision, it has objectively either no shape at all or an infinity of shapes."[31] Most historians, as John Tosh wrote in his study of the profession, disregarded the extreme view.[32] John Lewis Gaddis in his *Landscape of History* shrugged off the claims of postmodernism. He wrote, "Post modernist insights about the relative character of all historical judgments – the inseparability of the observer from the observed – ... some of us feel that we've known this all along."[33] In sum, as the historian Sarah Maza observed, "The crisis around postmodernism was merely the final stage in a longer evolution away from an earlier belief that a stance of complete objectivity toward their material was, for historians, both possible and the ultimate professional goal."[34]

---

[31] Richard J. Evans, *In Defense of History* (New York: W. W. Norton, 1999), p. 193.

[32] Tosh, *The Pursuit of History*. See especially pp. 176–177.

[33] John Lewis Gaddis, *The Landscape of History: How Historians Map the Past* (New York: Oxford University Press, 2002), pp. 9–10.

[34] Sarah Maza, *Thinking about History* (Chicago: University of Chicago Press 2017), p. 100.

THE HISTORIAN'S CRAFT

Coming to accept the obstacles to a pure objective recounting of the past, historians recognized that knowledge of the past could advance by defending their interpretation within a community of scholars in which they could discuss, debate, and persuade others of their views. They formed professional institutions and set norms and practices to govern their profession. To hold themselves accountable, they established journals in which peer reviews of their work were published. Conferences were organized where interpretations could be debated and discussed. In such ways, the craft accepted that historical knowledge would progress through the work of a community of scholars.

Today, few, if any, historians would disagree that objective reality is an unattainable goal. None, wrote Bernard Bailyn, would be so naive as to "dream that a historian can contemplate the past from some immaculate cosmic perch, free from the prejudices, assumptions, and biases of one's own time, place, and personality; none of whom deny that facts are inert and meaningless until mobilized by an inquiring mind, and hence that all knowledge of the past is interpretive knowledge."[35] While acknowledging that their work cannot recapture the past as it actually happened, the vast majority of historians reject the skepticism of those who argue that all accounts of the past are simply individual inventions. As we trace the debate over the Hiroshima decision, we will have opportunity to see how interpretations are argued and critiqued by other historians and how that process advances historical knowledge.

[35] Bailyn, *Sometimes an Art*, p. 21.

An Argument without End

For the theologian Soren Kierkegaard, "the pure truth is for God alone. What is given to us is the pursuit of truth."[36] Similarly, the eminent Dutch historian Pieter Geyl described the search for historical "truth." Early in World War II when Europe fell to the Nazis, Geyl began thinking of the parallels between Napoleon and Hitler. Because he was under German surveillance, Geyl could not write about Hitler. Instead, he wrote a remarkable book, *Napoleon For and Against*, studying how a succession of leading French historians over more than a century had interpreted Napoleon differently. His study of the historical debates over Napoleon from his fall in 1814 down to Geyl's day found how the divergent portraits of Napoleon were influenced by the personal background of historians and their views on the political and ideological controversies of their own times – in short, the influence of the present on the past in the writing of history. Geyl wrote that the scientific method can help to establish a substantial factual basis about which historians can agree. But once the historian turns to interpretation, it is unavoidable that "the personal element [of the historian] can no longer be ruled out, that point of view which is determined by the circumstances of his time and by his own preconceptions." One should not find it disillusioning or even surprising, Geyl wrote, that there seemed no finality or agreement in viewing Napoleon's character and achievements. "No human intelligence could hope to bring together the overwhelming multiplicity of data and of

---

[36] Quoted in John Lukacs, *Remembered Past: On History, Historians, and Historical Knowledge* (Wilmington, DE: ISI Books, 2005), p. 17.

factors, of forces and of movements, and from them establish the true, one might almost say, the divine, balance.... Truth, though for God it may be One, assumes many shapes" to mere mortals. Truth would always be partial and relative. "History," Geyl concluded, "is indeed an argument without end."[37]

We will approach the decision to use the atomic bomb much as Geyl approached the historiography of Napoleon. We will see how historians' views of the Hiroshima decision have been influenced by their personal background and the political and ideological controversies of their own times. And we will find many reasons to agree with Geyl's conclusion that history is an "argument without end." That, we will discover, is the way historical knowledge progresses. From the clash of conflicting interpretations comes deeper understanding of the issues and problems, but historians' debates will not achieve ultimate truth. Historians must be committed to the pursuit of objective truth even while acknowledging that it is elusive, and that perfect objectivity is impossible.

---

[37] Pieter Geyl, *Napoleon: For and against*, translation by Olive Renier (New Haven: Yale University Press, 1949), pp. 15–16.

2

The Hiroshima Decision

Before considering the competing interpretations of the Hiroshima decision, which we will do in the succeeding chapters, we need to first provide the reader with a simple chronicle of factual details that most historians could agree upon. We begin by briefly recalling the bare outlines of the events leading up to the decision to use the atomic bomb. This will not give us an understanding of the meaning of events. That will come only when historians adopt a point of view and build an interpretation that finds a pattern of explanation. Then the debates among historians over the meaning of the facts begin. As the historian William McNeil writes,

> facts that could be established beyond all reasonable doubt [remain] trivial in the sense that they do not, in and of themselves, give meaning or intelligibility to the record of the past. A catalogue of undoubted and indubitable information, even if arranged chronologically, remains a catalogue. To become a history, facts have to be put together into a pattern that is understandable and credible.[1]

Facts do not speak for themselves. Facts are inert until historians interpret them. Certain limited aspects of the Hiroshima decision can be written in a definitive way, but

---

[1] William H. McNeill, "Mythistory, or, Truth, History, and Historians," *American Historical Review* 91, no. 1 (February 1986): 1–10.

such great transitional developments will inevitably be subject to changing times, interests, and questions. "When you go beyond factual reestablishment into the interpretation of large subjects, there is no definitive history."[2] Only with the human intellect and the historian's reflection and conceptualization do we move beyond the factual and enter the realm of knowledge and understanding. We will see that those historians dealing with the sequence of events, which we tell in this chapter, will come to a wide range of interpretations of their meaning. They will differ in a host of ways depending on what facts they choose to emphasize, the questions they ask, their generational and national perspectives, and their personal background. Before we see these differences play out in competing interpretations, let us establish the definitive facts. As we begin to narrate just the factual barebones, it is still well to remember, as the historian Lynn Hunt cautions, "facts are necessarily provisional because there is always the possibility that the discovery of evidence in the future might call today's facts into question."[3]

The Manhattan Project

On the eve of the Nazi invasion of Poland, Albert Einstein wrote a letter with the help of another Jewish émigré physicist, Leo Szilard, to President Franklin Roosevelt on August 2, 1939, describing the possible military applications of nuclear fission and its likely use by Germany. The letter engaged Roosevelt's immediate attention and led to the largest scientific-industrial

---

[2] Bailyn, *On the Teaching and Writing of History*, pp. 67–68.
[3] Hunt, *History*, p. 32.

project in history. America's decision to embark on a massive project to build an atomic bomb had little to do with Japan. In a momentous coincidence of timing, Roosevelt set the United States on a course to build an atomic bomb in the months before Pearl Harbor. He made this decision amidst the greatest secrecy. His concern was not Japan, but rather the alarming likelihood that Hitler was already pursuing the same goal. Not until late 1944 did the United States learn that the German nuclear project had made only limited progress, but by that time the US effort to make an atomic bomb known as the "Manhattan Project" had become a massive top-secret undertaking, employing as many as 150,000 people at a staggering cost of $2 billion (more than 30 billion in 2021 dollars). It absorbed a large proportion of the nation's scientific and engineering talent, including some one hundred émigré physicists who had fled Germany and Austria in the preceding years.[4]

The Manhattan Project was led by four men. There were two science administrators: Vannevar Bush, formerly dean of the MIT School of Engineering, who headed the newly formed Office of Scientific Research and Development, and James B. Conant, the president of Harvard, who came to Washington to head the National Defense Research Committee. The army was to be responsible for the project and Brigadier General Leslie R. Groves was the officer-in-charge. He was the driving force behind the operational side of the project. Groves had headed the Army Corps of

---

[4] This chapter draws on Kenneth B. Pyle, *Japan in the American Century* (Cambridge, MA: Harvard Belknap Press, 2018).

Engineers, which had just finished building the Pentagon when he was put in charge of the Manhattan Project. Less than six feet tall but almost 300 pounds, Groves was, according to his closest subordinate, "the biggest sonovabitch I've ever met in my life, but also one of the most capable individuals. He had an ego second to none, he had tireless energy ... and he was absolutely ruthless in how he approached a problem to get it done .... I hated his guts and so did everybody else."[5] Groves himself chose the complex and cerebral Robert Oppenheimer as the lead scientist in the project (Figure 2.1). These four men ran the project and overall supervision was given to the venerable Henry Stimson, Secretary of War, a man of unquestioned integrity and rectitude and a pillar of the establishment.

Roosevelt kept the critical policy decisions involved in the bomb's future use entirely in his own hands. As a consequence, careful, extended deliberation was put off and there never really was the broad attention to the important questions that so momentous an issue clearly deserved. Roosevelt pondered the bomb's use largely in solitude when time might have permitted a deep and careful assessment of the new weapon. A small circle of military and political leaders was privy to the details of the project but was not gathered by the president to consider the possible use of the weapon.

Britain shared in the details of the Manhattan Project and in a secret aide-mémoire, which even Stimson did not

---

[5] Richard Rhodes, *The Making of the Atomic Bomb* (New York: Simon & Schuster, 1986), p. 426.

Figure 2.1 General Leslie Groves and Robert Oppenheimer at Alamogordo, NM, view the base of the steel tower on which the first atomic bomb hung was tested on July 16, 1945. The intense heat of the bomb melted the tower.
Source: Bettmann/Getty Images

know of, signed by the president and Prime Minister Churchill on September 18, 1944, they agreed that "when a 'bomb' is finally available, it might perhaps, after mature consideration, be used against the Japanese, who should be warned that this bombardment will be repeated until they surrender."[6] By that time, they knew that a bomb would not be ready for use against Germany. Three days later the president summoned Vannevar Bush to the White House for talks that included the future of the atomic bomb. They had an extended conversation over whether the bomb should actually be used against the Japanese or tested and held as a threat. The two men agreed that the question should be carefully discussed, but Roosevelt also accepted Bush's argument that it could be "postponed for quite a time" because "it would be inadvisable to make a threat unless we were distinctly in a position to follow it up if necessary."[7] At the end of December 1944, Stimson and Groves informed Roosevelt that a uranium bomb, which did not require testing, would be ready by August 1, 1945, and a plutonium bomb would be ready for testing in July.[8] The aide-mémoire with Churchill

---

[6] Kort, *The Columbia Guide to Hiroshima*, p. 175.
[7] Sherwin, *A World Destroyed*, p. 123.
[8] "Until the atomic bomb could be tested, doubt would remain about its effectiveness. The world had never seen a nuclear explosion before, and estimates varied widely on how much energy would be released. Some scientists at Los Alamos continued privately to have doubts that it would work at all. There was only enough weapons-grade uranium available for one bomb, and confidence in the gun-type design was high, so on July 14, 1945, most of the uranium bomb ('Little Boy') began its trip westward to the Pacific without its design having ever been

was the only policy guideline on the use of the bomb that FDR left behind when he died on April 12, 1945, and Harry Truman knew virtually nothing of the project until he became president.

Total War: Unconditional Surrender

World War II was the most extreme example of total war that the world has ever experienced. Nations were fully mobilized for an all-out struggle. Ordinary citizens were rallied and summoned to the war effort. In the early months of the war, Roosevelt had privately determined that the war should be fought to unconditional surrender and not to a negotiated peace. Then, on January 24, 1943, in a press conference at the end of his meeting with Churchill at Casablanca, he explained to the press: "I think ... peace can come to the world only by the total elimination of German and Japanese war power.... The elimination of German, Japanese and Italian war power means the unconditional surrender by Germany, Italy and Japan"[9] (Figure 8.1).

Although none of America's foreign wars had ever been fought to unconditional surrender, Roosevelt's purpose in this policy was to galvanize public support and avoid the

> fully tested. A test of the plutonium bomb seemed vital, however, both to confirm its novel implosion design and to gather data on nuclear explosions in general. Several plutonium bombs were now 'in the pipeline' and would be available over the next few weeks and months. It was therefore decided to test one of these."

The Manhattan Project: An Interactive History (US Department of Energy)
[9] See Robert Dallek, *Franklin D. Roosevelt and American Foreign Policy, 1932–1945* (New York: Oxford University Press, 1979), pp. 374–376.

political criticisms that President Woodrow Wilson had received in World War I for his efforts to achieve "peace without victory" through an armistice and a negotiated peace. In addition, FDR wanted to hold the alliance with Stalin together by deferring likely disagreements over war settlement. Finally, he also wanted a free hand to shape a postwar American-led international order.

The American determination to achieve unconditional surrender led to the most extreme measures including the targeting of civilians to break enemy morale. Americans saw this war as a crusade against evil and so daunting was their industrial and technological capacity that they might well feel that they had no reason to compromise. By 1944, US industrial and technological capacity made the American war machine overwhelming. Nothing symbolized its prowess better than the B-29 super fortress, which came into use in the last year of the war. With a tail as tall as a three-story building, the largest propellers ever mounted on a plane, capable of flying nonstop four thousand miles, it was an "aerial battleship."[10] When Saipan fell to American troops in July 1944, the Japanese home islands came within range of the new B-29 and the firebombing of Japanese cities began.

Prior to American entry into the war, FDR had publicly called on the combatants to avoid bombing of civilians,[11]

---

[10] James M. Scott, *Black Snow: Curtis LeMay, the Firebombing of Tokyo, and the Road to the Atomic Bomb* (New York: W. W. Norton, 2022), pp. 22–23.

[11] On September 1, 1939, Roosevelt addressed an "urgent appeal to every Government which may be engaged in hostilities publicly to affirm its determination that its armed forces shall in no event, and under no

TOTAL WAR: UNCONDITIONAL SURRENDER

but by the latter part of the war, the US Air Force had changed from aiming at military targets to carpet bombing of cities. Major General Curtis LeMay, commander of the XXI Bomber Command, devised a strategy of firebombing which brought stunning results in 1945. Rather than flying at high altitudes where the jet stream could blow bombs off target, LeMay had bombers fly at low altitudes using a form of napalm to ignite fires in Japanese dwellings, which were predominantly wood. The bombing of civilians was justified by the necessity to hit military production, which was often subcontracted to small shops in civilian neighborhoods. But soon it was also legitimated as necessary to break civilian morale. On the night of March 9–10, 1945, some 300 B-29s carried out a massive bombing of Tokyo in which upward of 100,000 residents of the Japanese capital died (Figure 6.1). During the last year of the war, incendiary bombing extended to more than sixty Japanese cities, which destroyed between 40 and 90 percent of those cities and took the lives of as many as several hundred thousand Japanese civilians.

There is no record that Roosevelt had second thoughts about the expanded bombing mission. In fact, when Churchill suggested at the Yalta conference in February 1945 that it might be of "great value" if a four-power ultimatum were issued

---

circumstances, undertake the bombardment from the air of civilian populations or of unfortified cities." Bundy, *Danger and Survival*, p. 63. Roosevelt said that "Ruthless bombing from the air ... which has resulted in the maiming and in the death of thousands of defenseless men, women, and children, has sickened the hearts of every civilized man and woman, and has profoundly shocked the conscience of humanity." Dower, *Cultures of War*, p. 220.

calling on Japan to surrender unconditionally, FDR dismissed the suggestion, observing that the Japanese "would be unlikely to wake up to the true state of affairs until all of their islands had felt the full weight of air attacks."[12]

Truman and the Momentum of History

When FDR died on April 12, 1945, his own vice president knew little of the Manhattan Project. Truman had met with FDR only twice since assuming the vice presidency. Shortly after Roosevelt's death, Stimson and Groves came to the White House and briefed the new president. Stimson told Truman: "Within four months we shall in all probability have completed the most terrible weapon ever known in human history, one bomb of which could destroy a whole city."[13]

In contrast to Roosevelt, who characteristically kept his own counsel and dominated policymaking, the new president drew heavily on his advisors. Stimson asked the new president for authorization to appoint an Interim Committee to advise him on the use of the weapon. The Committee that Stimson chaired included Bush; Conant; Karl Compton, the president of MIT; and James Byrnes, soon to be Secretary of

---

[12] Dale M. Hellegers, *We, the Japanese People: World War II and the Origins of the Japanese Constitution*, 2 vols. (Stanford: Stanford University Press, 2001), vol. I, p. 87.

[13] The memorandum discussed with the president in its entirety is in Henry L. Stimson and McGeorge Bundy, *On Active Service in Peace and War* (New York: Harper, 1947), pp. 635–636.

State;[14] and a panel of several leading scientists was also brought in to advise the Committee: Oppenheimer, E. O. Lawrence, Arthur Compton, and Enrico Fermi.

The new president was caught up in a surge of breathtaking events. Allied troops swept into Germany and on May 8, after the suicide of Adolf Hitler, Germany surrendered. The battle of Okinawa began on April 1. The eighty-two-day battle was so bloody that a third of the entire Okinawan population of 450,000 people lost their lives, many at the hands of a Japanese military nominally defending them. In all, "234,000 people were killed, including 147,000 Okinawans, over 72,000 mainland Japanese, and more than 12,000 Americans. The U.S. Navy lost more men at Okinawa than in any other battle in its entire history."[15]

At this late date, at the end of May 1945, just weeks after Germany's surrender, with the invasion of the Japanese homeland imminent and with the bomb about to be tested, at last discussion of the weighty issues was about to take place. Should the Japanese be warned that the new weapon would be used against them if they did not surrender? Should there be a demonstration to impress the Japanese leaders? Should it be used against civilians, noncombatants? In a conversation with Stimson on May 29, 1945, Army Chief of Staff General George Marshall expressed concern that use against civilians would leave the United States with a burden of "opprobrium

---

[14] Also included were George Harrison, William Clayton, and Ralph Bard. Malloy, *Atomic Tragedy*, p. 210, n54.

[15] Kent E. Calder, *Embattled Garrisons: Comparative Base Politics and American Globalism* (Princeton: Princeton University Press, 2008), p. 283.

which might follow from an ill-considered employment of such force." He urged Stimson to consider that the bomb "might first be used against straight military objectives such as a large naval installation and then if no complete result was derived from the effect of that, he thought we ought to designate a number of large manufacturing areas from which the people would be warned to leave."[16]

Two days later, on May 31, the Interim Committee came to the Pentagon for a momentous meeting to discuss how the bomb should be used. There, on Conant's recommendation, it was unanimously agreed that the bomb should be employed against Japan as soon as possible and that the target should be a vital war plant employing a large number of workers and closely surrounded by workers' houses. They briefly examined and ruled out the possibility of a warning or a demonstration. Oppenheimer could not think of a sufficiently spectacular demonstration other than "a real target of built-up structures." Furthermore, "if the Japanese received a warning that such a weapon would be exploded somewhere over Japan, their aircraft might create problems that could lead to the failure of the mission. If the test were conducted on neutral ground, it was hard to believe that the 'determined and fanatical military men of Japan would be impressed'."[17] In retrospect, the Interim Committee's deliberations about the use of the bomb seem surprisingly brief.

[16] Quoted in Barton Bernstein, "Understanding the Atomic Bomb and the Japanese Surrender," in Michael J. Hogan, ed., *Hiroshima in History and Memory* (Cambridge: Cambridge University Press, 1996), p. 78.

[17] Sherwin, *A World Destroyed*, p. 208. Also, see Appendix L for text of notes from the Interim Committee meeting, pp. 295–304.

Within days of receiving the Interim Committee's recommendation that the bomb should be used on Japanese cities with no prior warning or demonstration, the president also received the recommendation of the Joint Chiefs for the invasion of Japan. Given the immense prestige of his predecessor, the new president was inclined to be faithful to Roosevelt's war goal. The goal of unconditional surrender had become deeply implanted in American public opinion and military strategy. Memories of Pearl Harbor, the bitterness of fighting, Japanese atrocities, and wartime propaganda had built overwhelming public support for nothing short of all-out victory. In his first address to a joint session of Congress only four days after becoming president, Truman asserted that "our policy will continue to be unconditional surrender" and the entire chamber rose cheering. Congress reflected the overwhelming public sentiment. In one poll undertaken on June 1, 1945, American opinion favored by 9 to 1 an uncompromising stance in favor of unconditional surrender as against a negotiated peace, even though it meant a costly invasion of the Japanese islands.[18]

It was not only the legacy of Roosevelt and his policy of unconditional surrender that carried Truman along in his early decision-making, but it was also the momentum of the massive Manhattan Project, now close to its goal, that propelled his decisions. Even though American intelligence learned in late 1944 that the Germans had not made progress on building an atomic bomb, having assumed that the war

[18] Leon V. Sigal, *Fighting to a Finish: The Politics of War Termination in the United States and Japan* (Ithaca: Cornell University Press, 1988), p. 95.

would be over before it could be achieved, the Manhattan Project could not be stopped. Many of the scientists who had worked on the project motivated by a fear that Hitler might acquire the bomb now had second thoughts. Albert Einstein later said that "If I had known that the Germans would not succeed in constructing the atom bomb, I would never have lifted a finger."[19] A group of the scientists involved signed a document known as the "Franck Report," which was delivered to Stimson and the Interim Committee, urging that a demonstration of the bomb be attempted and if it were subsequently to be used in the war that a clear warning be issued. Their effort, however, made no headway in the rush of events.

A targeting committee had been choosing cities where the use of the first available bombs would make their greatest impact. Kyoto, which was Groves' favored target, was eliminated on the insistence of Stimson, leaving Hiroshima, Kokura, and Niigata. Nagasaki was added after Kyoto's elimination.

Potsdam

In July 1945, Stalin, Churchill, and Truman met at Potsdam, outside of Berlin, in the last of the "Big Three" wartime conferences, to discuss the contentious issues of Russian occupation of Eastern Europe as well as how to bring the war in the Pacific to an end (Figure 4.1). The planned invasion

---

[19] Quoted in Michael Walzer, *Just and Unjust Wars: A Moral Argument with Historical Illustrations* (New York: Basic Books, 1977), p. 263.

of Japan made Russian help essential. Truman was intent on ensuring that Stalin, who had signed a neutrality pact with Japan in 1941, would deliver on his earlier promise to Roosevelt that he would enter the war against Japan approximately three months after the war ended in Europe. In return, Roosevelt had agreed that Russia would be compensated with the restoration of the rights in Northeast Asia, which it had lost in the Russo-Japanese War. Stalin was now ready to break the neutrality pact with Japan and seize the territorial gains Roosevelt had promised him. He assured Truman of his intention to enter the war and the president wrote in his diary "fini Japs when that comes about" and to his wife, "I've gotten what I came for."[20]

While the Big Three were at Potsdam, Truman received word of the successful testing of the plutonium bomb at Alamogordo in the desert of New Mexico on July 16 and, as Churchill noted, the president was greatly energized by the news. Truman recorded in his diary: "Believe Japs will fold before Russia comes in. I am sure they will when Manhattan appears over their homeland."[21] At a break in their meetings, he casually mentioned to Stalin that the United States had developed a highly destructive new weapon and Stalin seemed indifferent, but we now know that

---

[20] Wilson D. Miscamble, *The Most Controversial Decision: Truman, the Atomic Bombs, and the Defeat of Japan* (Cambridge: Cambridge University Press, 2011), pp. 59–60.

[21] David Holloway, "Jockeying for Position in the Postwar World: Soviet Entry into the War with Japan in August 1945," in Tsuyoshi Hasegawa, ed., *The End of the Pacific War: Reappraisals* (Stanford: Stanford University Press, 2007), pp. 171–172.

he was fully aware from Soviet espionage precisely what the president was telling him.[22]

On July 26, Truman authorized the Potsdam Declaration, which he, Churchill, and Chiang Kai-shek (who was not present) signed. With the bomb successfully tested, Truman and his advisors were losing interest in Russia's joining in the war. Stimson had urged the president to have Stalin sign the Declaration. Stimson thought that the impact of the Soviet signature, indicating its breaking of the neutrality pact and impending entry into the war together with reference to a willingness to accept retention of the imperial institution, would offer the Japanese strong motivation to accept surrender terms. Churchill, as well, suggested that modification of terms might avert the need to invade and suffer massive casualties.[23]

His new Secretary of State James Byrnes, however, persuaded Truman not to soften the unconditional surrender policy and not to include the Russians in the Declaration. Stalin was not asked to sign it, although he had come to Potsdam with a draft of such a joint statement, which he had been led to expect he would sign, demanding Japanese surrender. He wanted such a statement since if rejected it would provide pretext for breaking the neutrality pact with Japan and going to war to recover territory lost in the Russo-Japanese War and the strategic positions he sought for future security.

---

[22] Tsuyoshi Hasegawa, *Racing the Enemy: Stalin, Truman, and the Surrender of Japan* (Cambridge: Harvard University Press, 2005), pp. 154–155.

[23] Winston S. Churchill, *The Second World War: Volume 6, Triumph and Tragedy* (Boston: Houghton Mifflin, 1953), p. 642.

The Potsdam Declaration, issued as a public proclamation, called on Japan to surrender unconditionally or face prompt and utter destruction.[24] The Allies would occupy Japan to disarm it and establish a new order in accord with the freely expressed will of the Japanese people. There were three significant omissions: it made no mention of the bomb, or of Russia's impending entry, or of the fate of the emperor. Truman and Byrnes decided that it was politically unacceptable to abandon the policy of unconditional surrender. Byrnes advised the president that there would be terrible "political repercussions," and that the president would be "crucified" by public opinion and accused of appeasement.[25]

Even before authorizing the Potsdam Declaration, Truman had given verbal approval to the military on July 24 to move ahead with plans to use the atomic bomb, apparently with the understanding that he could rescind the order if the Japanese accepted the ultimatum. Truman wrote in his diary on July 25 that the bomb would be used against Japan "between now and August 10th" and "the target will be a purely military one and we will issue a warning statement asking the Japanese to surrender and save lives. I'm sure they will not do that, but we will have given them the chance."[26]

---

[24] The Potsdam Declaration is sometimes also referred to as the "Potsdam Proclamation."

[25] Miscamble, *The Most Controversial Decision*, p. 101. See also Sigal, *Fighting to a Finish*, p. 128; Malloy, *Atomic Tragedy*, p. 130.

[26] Hasegawa, *Racing the Enemy*, p. 159. See also Barton J. Bernstein, "Writing, Righting, or Wronging the Historical Record: President Truman's Letter on His Atomic-Bomb Decision," *Diplomatic History* 16, no. 1 (Winter 1992): 163–173.

Having already verbally given his approval of its use before the issuance of the Potsdam Declaration, he largely ceded control of the bomb and its use to the military.

Japan's *Ketsugō* Strategy

After the fall of Saipan in July 1944, bringing the homeland within range of the new B-29 bombers, the cabinet headed by Tōjō Hideki resigned, and a new weak and uncertain government faced mounting difficulties. In October, the epic battle of Leyte Gulf, the biggest naval engagement in history, ended in the destruction of the Japanese carrier fleet, and "the once mighty Japanese navy would never again play an important role in the Pacific War."[27] The remaining Japanese holdings in Southeast Asia were effectively cut off from the homeland. Desperation gripped the Japanese leadership. It was not simply the rapidly deteriorating military situation that caused despair. Rather it was increasingly the "domestic situation." The leadership was apprehensive over the growing unrest at home brought on by wartime controls, the shortage of food, and the devastation caused by American carpet bombing of the cities. The records of the time are replete with references to the unrest and disaffection of ordinary Japanese. In these circumstances, an imposing group of conservative civilian leaders signed a memorial to the emperor urging surrender.

---

[27] Alvin D. Coox, "The Pacific War," in Peter Duus, ed., *The Cambridge History of Japan: Volume 6, The Twentieth Century* (Cambridge: Cambridge University Press, 1988), p. 364.

Their goal was to preserve the imperial reign in the homeland or what was simply known as the "national polity" or *kokutai*.

The emperor, however, chose to side with the army's determination to continue fighting and on April 5 he approved the appointment of the aging Admiral Suzuki Kantarō, his former grand chamberlain, to lead the government. Decision-making was now placed in a Supreme War Council made up of the prime minister, foreign minister, ministers of war and navy, and the chiefs of staff of the army and navy. Known as the Big Six, they would make decisions by unanimous vote, occasionally meeting in the presence of the emperor. Within the Big Six, Prime Minister Suzuki, the foreign minister, and the naval minister were inclined toward finding a way out of the war, while the other three sided with the army's defensive strategy, known as *ketsugō* ("decisive operation"). *Ketsugō* was a comprehensive battle plan to defend the homeland. It included a massive mobilization of troops rushed home from the continent, the preparation of suicide attacks, and the training of the civilian population to join in the decisive battle with the invaders. The expectation was that it would be so costly in casualties that the Allies would be compelled to negotiate a settlement. The Japanese belief that they could sap the will of the Americans for a prolonged war and bring about a negotiated settlement had been a part of the military's strategy from the outset of the war, but by 1945, with allied invasion imminent, it had come to focus on a decisive battle in defense of the homeland.

These circumstances of a deadlock in the Big Six led the peace party down a strange and unlikely path. They turned to the Soviet Union, with which Japan still had a neutrality treaty, to request its help in mediating a negotiated settlement. Foreign Minister Tōgō Shigenori recalled: "Had we not approached the Soviet Union, we would clearly have had to accept the terms of unconditional surrender. Only through Soviet mediation could we expect to turn unconditional surrender into conditional surrender."[28] On June 22, the day that Okinawa fell, the emperor sanctioned a direct approach to Moscow, even though the Soviet foreign minister had notified the Japanese government on April 5 that it would not renew the neutrality pact when it was due to expire a year hence. That fact alone should have discouraged an approach to Moscow. Ambassador Satō Naotake in Moscow was unambiguous in discouraging the approach, informing Foreign Minister Tōgō that it was unimaginable that Moscow would help in such an effort. Satō was extraordinarily direct in his criticism of the attempt, especially since Tokyo had been unable to come to any agreement on acceptable peace terms. The Japanese were banking on the tensions between the Soviets and the Anglo-American powers to aid in their effort. The hope was that Moscow might be detached from the Allied side, persuaded to maintain its neutrality, recompensed with territorial concessions in the Chinese northeast, and induced to mediate a peace that would leave Japan intact. Moreover, the army was willing to accept this one diplomatic strategy while still maintaining its own *ketsugō* strategy. It was a measure of Japanese desperation that civilian leadership, with the support of the emperor and the wary acquiescence of the military, hoped the Soviets might provide an alternative to unconditional surrender.

---

[28] Hasegawa, *Racing*, p. 110.

Hiroshima and Nagasaki

Having broken both the civilian and military codes of the Japanese, Washington was aware of the massive Japanese buildup for an Armageddon-like battle against the invasion as well as the attempt to persuade Moscow to mediate. When the Potsdam Declaration was broadcast, Prime Minister Suzuki, perhaps regarding the broadcast as propaganda, said that Japan would ignore it, using the word *mokusatsu*, literally meaning to kill by silence, which was interpreted in Washington as rejection. On August 6, the uranium bomb, nicknamed "Little Boy," was dropped at 8:15 a.m. on the center of Hiroshima, a major depot of the Japanese army. Some 80,000 people are estimated to have died at once and perhaps nearly that same number died later from radiation sickness and other injuries by the end of the year. On August 8, Russia entered the war and the Red Army swarmed into Manchuria, routing the Japanese army there and then moving down the Korean peninsula. Some 700,000 Japanese were taken as prisoners back to Russia where most were held in gulags, doing forced labor for years.[29] Stalin pressed his generals to move at top speed to seize all the spoils he had been promised at Yalta. Additionally, Stalin hoped to occupy Hokkaido.

On August 9 at 11:02 a.m. a plutonium bomb, nicknamed "Fat Man," was dropped on Nagasaki, home of the Mitsubishi shipyards, killing an estimated 38,000 people, and

---

[29] See Andrew Barshay, *The Gods Left First: The Captivity and Repatriation of Japanese POWs in Northeast Asia, 1945–1956* (Berkeley: University of California Press, 2013).

approximately that many more died by the end of the year. Kokura had been the intended target but was under cloud cover. Nagasaki was the backup target for the second bomb. Rather than wait for Japanese reaction to the first bomb, General Groves had decided that hitting a second city swiftly would maximize the psychological impact. This decision was left to the military. In all, a great many more than 200,000 died from the two horrific bombs. Moreover, the Air Force was preparing a list of several other cities for targeting as the atomic bombs became available.[30]

In the face of such utter disaster, an emergency meeting of the Supreme War Council was convened in the palace. The emperor in unprecedented action broke the deadlock among the Big Six on August 10 and expressed his will that the war be ended on the terms set forth by the Potsdam Declaration, with the sole reservation that the prerogatives of the emperor as sovereign ruler not be compromised. When the Americans received this response, Secretary of State Byrnes wanted to reject it and adhere to the unconditional surrender policy but, in the end, Truman sent an ambiguous reply stating that the emperor would be "subject to the Supreme Commander of the Allied Powers" and "the ultimate form of government of Japan shall be established by the freely expressed will of the Japanese people." Truman in the meantime ordered that there be no more use of the bomb without his permission, telling his Cabinet, as one member recorded, that "the thought of wiping out another 100,000 people was too horrible. He didn't like the idea of

---

[30] Michael D. Gordin, *Five Days in August: How World War II Became a Nuclear War* (Princeton: Princeton University Press, 2007), pp. 98–100.

killing, as he said, 'all those kids.'"³¹ In a second palace meeting with the Supreme War Council on August 14, the emperor insisted on accepting the reply from Washington. The next day at noon, in a recording of his Imperial Rescript calling on his people to "endure the unendurable," he announced acceptance of the Potsdam Declaration. Two days later in a second Imperial Rescript he called on the Japanese armed forces throughout Asia to peacefully surrender and lay down their arms. Both Rescripts were almost universally accepted by the people and the military.

Within days, American forces began landing in Japan to begin the occupation led by General Douglas MacArthur, the Supreme Commander of the Allied Powers appointed by the president. On September 2, 1945, the official surrender ceremony was held aboard the battleship USS *Missouri* anchored in Tokyo Bay. Soviet troops nevertheless continued fighting for two weeks to expand their control in the northern islands.

Interpreting the Facts

Having laid out the bare-bones facts of the events leading up to the use of the atomic bomb, we are ready to examine some of the major interpretations that historians have made of those facts and the details that they brought to bear. The interpretation of these events has engaged countless historians. We cannot discuss the entire corpus of interpretive

---

[31] Secretary of Commerce Henry Wallace recorded this in his diary. See Henry A. Wallace, *The Price of Vision: The Diary of Henry A, Wallace, 1942–1946* (Boston: Houghton Mifflin, 1973), p. 474.

work. Our purpose is to provide the anatomy of the contentious debates. What are the important fault lines in the controversy? What are its primary issues? Moreover, we can explore what the debates reveal about the nature of the historians' methods. What has influenced them to look at the same events and see them in a different way? In the following chapters we will see how professional historians seek to persuade others of their interpretations of the Hiroshima decision. The competing and discordant ways that the facts were interpreted will allow us to explore the nature of the historian's craft as it engages one of the most contentious issues in modern history.

3

Participants and Their First Draft of History

The participants in making the decision to use the atomic bombs on Hiroshima and Nagasaki were from a human point of view what people might consider "the best and brightest." They included the presidents of Harvard and MIT, four Nobel Prize-winning scientists, the highly admired army chief of staff, and the secretary of war, who was America's revered and longest-serving public servant. There were also seasoned politicians, including the president of the United States and Secretary of State. A rarely noted fact is that there were no women involved. In all aspects of the decision, there were only men. Perhaps that is taken for granted since at that time there were relatively few women in leadership of government or in science.[1]

One extraordinary Japanese *hibakusha* (atomic bomb survivor) later implied that the presence of women in decision-making could have made a difference. Yamaguchi Tsutomu, depending on how you look at it, was "either the

---

[1] There were hundreds of women who worked in staff positions as scientists, mathematicians, engineers, and technicians in the Manhattan Project. See Caroline C. Herzberg and Ruth H. Howes, *Their Day in the Sun: Women of the Manhattan Project* (Philadelphia: Temple University Press, 2003); see also "Women Scientists in the Manhattan Project," www.atomicheritage.org/women-scientists-manhattan-project.

world's luckiest man or the world's unluckiest man."[2] He survived the atomic blast in Hiroshima, but then in an unfortunate choice fled to Nagasaki. He survived that blast as well and lived another sixty-five years, passing away in 2010 at the age of ninety-three. A man who survived the only two nuclear strikes in history deserves our respectful attention, and before he died, he offered a prescription for peace in the nuclear age: "The only people who should be allowed to govern countries with nuclear weapons are mothers, those who are still breast-feeding their babies."[3] Only nursing mothers should command nuclear forces. They should be – Yamaguchi would have said they should have been – the participants in such decisions, not an elite, not the so-called best and brightest.

Securing Their Place in History

Makers of history want historians to treat them favorably. Those who wield power often wish to influence the way in which history will view them. They are concerned about securing their place in history. Participants in historic events hope their reputations will remain intact when they are gone. I am bemused when I hear politicians express concern about securing their place in history – as though historians come to

---

[2] Richard Lloyd Parry, "The Luckiest or Unluckiest Man in the World? Tsutomu Yamaguchi, Double A-bomb Victim," *London Times*, March 25, 2009.

[3] See Steven Pinker, *The Better Angels of Our Nature: Why Violence Has Declined* (New York: Penguin Books, 2012), p. 684. See also D. Garner, "After Atom Bomb's Shock, the Real Horrors Began Unfolding," *New York Times*, January 20, 2010.

final conclusive judgments that represent "the judgments of history." The judgments of historians are not fixed. Their work is always subject to debate and revision. Nothing demonstrates this better, as we shall see, than the controversy and diverging explanations of historians about the Hiroshima decision. Still, failing to realize this reality, politicians often go to great lengths to try to shape "the verdict of history." Participants in controversial history-making events are particularly sensitive to how they will be remembered for their part in the events. Henry Kissinger was a pro when it came to self-vindication as he admitted in the first volume of his memoirs: "By a selective presentation of documents one can prove almost anything.... The participant in great events is of course not immune to these tendencies when he writes his account. Obviously, his perspective will be affected by his own involvement; the impulse to explain merges with the impulse to defend."[4] Participants want to explain their motives and recount why they acted as they did. They may write memoirs, give interviews, even withhold evidence, or in some other way try to influence history's judgments. They may hope to suppress unfavorable details of events by classifying documents, limiting access to archives, and selective publication of archives.[5] In the waning days of Donald Trump's presidency, the historian Jill Lepore speculated as to what lengths he would go to try to control history. She described how past American presidents had often sought to control their papers, limiting access to their archives, and suppressing evidence

---

[4] Henry Kissinger, *White House Years* (Boston: Little, Brown, 1979), p. xxii.
[5] See Woodward, *American Attitudes toward History*, pp. 17–18.

unfavorable to them.⁶ Might Trump do the same? The answer proved to be "yes."

Churchill is famously said to have quipped: "History will treat me kindly because I propose to write it."⁷ Churchill was extraordinarily successful in writing an influential version of his life and times, giving it his own spin. Still, his was only a first draft of history. Inevitably, historians must grapple with the records, the diaries and letters, the memoirs, and writings of participants in major historical events. From these documents, historians try to reconstruct the motivations and inner thoughts of participants. Historians cannot take such remembrances at face value. The historian Barton Bernstein puts it well when he writes that such memoirs and remembrances

> become a way of reconstructing events, of refurbishing reputations, of turning defeats into victories, of concealing ugly matters, of giving new reasons for old decisions, of blaming others for past mistakes, and even of claiming remarkable prescience. Memoirists, like others, succumb to the frequent, all-too-human desire to rewrite their own past. Most of us have some need to claim victories that originally went unwon, to recall wise counsel ("I told you

---

[6] Jill Lepore, "Will Trump Burn the Evidence?" *New Yorker*, November 16, 2020.

[7] Quoted in Gaddis, *Landscape of History*, p. 137. His actual statement was, "For my part, I consider that it will be found much better by all Parties to leave the past to history, especially as I propose to write that history." Speech in the House of Commons (January 23, 1948; cited in Fred R. Shapiro, ed., *The Yale Book of Quotations*, (New Haven, CT: Yale University Press, 2006), p. 154.

so") that after the event we claim, incorrectly, to have given much earlier.[8]

There are many reasons why the reliability of firsthand accounts of events must be subjected to careful assessment. Legal scholars have told us how eyewitness testimony is notoriously unreliable. The famous *Rashomon* film, which we mentioned in Chapter 1, illustrates the problem of multiple conflicting yet equally plausible versions of events that humans can have. Some view the so-called *Rashomon* effect as demonstrating the relativism of knowledge or the unknowability of truth: There is no truth, only subjective perception of events. For the film's brilliant director, Kurosawa Akira, the issue is simpler. It is self-advocacy. His film, he wrote, was a parable on the addiction of humans to dishonesty.

> Human beings are unable to be honest with themselves about themselves. They cannot talk about themselves without embellishing. The script portrays such human beings – the kind who cannot survive without lies to make them feel they are better people than they really are. . . . Egoism is a sin the human being carries with him from birth; it is the most difficult to redeem.[9]

Another reason why firsthand accounts must be examined carefully is that memory can be faulty. Social psychologists have produced studies of the unreliability of the memory.

---

[8] Barton J. Bernstein, "Ike and Hiroshima: Did He Oppose It?" *Journal of Strategic Studies* 10, no. 3 (July 1987): 384.

[9] Akira Kurosawa, *Something like an Autobiography* (New York: Vintage, 1983), p. 183.

When Dean Acheson, the former Secretary of State, was writing his memoirs, he is said to have called a former colleague to confirm his memory of a particularly important meeting. His colleague confirmed all the details Acheson remembered of the meeting, except one: Acheson wasn't there.[10]

Participants' Wariness of Historians

It is often said that journalists provide the first draft of history. But in the case of the Hiroshima decision, it was the participants in the decision-making whose writings set the baseline for the future. Leaders of the Manhattan Project went to great lengths to explain and justify their motives and to recount why they acted as they did. Their efforts amounted to a first draft of history which endured for decades. Indeed, theirs may be one of the most successful efforts that one can find of decision-makers framing a lasting historical interpretation of their own activities. Acutely conscious of the history-making events they had overseen, knowing the likelihood of controversy, and aware that historians would be rendering interpretations that might be harshly unfavorable, they took the initiative to influence the public memory. Having made history, they were determined to write it. They would shape the first draft of history to justify their part.

The participants in the Hiroshima decision were distrustful of how historians might interpret their actions. They

[10] Cohen, *Making History*, p. 565.

Figure 3.1 James Conant (center front) with other leading scientists involved in the Manhattan Project (left to right): Ernest O. Lawrence, Arthur H. Compton, Vannevar Bush, Conant, Karl T. Compton, and Alfred L. Loomis at the University of California, Berkeley, in 1940.
Source: Gado Images/Alamy

were particularly concerned that historians would reach damaging moral judgments of their decision which would poison the minds of the next generation. Harvard President James Conant (Figure 3.1), one of the most significant figures in promoting and overseeing the making of the bomb and in deciding how it was to be used, wrote to a friend, regarding such moral concerns: "This type of sentimentalism, for so I regard it, is bound to have a great deal of influence on the next generation. The type of person who goes in to teaching, particularly school teaching, will be influenced a great deal by this type of [sentimental] argument."[11]

Secretary of War Henry Stimson, who wrote the participants' principal defense of the Hiroshima decision, was of the same mind as Conant. He confessed to President Truman that his written defense was intended "to satisfy the doubts of that rather difficult class of the community which will have charge of the education of the next generation, namely educators and historians."[12] Stimson worried that issues of the morality of the use of the bomb would arise in the future and that historians would misinterpret his intentions. He had doubts about historians' achieving objective truth. As he wrote in his memoirs *On Active Service in Peace and War* in 1948: "History is often not what happened but what is recorded as such."[13] He was of course right. Eventually historians do take over and, as John Lewis Gaddis writes, "replace altogether the firsthand memories people have of the events through which they've lived. Historical knowledge submerges participants' knowledge of what took place."[14] In time, the firsthand memory of the decision-makers would be replaced by the judgments and interpretations of historians. Perhaps in calling historians a "difficult class of the community," Stimson was thinking that they would impose their own biases in reconstructing the events. He had a point. How could they know what happened? They weren't there. They

---

[11] James G. Hershberg, *James B. Conant: Harvard to Hiroshima and the Making of the Nuclear Age* (New York: Knopf, 1993), p. 293–294.
[12] Hershberg, *James B., Conant: Harvard to Hiroshima*, p. 300.
[13] Stimson and Bundy, *On Active Service*, p. xi.
[14] Gaddis, *Landscape*, pp.136–137.

could never know the uncertainties of the time. How easy and safe it would be for historians writing at their desks, giving lectures in their classrooms, to simplify events. They knew how things turned out. They had the benefit of hindsight.

Preempting the "Difficult Class of the Community"

Anxious about how their decision to use the atomic bomb would be viewed in the future, leaders of the Manhattan Project set out to preempt the judgment of historians. It is remarkable how durable the Hiroshima decision-makers' version of history became. Perhaps, as we shall see, its durability was tied to the way in which it supported what Americans wanted to believe about themselves and their country. In the months after the end of the war, Americans celebrated the defeat of fascism. American power in the world was at its height and it should be no surprise that Americans reveled in their accomplishments. A war fought to change the world had been won and Americans were ready to remake the world in their own image. Public opinion polls recorded overwhelming support for the use of the bomb to save the American lives that would have been lost in an invasion. The tide of public opinion for a time submerged doubters of the decision to use the atomic bomb.

But the euphoria was short-lived. Realization that the world was changed forever with the advent of the new weapon soon set in. Celebration of the biggest scientific project in human history gave way to a rising wave of second thoughts. Many scientists who had been part of the Manhattan Project expressed deep regrets and often outrage that their work had led to its tragic use against civilians. The science administrators themselves often privately struggled with remorse and self-doubt. Robert Oppenheimer's reaction to the success of the Alamogordo test was memorable. He thought of lines from the Hindu scripture the *Bhagavad Gita*: "Now I am become death, the destroyer of worlds."[15] The following year, Oppenheimer wrote in the *Bulletin of the Atomic Scientists*: "Every American knows that if there is another major war atomic weapons will be used." He went on to explain that "[w]e know this because in the last war, the two nations which we like to think are the most enlightened and humane in the world – Great Britain and the United States – used atomic weapons against an enemy which was essentially defeated."[16]

Oppenheimer met with Truman in the Oval Office on October 25, 1945, weeks after the end of the war. It was a remarkable encounter of the scientist who oversaw the making of this terrible weapon and the politician who used it and opened a new era in human history. Oppenheimer spoke of his anguish over Hiroshima and Nagasaki. "Mr. President," he said, "I feel I have blood on my hands." Truman, taken aback, assured him: No, it was his responsibility, not Oppenheimer's. After an awkward silence, the president ended the meeting. Truman privately called Oppenheimer a "cry-baby scientist" and told an associate, "I don't want to see that son-of-a-bitch in this office ever again."

---

[15] Kai Bird and Martin J. Sherwin, *American Prometheus: The Triumph and Tragedy of J. Robert Oppenheimer* (New York: Vintage, 2006), p. 309.
[16] Bird and Sherwin, *American Prometheus*, p.348.

The president, with his own troubled thoughts, believed that Oppenheimer "hasn't half as much blood on his hands as I have. You just don't go around bellyaching about it." Oppenheimer had touched a raw nerve and the memory of the meeting stayed with the irritated Truman, who was known to occasionally embellish accounts of his response, as, for example, the president pulling a handkerchief from his breast pocket and telling Oppenheimer "Well, here would you like to wash your hands?"[17]

Some years later Winston Churchill at a formal dinner with Truman brought the subject up in a jocular (and utterly inappropriate) fashion, asking the president if he had prepared an explanation for the time when both stood before Saint Peter and were asked to account for having dropped the atomic bombs on Japan. Someone else at the dinner, sensing the delicate topic for the president, quickly changed the discussion before Truman could respond.[18]

No one of the Manhattan Project leaders was more conflicted, even "haunted," by his role in creating the new weapon than Conant.[19] When he returned to his position as president of Harvard in the fall of 1945, he was a deeply troubled man. Jennet Conant in her biography of her grandfather recorded the fear he felt over "his Frankenstein creation."[20] The responsibility for the bomb weighed heavily

---

[17] Bird and Sherwin, *American Prometheus*, p. 332.
[18] Dean Acheson, *Present at the Creation: My Years in the State Department* (New York: W. W. Norton, 1969), pp. 715–716.
[19] Hershberg, *Conant*, p. 752.
[20] Jennet Conant, *Man of the Hour: James B. Conant, Warrior Scientist* (New York: Simon & Schuster, 2017), p. 348.

on him. Whether it was thoughts of his reputation or his guilt over the role he had played or a combination of both, we cannot know, but his usual calm, unemotional exterior now masked profound misgivings. We do know that he was fearful of the atomic future. In September he summoned the head of the Harvard libraries to his office with an odd proposal. Fearful that a future world war would bring the end of civilization, he told the startled librarian that he thought it advisable "to select the printed material that would preserve a record of our civilization for one we can hope will follow, microfilming it and making perhaps ten copies, and burying these in ten different places throughout the country." Would the librarian, Conant asked, recommend what would be required to preserve the record of our civilization? How could we keep evidence of our literature, philosophy, fine arts, and other achievements? The librarian, shaken by the extraordinary request, privately thought Harvard's president had "temporarily lost his bearings." When he returned to Conant two weeks later, he advised him against such a project, which would be a monumental task and might create public alarm.[21]

Conant dropped his idea of preserving a record of human civilization and turned to his more immediate concern. How should the momentous events of the building of the bomb and its use on Hiroshima and Nagasaki be explained for posterity? How could it be justified? How could future generations appreciate the need to use this terrible weapon against Japan? As public criticism and doubts

---

[21] Conant, *Man of the Hour*, pp. 348-349.

mounted in various quarters in the year after Japanese surrender, it was Conant more than anyone else who took the lead in organizing a defense of the Hiroshima decision and arranging a self-vindicating first draft of its history.

Moral objections to the use of the new weapon were widely expressed. The Vatican as well as the leading American Catholic press were critical of the decision. "The name Hiroshima, the name Nagasaki," declared *Commonweal*, "are names for American guilt and shame."[22] The Protestant response was especially galling to Conant. On March 6, 1946, a blue-ribbon panel of the Federal Council of Churches published a report in which Reinhold Niebuhr and twenty-one other Protestant leaders condemned the atomic bombings as "morally indefensible." Regardless of whether the war had been shortened, the theologians said, by using the bomb without issuing a warning, the United States had acted irresponsibly and had "sinned grievously against the law of God and against the people of Japan." Conant, who had greatly admired Niebuhr for his prewar opposition to isolationism and his cerebral Christian realism, was stung by these words and fired off a letter to Niebuhr telling him that the decision to use the bomb was "part and parcel" of the war effort and "it made no sense to condemn the A-bomb as morally more egregious than strategic bombing." Niebuhr responded that, although it was America's "first task" to win the war, there was a need to "establish moral checks upon its power lusts" and inculcate "self-criticism ... informed by the humble realization of the fact that the possession of great power is

---

[22] Bird and Lifschultz, *Hiroshima's Shadow*, p. 245.

a temptation to injustice for any nation."[23] Niebuhr concluded: "We would have been in a stronger moral position had we published the facts about this instrument of destruction, made a demonstration of its effects over Japan in a nonpopulated area, and threatened the use of the bomb if the Japanese did not surrender."[24]

What further alarmed Conant and other leaders of the Manhattan Project was the astonishing public reaction generated by an essay in the sophisticated, highbrow *New Yorker* magazine by the young journalist John Hersey (Figure 3.2). The *New Yorker* gave over its entire August 1946 issue to his essay. It was an immediate sensation. Reprinted as a book, simply entitled *Hiroshima*, it became a runaway bestseller. It brought the horror of ground zero home to the American public and the sober reality of the cruel suffering wrought on civilians. In the first weeks of the Occupation, several war correspondents had managed to evade MacArthur's controls to report briefly on conditions in Hiroshima and Nagasaki. Wilfred Burchett, an Australian journalist, filed a story that spoke of a plague still sickening inhabitants.[25] The reference was to radiation sickness that General Groves and MacArthur's officials denied. But it was Hersey who came months later and was able to write the lengthy account that gained world attention to the plight of survivors.

[23] Hershberg, *Conant*, p. 285.
[24] Barton J. Bernstein, "Seizing the Contested Terrain of Early Nuclear History: Stimson, Conant, and Their Allies Explain the Decision to Use the Atomic Bomb," *Diplomatic History* 17, no. 1 (Winter 1993): 38–39.
[25] Wilfred Burchett, *Shadows of Hiroshima* (London: Verso, 1983).

Figure 3.2 War correspondent John Hersey, author of the bestselling *Hiroshima* (1946), which described the suffering of the bomb's victims.
Source: Bettmann/Getty Images

Hersey, born in China to missionary parents, was thirty-two when his essay appeared. He had been a war correspondent writing for *Time* and *Life* magazines and won the Pulitzer Prize in 1944 for his novel *A Bell for Adono* about a Sicilian village occupied by the Americans. Having such fame, his next writings were bound to gain immediate notice. In the spring of 1946, he went to Hiroshima to write a firsthand account of experiences of the bomb survivors – the Japanese called them *hibakusha*. Hersey sought to humanize the *hibakusha* after years of wartime propaganda dehumanizing the Japanese enemy. Bringing to journalism the techniques of a novelist, he allowed the victims of the bomb to speak for themselves. He placed them in their quotidian activities in the hours before "a busy city of two hundred and forty-five thousand that morning [was reduced] to a mere pattern of residue in the afternoon."[26] He chose six Hiroshima residents with whom Americans might readily identify: two doctors, a Japanese Methodist minister, a German Jesuit missionary, a secretary, and a widowed seamstress. "At exactly fifteen minutes past eight in the morning, on August 6, 1945, Japanese time," Hersey's narrative began, "at the moment when the atomic bomb flashed above Hiroshima, Miss Toshiko Sasaki, a clerk in the personnel department of the East Asia Tin Works, had just sat down at her place in the plant office and was turning her head to speak to the girl at the next desk."[27] Hersey described the horrific suffering of residents in unsparing graphic detail: "Their faces were wholly burned, their eye sockets were hollow, the fluid from their melted eyes had run down their cheeks. (They must have had their faces upturned when the bomb went off; perhaps they were anti-aircraft personnel.) Their mouths were mere swollen, pus-covered wounds, which they could not bear to stretch enough to admit the spout of the teapot."[28] Hersey also described the shocking effects of radiation poisoning, which were not generally known. Even the lead scientists, including Oppenheimer, had vastly underestimated the effects of this danger. In a May 1945 memo, he had written that radiation

---

[26] John Whittier Treat, *Writing Ground Zero: Japanese Literature and the Atomic Bomb* (Chicago, IL: University of Chicago Press, 1995), p. 56.
[27] John Hersey, *Hiroshima* (New York: Vintage ed, 1989), p. 1.
[28] Hersey, *Hiroshima*, pp. 51–52.

would be "injurious within a radius of a mile and lethal within a radius of about six-tenths of a mile."[29]

Hersey did not directly give his own view of the morality of the use of the bomb, but at the end of the essay left it to a Jesuit priest to express it in a letter sent to the Vatican asking guidance for answers to his questions. "The crux of the matter," the priest wrote, "is whether total war in its present form is justifiable, even when it serves a just purpose. Does it not have material and spiritual evil as its consequences which far exceed whatever good might result? When will our moralists give us a clear answer to this question?"[30]

Hersey's essay was journalism with the flair of a novelist and as such it captivated readers with its vividness and immediacy. His colleagues called it "a radically new form of journalism" and the "first nonfiction novel."[31] By recording the reactions and experiences of the first victims of the bomb, Hersey was providing a journalist's first draft of history. To describe the popular reaction in today's terms, Hersey's essay "went viral." The issue sold out immediately. Albert Einstein wanted a thousand copies to send to scientists. The essay was

---

[29] Conant, *Man of the Hour*, p. 377. See also Susan Southard, *Nagasaki: Life after Nuclear War* (New York: Penguin, 2015), p. 107.

[30] Hersey, *Hiroshima*, pp. 89–90.

[31] Nicholas Lemann, "John Hersey and the Art of Fact," *New Yorker*, April 22, 2019. See also Russell Short, "John Hersey: The Writer Who Let 'Hiroshima' Speak for Itself," *New Yorker*, August 31, 2016; Dan Gerstle, "John Hersey and Hiroshima," *Dissent* 59, no.2 (Spring 2012); Michael J. Yavenditti, "John Hersey and the American Conscience: The Reception of 'Hiroshima'," *Pacific Historical Review* 43, no. 1 (February 1974): 24–49; Lesley M. M. Blume, *Fallout: The Hiroshima Cover-up and the Reporter Who Revealed It to the World* (New York: Simon & Schuster, 2020).

excerpted in newspapers, widely discussed on radio, and when it was printed in book form under the simple title *Hiroshima*, it sold millions of copies.

Agitated by the rising hue and cry, Conant wrote to his wartime colleague Harvey Bundy, who had been Stimson's wartime aide, urging that Stimson write an explanation of the decision. Expressing concern that the reaction was coming not just from the "professional pacifists and ... certain religious leaders," not just from "verbally-minded" academics and repentant scientists but now increasingly from the general public, his letter worried that the result would be "a distortion of history." Conant wrote that there needed to be, as his biographer put it, "an aggressive public relations offensive."[32] Intent on staking out moral high ground while shaping the judgment of posterity, Conant, always confident in his own judgment and dogged in his determination, at once became the moving force behind such an offensive. What motivated Conant in organizing a "media blitz" were painful thoughts of his role in the use of the horrific weapon. Jennet Conant in her biography of her grandfather concluded that his "insistence that he felt no guilt for the bombings – suggests that he doth protest too much, that he was perhaps a man in desperate search of vindication."[33]

To quiet the growing doubts about the use of the bomb, Conant approached two leaders of the Manhattan Project whose views he thought would carry great weight in the public discourse. He engaged Karl Compton, the long-time

---

[32] Conant, *Man of the Hour,* p. 384.
[33] Conant, *Man of the Hour,* pp. 384–385.

president of MIT, who had served on many governmental bodies during the war, including the Interim Committee, and who had just returned from Japan, to write a vigorous defense of the decision. Compton, a highly respected physicist, complied with an article in the December 1946 *Atlantic* magazine. Dismissing "the wishful thinking among those after-the-event strategists who now deplore the use of the atomic bomb on the ground that its use was inhuman or that it was unnecessary because Japan was already beaten," Compton asserted "that the use of the atomic bomb saved hundreds of thousands – perhaps several millions – of lives, both American and Japanese." He further implied that Nagasaki was equally necessary because "it was not one atomic bomb, or two, which brought surrender; it was ... *the dread of many more*, that was effective."[34] Truman praised Compton for the article, which, the president wrote, was "the first sensible statement I have seen on the subject."[35]

Conant also succeeded in persuading a reluctant Stimson, who had overseen the Manhattan Project, to write a full-scale defense of the decision. Stimson was one of the most remarkable American public servants in the twentieth century (Figure 3.3). Regarded as a Republican elder statesman, he had been Secretary of War under President William Howard Taft and Secretary of State under Herbert Hoover. Franklin Roosevelt brought him into his cabinet in a bipartisan gesture in 1940 as Secretary of War. Although

---

[34] Karl T. Compton, "If the Atomic Bomb Had Not Been Used," *Atlantic Monthly*, December 1946. Italics in original.
[35] Bernstein, "Seizing the Contested Terrain," p. 44.

Figure 3.3 President Truman and Secretary of War Henry Stimson in the Oval Office on August 8, 1945, discussing prospects for Japanese surrender after the atomic bombing of Hiroshima.
Source: Bettmann/Getty Images

"Victorian" in his views on race and gender,[36] his integrity was legend. As Hoover's Secretary of State, he had ended a successful program of decrypting Japanese diplomatic because "gentlemen do not read each other's mail."[37] If that seemed soft-hearted, it should be remembered that he also as Secretary of State had unsuccessfully urged Hoover to confront Japan over its seizure of Manchuria in 1931.

[36] Malloy, *Atomic Tragedy*, p. 4.
[37] Stimson and Bundy, *On Active Service*, p. 188.

Conant believed that Stimson's views would carry great moral authority. The eighty-year-old Stimson lent his name to an essay that was in reality drafted by McGeorge Bundy, a twenty-seven-year-old Harvard scholar whose father, Harvey Bundy, was a long-time associate of Stimson. Conant, General Groves, and other participants in the decision were also heavily involved in the work of drafting. Stimson, moved by loyalty and service, agreed not only to lend his name and reputation to the defense of the bomb's use but also to allow others with their own interests in mind to shape and craft the defense. General Marshall later observed that Stimson "generously took a greater share of the responsibility than was fair" in lending his name to what became the "the single most influential account of the use of the bomb."[38] Stimson was reluctant to lend his name to what he called "the product of many hands."[39] Describing himself as the "victim" chosen to defend the president's decision, he sought the advice of his friend Supreme Court Justice Felix Frankfurter. "I have rarely been connected with a paper about which I have so much doubt at the last moment." Wouldn't it be better, he wondered, to wait for the completion of his memoirs where he could more fully describe his thoughts? "I think the full enumeration of the steps in the tragedy will excite horror among friends who heretofore thought me a kindly-minded Christian gentleman but who will, after reading this, feel that I am cold blooded and cruel."[40] Frankfurter urged him to

---

[38] Conant, *Man of the Hour*, p. 391. [39] Conant, *Man of the Hour*, p. 388.
[40] Hershberg, *Conant*, p. 295. Conant, *Man of the Hour*, p. 388 offers a slightly different quotation.

move forward with it, telling Stimson that the longer "sloppy sentimentality" is "allowed to make its way, the more difficult it is to overtake it."[41] Finally, Truman himself, bothered by speculation that the decision to use the bomb had not been carefully considered, wrote Stimson telling him that he knew the facts better than anyone else and urged him "to straighten out the record on it."[42] By this time Stimson felt duty-bound.

The *Harper's* Article

Stimson's essay published in the February 1947 issue of *Harper's Magazine* became the cornerstone of the participants' defense and the first draft of history. Considering all who had a hand in this article, it would not be too much to say that the Washington establishment had lent its hand in providing the official defense of the decision. It became American orthodoxy. The *Harper's* article was designed to quiet growing doubts among Americans, to reassure them of their self-identity as a virtuous nation and the morality of their leaders. Of notable importance was the style of the article. Conant urged that the article adopt a calm and nonargumentative style. A straightforward, objective recital of the facts would be the most compelling and persuasive.

The essay gave many reasons why the atomic bomb had been used. First, the article stressed that American leaders made the only acceptable choice open to them. Stimson explained that the decision to build the bomb was entirely

---

[41] Bernstein, "Seizing the Contested Terrain," p. 50.
[42] Hershberg, *Conant*, p. 295.

defensive and unavoidable to protect American security. Developing the bomb was forced on America because of the knowledge that the Germans had already embarked on its development, and should the Nazis succeed in being the first to build a nuclear weapon the allies would likely be defeated. Moreover, from the start of the Manhattan Project it was assumed by all involved that it would be used because "if we should be the first to develop the weapon, we should have a great new instrument for shortening the war and minimizing destruction." Stimson concluded that there was ultimately no avoiding the use of the bomb:

> I believe that no man, in our position and subject to our responsibilities, holding in his hands a weapon of such possibilities for accomplishing this purpose and saving those lives, could have failed to use it and afterwards looked his countrymen in the face ... [It] was our least abhorrent choice. The destruction of Hiroshima and Nagasaki put an end to the Japanese war. It stopped the fire raids, and the strangling blockade; it ended the ghastly specter of a clash of great land armies.

The article presented the decision as a binary choice – either invade or use the bomb. It made no mention of other alternatives, such as a blockade, which the Navy favored, or negotiation with Japan, as several of Truman's advisors favored, or waiting for Soviet entry into the war, as some historians later suggested should have been considered. The article, in fact, made no mention of the administration's extensive discussions of how to involve Russia in the war against Japan and whether to share atomic secrets with Russia. It also omitted the role that the politics of public opinion had in determining Truman's thinking and the advice of Secretary of State Brynes that any easing of surrender terms or attempt to negotiate with Japan would lead him to be "crucified" by public opinion.

Second, the *Harper's* article stressed that by averting an invasion the bomb, as awful as it was, had been the only moral choice to make. The bomb had avoided the greater loss of life that would have resulted from an invasion or the prolonging of the war. It was a necessary choice to "end the war in the shortest possible time and to avoid the enormous losses of life which otherwise confronted us." It had saved American and Japanese lives. Stimson wrote that before the bomb was used, the expectation had been that with the planned invasion first of Kyushu and then of the Kanto plain (the Tokyo area), the war was likely to continue for at least another year and "I was informed that such operations might be expected to cost over a million casualties to American forces alone." It is not clear where Stimson got the figure of "a million casualties" (by casualties he presumably meant dead, wounded, and missing). Former president Hoover had met with Stimson and Truman and given them a memo in May 1945 urging negotiations with the Japanese to avert an invasion that might cost "the lives of 500,000 to a million boys."[43] A study by a scientist W. B. Shockley commissioned by one of Stimson's staff suggested that an invasion might cost the Japanese 5–10 million deaths and the United States between 1.7 and 4 million casualties, including

---

[43] Kort, *Columbia Guide*, pp. 186–188.

400,000–800,000 deaths. It is not certain that Stimson saw this study.[44] The figure of a "million casualties" became the source of much controversy. Truman later in his memoirs used the figure of a half million. As the historian Barton Bernstein observed, "the over a 'million' number skillfully helped to legitimize the use of the bomb and to foreclose debate."[45] The truth was no one knew, but for the subsequent defenders of the bomb's use "the over 'a million' number" became an oft-cited figure.[46]

Third, Stimson argued that the atomic bomb was "as legitimate as any other of the deadly explosive weapons of modern war." In the conventional bombing of Tokyo in March 1945, "more damage was done and more casualties were inflicted than was the case at Hiroshima. ... Similar successive raids burned out a great part of the urban area of Japan." The essay reflected Conant's view, which he had expressed to Reinhold Niebuhr – that "it made no sense to condemn the A-bomb as morally more egregious than strategic bombing." In arguing that it was a "legitimate" weapon,

---

[44] Richard B. Frank, *Downfall: The End of the Imperial Japanese Empire* (New York: Random House, 1999), pp. 340, 342.

[45] See the essay Barton Bernstein, "The Struggle over History: Defining the Hiroshima Narrative," in Philip Nobile, ed., *Judgment at the Smithsonian: The Bombing of Hiroshima and Nagasaki*, pp. 139–140, 178–185. See also Bernstein's more recent essay in *The End of the Pacific War: Reappraisals*, pp. 14–15.

[46] Kort, *The Columbia Guide*, pp. 96–104, provides a detailed overview of the literature and concludes: "No reader of this overview can fail to notice how widely these casualty estimates vary. This in part is because at the time there was no single accepted methodology for projecting casualties. Nor has one emerged."

Stimson seemed to be saying that it was not a revolutionary weapon. Yet, at other times he clearly regarded it as a wholly new and different weapon in its implications for the future. Stimson left unsaid how he himself had agonized over the conventional bombing and the targeting of civilians. Nor did he mention that prior to American entry into the war, FDR had publicly called on the combatants to avoid bombing of civilians, which the United States was deliberately doing by the end of the war. Some historians subsequently saw the use of the bomb as a violation of international law, including the Hague convention, which outlawed use of weapons of indiscriminate cruelty.

Fourth, he characterized the bomb as a "psychological weapon" used to apply a shock to the military leaders, breaking the deadlock in the Japanese government and "strengthening the position of those who wished peace." Stimson wrote: "I felt that to extract a genuine surrender from the Emperor and his military advisers, they must be administered a tremendous shock which would carry convincing proof of our power to destroy the Empire. Such an effective shock would save many times the number of lives, both American and Japanese, that it would cost." Stimson left untold that Truman had ignored his recommendation that offering to preserve the emperor in the Potsdam Declaration and even having the Russians sign that document could open the path to a negotiated surrender.

Finally, Stimson made the dubious claim that use of the bomb had been "carefully considered." A demonstration was ruled out on the advice of leading scientists because of the limited number of bombs available and the possibility that a demonstration might well be a "dud." Stimson offered no further explanation for the swift use of the second bomb on Nagasaki, rather than pause to wait for possible surrender, other than to repeat Compton's assertion that it helped convince the Japanese that there could be "many more."

When the article was published, the self-satisfied, young Bundy, who was the unacknowledged coauthor, crowed to Stimson that the dissenters from the use of the bomb had been quieted. "We deserve some sort of medal," he added, because "the chatterers" had been reduced to silence.[47] However, reflecting on the essay decades later Bundy had second thoughts and wrote that the essay had been "intended to demonstrate that the bomb was not used without a searching consideration of the alternatives. That some effort was made, and that Stimson was its linchpin, is clear. That it was as long or wide or deep as the subject deserved now seems to me most doubtful."[48] A more considered study of the use of the bomb might have led to a different decision. For example, recent research by the historian Sean Malloy shows that, while scientists had some understanding of the lethal properties of the bomb's side effects, those who made the decision, including Truman, Byrnes, and Stimson, were not aware of the radiation effects and "that the weapon would continue to sicken and kill its victims long after use" (Figure 5.1). The stove-piping of knowledge, together with the secrecy of the Manhattan Project, kept awareness of the biological effects of radiation from the decision-makers, who were only impressed

---

[47] Bernstein, "Seizing the Contested Terrain," p. 55.
[48] Bundy, *Danger and Survival*, pp. 92–93.

by the blast potential of the bomb: "If American leaders had had even a rough understanding of radiation effects, that knowledge might well have affected decisions about *how* the bomb was used ... such as the choice of targets, the possibility of an explicit warning or demonstration, and the pursuit of various diplomatic options."[49] If there is one thing about which most historians could agree, it was that the decision to use the bomb had not been carefully and fully considered. The secrecy of the Manhattan Project together with Roosevelt's inclination to hold consideration of the use of the bomb largely to himself kept it from the deliberation such a momentous decision deserved.

The Lasting Influence of the Participants' Version of History

The participants in the Hiroshima decision knew that academic historians (Conant called them "verbally minded academics") would debate the interpretation of the momentous events. They knew that in time academic historians would reconstruct the events according to their own biases and perspectives. So, the participants took it upon themselves to construct an account that would justify their decision-making and present it in such a way that it would reassure the self-identity of the American people. They were shrewd not only in making their arguments but also in choosing

---

[49] Sean L. Malloy, "'A Very Pleasant Way to Die': Radiation Effects and the Decision to Use the Atomic Bomb against Japan," *Diplomatic History* 26, no. 3 (June 2011): 544. See also Malloy, *Atomic Tragedy*, p. 53.

a straightforward, matter-of-fact style, as Conant advised, that would convince Americans of the reasonableness of the decision.[50]

Conant was pleased by the receptivity of the American people to Stimson's article. It had "helped a great deal," he said. "You have to get the past straight before you do much to prepare people for the future."[51] In retrospect, the surprise was how successful this first draft of history was in laying the foundation for an enduring interpretation. It was, Malloy writes, "stunningly effective at shaping public and scholarly understanding of the subject."[52] Stimson's essay did in fact stand for two decades as the authoritative, largely unchallenged historical interpretation of the use of the bomb.

Important works by major historians, of which there were only a few in the first two postwar decades, supported the orthodox interpretation. The Harvard historian Samuel Eliot Morrison's monumental study of naval operations in the war found the use of the bomb justified in speeding the end of the war.[53] Likewise, Herbert Feis, the prolific diplomatic historian of the war, agreed that it was necessary to obtain an early end to Japanese resistance.[54] The most important book published in the two postwar decades was the historian Robert Butow's *Japan's Decision to Surrender* (1954), but it

[50] Bernstein, "Contested Terrain," pp. 36, 49.
[51] Hershberg, *Conant*, p. 304.   [52] Malloy, *Atomic Tragedy*, p. 163.
[53] Samuel Eliot Morison, *Victory in the Pacific, 1945: History of United States Naval Operations in World War II, Vol. XIV* (Boston: Atlantic-Little, Brown, 1960).
[54] Herbert Feis, *Japan Subdued: The Atomic Bomb and the End of the War in the Pacific* (Princeton: Princeton University Press, 1961).

was focused largely on Japanese politics rather than primarily the Hiroshima decision. We will consider it in Chapter 7 when we turn to the responsibility that Japan itself bears for the tragedy.

The broad acceptance of the orthodox defense owed much to its success in fortifying the self-image of Americans. It quieted the moral doubts raised by being the first to use the nuclear bomb and the killing of more than a quarter million Japanese. It satisfied most Americans that the decision had been reached only with the greatest reluctance and done to bring an early end to a brutal war, save lives by averting an invasion, replace a depraved militarist regime, and remake Japan into a peaceful, disarmed democracy that would no longer be a threat to world peace. Confidence in the virtue of America's role in the world was kept intact. Stimson's defense of the Hiroshima decision became the orthodox view because it fit the worldview of the World War II generation.

The responsibility fell to subsequent generations of historians to debate the accuracy of this first draft of history. Custodians of the public memory, they were charged with maintaining an independent, open-ended inquiry. It was their role to question popular and idealized versions of these momentous events and, if necessary, save the public from myths and cherished illusions. The orthodox view became the starting point for what became one of the most intense and fraught controversies in American history.

4

The Revisionists

Participants in the Hiroshima decision feared, as Stimson wrote, that "ill-informed criticism" by "the teachers of our next generation" might have "rather poisonous effects."[1] They were right to worry. An unruly new generation emerged in the 1960s. Young historians reached highly critical judgments of the Hiroshima decision and the orthodox defense of it. Known as "revisionists," they found many reasons to challenge the participants' first draft of history. The 1960s was a decade of upheaval in American society. Motivated by urgent issues from their own time and by their own political commitments, the revisionists made a sharp break with the orthodox interpretation of the use of the bomb as well as with the prevailing view of the entire American past.

Revisionism is fundamental to the historian's craft.[2] Sometimes "revisionist history" is a derogatory term used to discredit critics who are proposing a new view of the past and to suggest that they are falsifying history. Nevertheless, revisionism is a legitimate and necessary activity of historians. The historian's craft by its very nature invites new views of the past. The meaning of history is not fixed. The perspective on the past is forever changing. Different perspectives, new

---

[1] Malloy, *Atomic Tragedy*, p. 161.
[2] James M. Banner, Jr., *The Ever-Changing Past: Why All History Is Revisionist History* (New Haven: Yale University Press, 2021).

insights, and new evidence impel new interpretations. As the American historian James McPherson observed,

> revision is the lifeblood of historical scholarship. History is a continuing dialogue between the present and the past. Interpretations of the past are subject to change in response to new evidence, new questions asked of the evidence, new perspectives gained by the passage of time. There is no single, eternal, and immutable "truth" about past events and their meaning. The unending quest of historians for understanding the past – that is "revisionism" – is what makes history vital and meaningful.[3]

Revisionism and Generational Change

One of the principal drivers of revisionism is generational change. Every generation reexamines the past from the perspective of its own experience and concerns. Typically, revisionism that is politically and ideologically motivated will emerge from younger historians whose formative experiences are shaped by major new events in their lifetime. They constitute ideological generations. It is sometimes said that history must be written for each new generation to respond to its concerns. The historian Bernard Bailyn observed that

> [e]very generation will have its own approach and questions, since history is, in the end, an inquiry about the past. History is not an inert reconstruction of the past that gets set once and for all; it is a form of inquiry; and those

---

[3] James McPherson, "Revisionist Historians," *Perspectives on History* (American Historical Association, September 1, 2003)

REVISIONISM AND GENERATIONAL CHANGE

inquiries will shift and renew and grow in time. Succeeding generations will write different kinds of histories – and should.[4]

In modern history, the rapid tempo of change tends to produce marked differences of outlook between generations. More than any other country, America has been prone to intense generational conflict.[5] But there were few times in American history that generational change was so marked as it was in the 1960s when political violence, domestic upheaval, and a contentious war in Vietnam shook American society. A new generation brought a radical break from the World War II generation's heroic view of an America leading the forces of light in a world struggle against totalitarianism. An era of good feelings gave way to an angry passion for radical reform; affirmation of American institutions gave way to distrust in their workings. The result was a new view of the American past. In this sharp generational divide, the orthodox view of the Hiroshima decision could not escape a revisionist interpretation.

When the Cold War began in the late 1940s, the wartime generation saw its hope for a peaceful world dashed by Soviet expansionism. To the wartime generation the origins of the Cold War would require "the brave and essential response of free men to communist aggression."[6] NSC 68

---

[4] Bernard Bailyn, *On the Teaching and Writing of History*, p. 95
[5] Samuel Huntington, "Paradigms of American Politics: Beyond the One, the Two, and the Many," *Political Science Quarterly* 89, no.11 (March 1974): 1–26.
[6] Arthur Schlesinger Jr., "Origins of the Cold War," *Foreign Affairs* 46, no.1 (October 1967): 23.

(National Security Council 68), a policy paper drafted in 1950, was one of the fundamental US Cold War strategic policy documents. It described the foe as animated by a "new fanatic faith, antithetical to our own" and determined to impose its "absolute authority over the rest of the world." The stakes in the struggle were existential: "The issues that face us are momentous, involving the fulfillment or destruction not only of this Republic but of civilization itself."[7] This apocalyptic view depicted a struggle between slave and free societies and reflected the wartime generation's view of the Cold War.

The outlook of the new generation that came of age in the turbulent 1960s, in contrast, was marked by radical rejection of the culture of consensus which celebrated American ideals and institutions. Known as "the baby boom generation," the result of the economic prosperity and the demographic surge that followed the hardships of the Great Depression and World War II, they were stirred by events in their formative years, angry that their country was betraying its ideals. The alienation of this new generation expressed itself, as the historian Gordon Wood described it, by "a multitude of radical changes ... in politics, civil rights, race relations, sexual habits, family life, women's roles, cultural attitudes. All these changes ... resulted in a series of challenges to our traditional identity as an optimistic,

---

[7] Ernest May, ed. *American Cold War Strategy: Interpreting NSC 68* (Boston, MA: Bedford/St. Martin's, 1993), pp.25–26; see also Melvyn Leffler, *A Preponderance of Power: National Security, the Truman Administration, and the Cold War* (Stanford: Stanford University Press, 1992), pp.355 ff.

enterprising, and progressive nation."[8] At home, this generation's new consciousness focused on the civil rights movement and the unmet demands for racial equality. America, the historian Richard Hofstadter observed, has sporadically had an "extraordinary penchant for violence,"[9] but rarely to the extent of the 1960s. The assassinations of John Kennedy and civil rights activist Medgar Evers in 1963, leader of the Islamic Nation Malcolm X in 1965, Martin Luther King, Jr., and Robert Kennedy in 1968, all bespoke a society rent by racial tensions. Race riots inflamed Washington, Newark, Cleveland, Detroit, Los Angeles, and other cities.

Abroad, America's Cold War strategy and the runaway arms race, the militarization of foreign policy, and the compromises that the Cold War strategy made with American ideals enraged the new generation. Together with the domestic turbulence, this postwar generation was galvanized by a new chapter in the Cold War. The escalating war in Vietnam in 1965 began with ground combat and bombing on a large scale. By the end of the year the United States had 184,000 troops in Vietnam. Anti-war demonstrations disrupted over 200 campuses.

The consensus and the triumphalism of the wartime generation was shaken by the decade's turbulence. The historian Arthur Schlesinger, Jr., a member of the World War II generation who had been one to celebrate the American

---

[8] Gordon S. Wood, *The Purpose of the Past: Reflections on the Uses of History* (New York: Penguin Press, 2008), p.249.

[9] Hofstadter, *The Progressive Historians: Turner, Beard, Parrington* (New York: Knopf, 1968), p.462.

experience, shaken by the turbulence in domestic life, the Vietnam debacle, and the assassination of the Kennedy brothers and Martin Luther King, had to admit that national self-righteousness could not withstand the spectacle of such national violence:

> We are indeed a frightening people – because in this decade we have killed three leaders who stood preeminently before the world as embodiments of American idealism. We are a frightening people – because for three years we have been devastating a small country on the other side of the world in a war which bears no proportionate relationship to our national security or national interest. We are frightening – because many in the world suspect the connection suggested by that devoted friend and student of America, Sir Denis Brogan: "Are we sure it is merely an accident that the most domestically murderous nation in the world was the first – and only – nation to drop the atom bomb?"[10]

Revisionist Historians

This tumult gave rise to a revisionist view of American history. Events came to a head in the rancorous presidential election of 1968 and a full-fledged generational rebellion. "A midcentury era of political consensus," the historian Jill Lepore wrote,

> had come to an almost unfathomably violent end. After 1968, American politics would be driven once again by

[10] Arthur Schlesinger, Jr., *Violence: America in the Sixties* (New York: Signet Boks, 1968), pp.24–25.

division, resentment, and malice. . . . The civil rights movement and the war in Vietnam called attention to aspects of American history that have been left out of American history textbooks from the very start. . . . A revolution on the streets produced a revolution in scholarship: a new American past.[11]

Pointing to America's growing empire of bases, alliances with authoritarian regimes, interventions in the domestic politics of other nations, all culminating in the deepening involvement in Vietnam, young historians began to question the origins of the Cold War. Writing in 1968, the revisionist historian Christopher Lasch observed that

> a growing number of historians and political critics . . . are challenging the view, once so widely accepted, that the cold war was an American response to Soviet expansionism, a distasteful burden reluctantly shouldered in the face of a ruthless enemy bent on our destruction, and that Russia, not the United States, must therefore bear the blame for shattering the world's hope that two world wars in the 20th century would finally give way to an era of peace.[12]

The revisionists believed many things and were a fractious group, but one thing that did unite them was a belief that the United States exaggerated and misrepresented the Soviet threat. The Stanford historian Barton Bernstein later recalled that his fellow revisionists believed that

---

[11] Jill Lepore, *These Truths: A History of the United States* (New York: Knopf, 2018), pp.633–635.

[12] Christopher Lasch, "The Cold War, Revisited and Re-Visioned," *New York Times*, January 4, 1968.

> the United States was substantially or primarily responsible for the Cold War. ... Different American policies – involving opening the second front in Europe earlier, providing postwar economic aid to the Soviet Union, acceding without protest or pressure to Soviet dominance of eastern Europe, and providing substantial reparations to the USSR from West Germany – might well have avoided the Cold War.[13]

Bernstein and some of the other revisionists were older than the baby boom generation, but their work prefigured its concerns and naturally drew its strongest support from that emerging generation. Where the wartime generation had characterized the American nation as having come reluctantly to its role in the world, to fulfilling its world responsibilities in the face of a totalitarian menace, the revisionists began to see a nation that from its early times had shown an expansionist and imperialist bent as it expanded across the North American continent.

The new generation of historians believed that history should not be written to fortify American policy. History should be used to confront contemporary problems. The urgency of their time required that historians be *engagé*. Their writings promoted political mobilization, anything but a detached and disinterested approach to the past. They brought to history an activist temperament. History was a tool for change. To them, devotion to "disinterested scholarship" and "objectivity" made historians apologists for the past. The historian Howard Zinn called for "socially relevant,

---

[13] Hasegawa, *The End of the Pacific War*, p. 20.

value-motivated, action-inducing historical work." Historians should be critics in the interest of progress. They sought moral lessons and concrete policy recommendations for the future. "Should not the historian thrust himself and his writing into history, on behalf of goals in which he deeply believes? Are we historians not humans first, and scholars because of that?"[14] Young historians attracted by this mission in a time of social upheaval challenged the prevailing view of the origins of the Cold War.

Often it has happened that because "revisionist" is a label to describe a radical break with previous versions of the past, revisionism tends to be the work of a polemical point of view. There is of course danger that history for political purpose begins with a point of view rather than with evidence. While it may open new paths, revision that is ideologically motivated often lacks balance because it permits bias to exaggerate its arguments. Gordon Wood writes in this connection that "when politics comes in the door, truth flies out the window. Historians who want to influence politics with their history writing have missed the point of the craft; they ought to run for office."[15] There were dangers that the complexity of the past would be cast aside for clarity and a tendency to simplify.

Nevertheless, with a time lag that allows for debate and reflection and testing of its thesis, such revisionism can help shape a fuller understanding of the past. In other words,

---

[14] Norman M. Wilensky, "Was the Cold War Necessary? The Revisionist Challenge to Consensus History," *American Studies* 13, no.1 (Spring 1972): 183–184.

[15] Wood, *Purpose of the Past*, p. 308.

the ideological concerns can fuel research, generate new knowledge, promote debate, and contribute to more persuasive interpretations. Still, the stricture of Bailyn is essential:

> Political and ideological concerns have undoubtedly stimulated historical research and writing.... Historians motivated chiefly by political and ideological concerns ... commonly do have a stake in the outcome. They are not simply satisfying their curiosity or the desire to reveal lost worlds. They want the story to prove something, to support certain policies, to send certain messages. They are likely, therefore, if only unconsciously, to exaggerate or otherwise bias the stories they tell.... Still, political commitments generate enormous power in historical study.... Are not historians supposed to be concerned with things that are urgent issues in their own time, seen historically? Yes, of course, but in a way that does not violate the texture of the past, that does not telescope past and present.[16]

Atomic Diplomacy

The new revisionist generation of historians ranged widely over American foreign relations dismissing the upbeat views of the previous generation. The fact that America had been the first nation to use the bomb and to use it on an Asian nation which was seemingly already defeated confirmed their view, perhaps more decisively than any other event, that American foreign policy had a history of immoral behavior. The radicalism of the new generation was made to order for

---

[16] Bailyn, *Teaching and Writing of History*, pp. 40–41.

a critical reexamination of the orthodox interpretation of the Hiroshima decision. In 1965, in the very midst of the domestic turmoil and the escalation of the Vietnam War, a book with the provocative title *Atomic Diplomacy* by the twenty-nine-year-old Gar Alperovitz charged that the United States had used its possession of nuclear weapons to gain leverage with the Russians in disagreements over the postwar settlement in Eastern Europe.[17] It thereby connected the use of the bomb to the origins of the Cold War.

The first question I always put to the students in my Hiroshima seminar when they had been assigned a new interpretation to read is "Tell me about the author's background." Historians are shaped by their own environment. History does not come to us as pure facts. It comes refracted through the mind of a historian and the issues and concerns of her or his own time. In his widely read *What Is History?*, the English historian E. H. Carr wrote that "when we take up a work of history, our first concern should be not with the facts which it contains but with the historian who wrote it. . . . Study the historian before you begin to study the facts. . . . By and large, the historian will get the kind of facts he wants. History means interpretation."[18] Upon further reflection, Carr added that even "before you study the historian, study his historical and social environment."[19] Historians reflect their own time and its spirit and concerns.

---

[17] Gar Alperovitz, *Atomic Diplomacy: Hiroshima and Potsdam: The Use of the Atomic Bomb and the American Confrontation with Soviet Power* (New York: Simon and Schuster, 1965).

[18] E. H. Carr, *What Is History?* (New York: Penguin Press, 1990), pp. 22–23.

[19] Carr, *What Is History?*, p. 44.

Alperovitz is a good example of why one must inquire about the historian's background before reading their interpretations. His teachers strongly influenced Alperovitz's approach to history. He was a student of William Appleman Williams, a historian at the University of Wisconsin, whose reconceptualization of the history of American foreign policy made him the advance guard of the new generation. Williams challenged the prevailing views of American history, asserting that the Cold War was the latest phase of American capitalism's need for foreign markets that had motivated a pattern of expansionist and counterrevolutionary undertakings. The neo-Marxian view of Williams influenced other revisionists. In his defining 1959 work *The Tragedy of American Diplomacy*, Williams asserted that "the United States dropped the bomb to end the war against Japan *and thereby stop the Russians in Asia, and to give them sober pause in eastern Europe.*"[20] From Wisconsin, Alperovitz went on to Cambridge University where he chose to write his doctoral dissertation on the use of the atomic bomb. There, he was influenced by the left-leaning Nobel Prize physicist P. M. S. Blackett, who had recently published a controversial book in which he argued that "the dropping of the atomic bombs was not so much the last military act of the second World War as the first major operation of the cold diplomatic war with Russia now in progress."[21]

---

[20] Quoted in Robert James Maddox, *The New Left and the Origins of the Cold War* (Princeton: Princeton University Press, 1973), p.32. Italics in Williams.

[21] Malloy, *Atomic Tragedy*, pp. 171–172.

The timing of the publication of *Atomic Diplomacy* in the very midst of the upheaval in American domestic and foreign politics brought Alperovitz immediate attention. Its thesis resonated with the times. The historian Richard Hofstadter once counseled historians, "if a new or heterodox idea is worth anything at all it is worth a forceful overstatement."[22] Alperovitz took a new idea and gave it a forceful overstatement. He built on his teachers' ideas and offered a rather simple, straightforward thesis to explain the Hiroshima decision. He argued that use of the atomic bomb was not a military decision to avoid an invasion and bring the war to an early end to save American lives as the orthodox view held but was rather a political decision designed to intimidate the Soviets and make Russia more tractable in disagreements over the postwar settlement in Europe. His interpretation depicted Truman following a devious strategy of deliberately delaying the Potsdam conference until the bomb had been successfully tested to give him the edge in negotiations with Stalin over their disagreements on Eastern Europe and other issues. Furthermore, Truman purposely avoided asking Stalin to sign the Potsdam Declaration, believing that it might bring Japan's surrender before the bomb could be used. Alperovitz implied that with such ulterior motives, Truman rejected viable alternatives, including pursuing possible Japanese peace feelers, or a noncombat demonstration of the bomb, or most important, waiting for Soviet entry into the war forced Japanese surrender. He claimed that Japan was on the verge of surrender and that Truman knew

---

[22] Novick, *That Noble Dream*, p. 451.

this from intercepted Japanese messages. "*It is very clear that well before atomic weapons were used both the Japanese and American governments had arrived at the same understanding of acceptable terms of surrender*" and that all that stood in the way was a guarantee of the emperor.[23] If the United States had assured Japan of the emperor's future, Japan was prepared to surrender.

Alperovitz argued that the president hastened to employ the bomb to impress Stalin and assert American dominance in the postwar world. Possession of the new weapon had given the Truman administration opportunity to pursue "atomic diplomacy." Truman reversed the Roosevelt administration's accommodation of Stalin and its plans for a postwar partnership and instead used the bomb to end the war before Russia entered. Once the bomb was perfected, American leaders no longer needed Russian help in an invasion of Japan. Using the bomb would compel Japan's surrender before Russia could share in the occupation of Japan and claim a sphere of influence in the Pacific. In Europe, Truman and Secretary of State Byrnes were determined to confront Stalin's plans to impose pro-Soviet regimes in Poland and other countries in Eastern Europe.

Several factors prompted Alperovitz's challenge to the orthodox interpretation. First, in his *Harper's* article Stimson chose not to make any reference to US discussions

---

[23] Gar Alperovitz, *Atomic Diplomacy: Hiroshima and Nagasaki: The Use of the Atomic Bomb & the American Confrontation with Soviet Power* (New York: Penguin, 1985 expanded edition), p. 30. Italics in original. See also Malloy, *Atomic Tragedy*, p. 214n31.

of the Soviet Union in its thinking about the use of the bomb because relations with Russia over international control of nuclear weapons were at a delicate stage. But Alperowitz, working in the newly opened Stimson papers, found abundant evidence that American leaders were keenly conscious of how the prospect of possession of the new weapon could give the United States the upper hand in its disagreements with the Soviets. For Alperovitz, with his personal biases shaped by his mentors, the discovery of these strategies, which had gone unmentioned in Stimson's article, provided the ammunition to attack the orthodox interpretation and offer a new interpretation of the Cold War. Alperovitz contended that the Hiroshima decision was a political decision which reversed FDR's policy of accommodating Stalin and contributed to the start of the Cold War.

Second, availability of other new materials fortified his reappraisal. Alperovitz had access to Japanese diplomatic messages intercepted by the Americans during the war. The decrypted messages seemed to him to show that Japan was near surrender if guarantee of the emperor's position were offered. Yet Truman had made no effort to pursue that possibility. Because the United States had cracked the Japanese diplomatic code and was fully apprised of Japan's willingness to surrender so long as the imperial institution was retained, he reasoned, why drop the bomb if Japan was on the verge of surrender? Why no demonstration of the bomb? Why not wait for Russian entry into the war before using the bomb?

Third, perhaps most persuasive to many readers of *Atomic Diplomacy* was Alperovitz's citing of American military figures whose views broadly suggested that the bomb was unnecessary. Dwight Eisenhower in his memoirs recalled that when Stimson told him that the bomb would be used against Japan,

> I voiced to him my grave misgivings, first on the basis of my belief that Japan was already defeated and that dropping the bomb was completely unnecessary, and secondly because I thought that our country should avoid shocking world opinion. ... It was my belief that Japan was, at that very moment, seeking some way to surrender with a minimum loss of "face".[24]

Eisenhower concluded that "[i]t wasn't necessary to hit them with that awful thing."[25] Alperovitz also cited Admiral William Leahy, Roosevelt and Truman's Chief of Staff, who wrote in his memoir:

> It is my opinion that the use of this barbarous weapon at Hiroshima and Nagasaki was of no material assistance in our war against Japan. The Japanese were already defeated and ready to surrender because of the effective sea blockade and the successful bombing with conventional weapons. ... My own feeling is that in being the first to use it, we had adopted an ethical standard common to the barbarians of the Dark Ages.[26]

[24] Alperovitz, *Atomic Diplomacy*, pp. 236–237.
[25] Alperovitz, *Atomic Diplomacy*, pp. 236–237.
[26] William D. Leahy, *I Was There: The Personal Story of the Chief of Staff to Presidents Roosevelt and Truman Based on His Notes and Diaries Made at the Time* (New York: McGraw-Hill Book, 1950), p.441. See also *Atomic Diplomacy* (1965), p. 238. A recent biography of Leahy implies that he had moral objections before the use of the bomb. See Phillips Payson O'Brien, *The Second Most Powerful Man in the World: The Life of*

Here it appeared Alperovitz had found persuasive support for his contention. If two such major and universally respected military figures in their postwar recollections saw it as unnecessary, then why was the bomb used?

Historians must always treat memoirs carefully. Subsequently, the historian Barton Bernstein through painstaking research cast doubt on the reliability of these after-the-fact remembrances. He found no convincing evidence that Eisenhower and Leahy had expressed moral opposition to the use of the bomb prior to its use. Eisenhower in his 1948 memoir said that at Potsdam he had opposed its use, but the diaries of Stimson and Truman make no mention of such advice. By 1963, Eisenhower had expanded his own remembrance, but Bernstein concluded that "Ike's postwar claims [are] dubious at best.... Nor is there any evidence that any high-ranking American military leader, other than General George C. Marshall on *one* occasion, expressed any moral objections before Hiroshima to the use of the atomic bomb on Japanese cities."[27] Leahy was skeptical about the effectiveness of the bomb when it was discussed before it was tested, but did not express his moral opposition to its use until after the war.

William D. Leahy, *Roosevelt's Chief of Staff* (New York: Dutton, 2019), pp.298–299.

[27] Barton J. Bernstein, "Ike and Hiroshima: Did He Oppose It?" *Journal of Strategic Studies* 10, no.3 (July 1987): 377–389. Despite Bernstein's contention, Alperovitz continued to weigh heavily Eisenhower's and Leahy's views in an expanded version of his interpretation for the fiftieth anniversary of the use of the bomb. See Gar Alperovitz, *The Decision to Use the Atomic Bomb and the Architecture of an American Myth* (New York: Knopf, 1995), pp.3–4.

Although the revisionists did not accept the orthodox defense of the Hiroshima decision, there was no uniform revisionist interpretation. Their views covered a broad span of opposition to the orthodox defense. Many disagreed with the rather simple primacy of anti-Soviet motives of Truman's use of the bomb that Alperovitz argued. While agreeing that Soviet–American relations had played a role in the administration's thinking, they parted ways with his contention that Truman had contrived the use of the bomb to impress the Russians and gain the upper hand in growing disagreements over Eastern Europe. Some revisionists rejected the view that Japan was close to surrender and that only an Allied guarantee of the emperor system stood in the way. Many revisionists saw Alperovitz's view as flawed in its obsessive focus on the use of the bomb as central to the origins of the Cold War. They were more inclined to see it as secondary to a larger picture of long-term American opposition to Bolshevik influence.[28]

Consider the revisionist Barton Bernstein, who has studied the Hiroshima decision more than any other historian. A Stanford professor, he devoted the greater part of his career to writing a remarkable number of studies of the many aspects of the decision. He began his career as a "new left" historian who rejected the prevailing interpretations of the origins of the Cold War. He arrived at his new left position prior to the Vietnam War.[29] But he parted company with

[28] See the analysis of revisionists by Charles Maier, "Revisionism and the Interpretations of Cold War Origins," *Perspectives in American History* IV (1970): 313–347.

[29] Peter Novick writes: "Best described as 'left liberals,' [they were] young historians like Barton Bernstein and Christopher Lasch, critical of

Alperovitz's thesis that the use of the atomic bomb to intimidate Russia had been the cause of the Cold War. Instead, Bernstein found Alperovitz's work "deeply flawed both in conception and in its use of evidence." It was mistaken in its assumption that Truman "had engaged in carefully weighed and calculated considerations" in determining to use the bomb for anti-Soviet purposes rather than wait for a likely Japanese surrender. Paying little attention to developments in Japan, Alperowitz's book was, "in short, about US-Soviet relations." Bernstein as well as some other revisionists did not agree that the A-bomb decision was "significantly motivated by anti-Soviet purposes."[30] For them, "ending the war speedily was the primary purpose; impressing the Soviet Union was secondary."[31] As he continued to pursue his research and writing, Bernstein, according to one of his former students, "attempted to find a middle ground" between orthodoxy and revisionism.[32] Summing up his extensive

American liberals' accommodation to the cold war and to McCarthyism. But without, at this stage, anything that could be called a socialist commitment. There is no hard-and-fast line to be drawn between this cohort of left historians and those who came along a few years later, but there were, overall, some distinctions worth noting. The sensibility of the former group had been shaped in the fifties and they were, for the most past, culturally very 'straight,' whereas those who came along later, attending college or graduate school during the tumultuous late sixties, were more likely to display a countercultural sensibility, and were more likely than those in the previous group to have an activist orientation." Novick, *That Noble Dream*, pp. 419–420.

[30] Hasegawa, *The End of the Pacific War*, pp. 20–23
[31] Barton J. Bernstein, "Roosevelt, Truman, and the Atomic Bomb, 1941-1945,' *Political Science Quarterly* 90, no.1 (Spring 1975): 24.
[32] Malloy, *Atomic Tragedy*, p. 172.

research and writing on the issues regarding how the use of the bomb might have been avoided, Bernstein wrote that

> it was quite possible, though less than definite, that both use of the A-bomb and an invasion could have been avoided and a Japanese surrender achieved before November 1945 if the United States had awaited the impact of Soviet entry, continued its blockade and heavy bombing of Japan, and modified its unconditional surrender policy to allow a constitutional monarchy.... The Nagasaki bomb was very probably unnecessary.[33]

The Reaction to Revisionism

The reaction to the revisionism of the younger generation from older scholars was often shrill and vindictive. They "invoked the authority of their gray hairs" to scold the younger revisionists for their views that came from not having lived through the trying struggles of World War II.[34] To outraged mainstream historians who viewed Soviet expansionism as originating the Cold War, "revisionism" was an epithet intended to denigrate critics by imputing to them a falsification or distortion of history. Arthur Schlesinger, Jr., exploded, "[s]urely the time has come to blow the whistle before the current outburst of revisionism regarding the origins of the cold war goes much further." He found Alperovitz "hopelessly shallow" in his interpretation.[35] Schlesinger later

---

[33] Hasegawa, *The End of the Pacific War*, pp. 23–24.
[34] Novick, *That Noble Dream*, p. 452.
[35] Letter to the *New York Review of Books* (October 20, 1966)

admitted his reaction had been "intemperate" and allowed that it was normal that younger historians should want to reappraise the orthodox view.

> There is a natural tendency, especially on the part of the generation which grew up during the Cold War, to take a fresh look at the causes of the great contention between Russia and America. ... Revisionism is an essential part of the process by which history, through the posing of new problems and the investigation of new possibilities, enlarges its perspectives and enriches its insights.[36]

Nevertheless, the controversy over the Hiroshima decision often lost the civility that usually characterized disagreements among historians.

Alperovitz's bold and sweeping contention made him a ready target for mainstream historians. It was not only the overeagerness to make his point but also his careless scholarship. He was accused of misrepresenting his sources and violating professional standards of the historian's craft. One of his milder and forbearing critics found him

> careless in the use of quotations. He stretches conclusion over gaps in the evidence and assumes every chance remark was part of a grand design. In his speculations about the Russians, his portrait of Stalin errs in the direction of the benign. These, however, are flaws common to many young historians eager to prove a case. He is

---

[36] Schlesinger, "Origins of the Cold War," pp. 22–23.

certainly far from a model of meticulousness, but his mistakes are relatively minor. They tarnish his argument but do not destroy it.[37]

The diplomat and authority on Russian-US relations George Kennan viewed the author of *Atomic Diplomacy* as "careless and inaccurate," and his "unscrupulous use of reference material" in a book "so slippery & dishonest that its very publication is a disgrace."[38] For his harshest critic, Robert James Maddox, his "shenanigans" amounted to "patent nonsense," and "the greatest hoax in American history."[39] His critics sometimes concentrated more on mocking his flawed use of sources and other technical mistakes than on analyzing his thesis. Alperovitz himself, while clinging to his original thesis, eventually conceded that he had been guilty of "some obvious graduate-student errors."[40]

Interpretive disagreements among historians generally stay within the scholarly community because the terms of the debates are not well understood outside of academia. But the Hiroshima decision was different. Alperovitz's view and

---

[37] Gaddis Smith, "Was Moscow Our Real Target?" *New York Times*, August 18, 1985.
[38] Frank Costigliola, *Kennan: A Life between Worlds* (Princeton: Princeton University Press, 2023), p.434.
[39] The Pennsylvania State University historian Robert James Maddox wrote many books and articles excoriating revisionists, especially Alperovitz. See, e.g., Victor Fic, "Hiroshima Revisionism: An Interview with Robert Maddox," History News Network, accessed January 18, 2022. See also Maddox, *The New Left and the Origins of the Cold War*.
[40] Alperowitz, *The Decision to Use the Atomic Bomb and the Architecture of an American Myth* (New York: Knopf, 1995), p. 6.

the broader revisionist critique at first made waves in the academic world and drew some media attention, but later, at the time of the fiftieth anniversary of the end of the war in 1995, the implications of revisionist historians' views burst into national controversy. The intention of the Smithsonian Institution's exhibition was to "tell the whole story, from the American as well as the Japanese side."[41] The curators underestimated the degree to which the public memory was wedded to the conviction that World War II had been a "good war." Studs Terkel's 1984 book *The Good War* won the Pulitzer Prize and by the fiftieth anniversary of the end of the war in 1995 the journalist Tom Brokaw identified the war's veterans as "the greatest generation any society has ever produced," foreshadowing his forthcoming bestselling book.[42] The Smithsonian curators were blindsided by the wave of public outrage. Veterans groups, believing that revisionism denigrated the heroic role of GIs fighting in the Pacific, angrily lobbied Congress to have the text revised in accordance with the orthodox view. Nevertheless, the public controversy, "with heated passions, with feverish polemics, with Congressional hearings," helped make the Hiroshima decision a lasting issue of interest for many more Americans.[43] The passing of the World War II generation, according to polls, led to steadily

---

[41] Gregg Herken, "The Smithsonian's Decision to Exhibit the 'Enola Gay,'" *Public History Weekly*, October 6, 2022.

[42] Tom Brokaw, The Greatest Generation (New York: Random House, 2001).

[43] Barton Bernstein, "The Struggle Over History: Defining the Hiroshima Narrative," Philip Nobile ed., *Judgment at the Smithsonian* (New York: Marlowe, 1995) p. 240.

rising doubts about the decision in the public mind after 1995 – most notably among younger Americans.[44]

A Neo-revisionist View

We come now to an important new marker in the anatomy of the debate over the Hiroshima decision. Alperovitz and the other revisionists had created controversy by arguing that rather than military factors as the orthodox view held, the decision was prompted by political strategy. They drew attention to the role that growing tensions with the Soviet Union played in American calculations about the Hiroshima decision, but they were notably handicapped in their analysis of international politics. They lacked the background and the language capability to use Japanese and Russian documents. Some revisionists like Alperovitz ignored the Japanese dimension, while others depended on spotty use of translated documents. What was also lacking more broadly was archival evidence of the Russian role. These shortcomings were addressed by the historian of Japanese–Russian relations Tsuyoshi Hasegawa. In his neo-revisionist view, he brought to bear several advantages. He was the first major historian of the Hiroshima decision with language capability in Japanese, Russian, and English and access to Soviet sources available after the Cold War. His 2005 book, coming forty years after

---

[44] See the Pew Research Center, "70 Years after Hiroshima, Opinions Have Shifted on Use of the Atomic Bomb," July 31, 2015, which showed declining support in both the United States and Japan for America's bombing of Hiroshima and Nagasaki.

Alperovitz's, was the first international history of the Hiroshima decision.

Again, as in the case of Alperowitz, understanding the author's background is important. Hasegawa had a diverse career which prepared him for his historiographic contribution. His purpose was different from the first wave of revisionists. Although he came later and from an entirely different background and by a unique route, he is properly considered a revisionist – or shall we say a neo-revisionist – because of his rejection of the orthodox view and his focus on US-Soviet relations in explaining the Hiroshima decision. He had an international background, multilingual ability, and access to new materials. Born in Tokyo in 1941, his childhood memory of the March 9–10, 1945, carpet bombing of the city which took 100,000 lives lingered with him. He graduated from the University of Tokyo, but he was not active in the student upheavals there. He came to the University of Washington in 1964 to pursue a doctorate in modern Russian history.[45] While doing his dissertation on the Russian Revolution, he was a student in Robert Butow's seminar on the Asia Pacific War. (Hasegawa also was a student in one of the first times I taught a lecture course on modern Japanese history at the University of Washington.) Butow's 1954 book *Japan's Decision to Surrender*, which we will discuss in Chapter 7, was universally admired and praised as the classic work on the

---

[45] Hibiki Yamaguchi, Fumihiko Yoshida, and Radomir Compel, "Can the Atomic Bombs on Japan Be Justified? A Conversation with Dr. Tsuyoshi Hasegawa," *Journal for Peace and Nuclear Disarmament* 2, no.1 (2019): 1–25.

end of the war. Butow's book made a lasting impression on Hasegawa. He became a naturalized American citizen in 1976 and taught Russian history for many years at the University of California at Santa Barbara. He wrote important works on twentieth-century Russian history with a special interest in Russo-Japanese relations. He brought all these attributes together in his book *Racing the Enemy: Stalin, Truman and the Surrender of Japan* (2005). It was widely acclaimed. Hasegawa believed that he had eclipsed Butow's classic work and many historians agreed.

Hasegawa built his complex interpretive framework around several distinctly original themes. First, he posited a race between Stalin and Truman during the last four months of the war. Each leader had his own goals. Stalin was hastening to enter the Pacific War before it ended to be able to claim the territorial gains promised to him at the Yalta conference in return for support of the invasion of Japan. News of Hiroshima stunned Stalin, who, fearing that the war might be over before Russia could come in, stepped up the timing of his planned entry. Truman, for his part, with knowledge of the successful test of the bomb, was in a hurry to use it and end the war before Stalin could join and participate in the occupation of Japan.

A second theme was the critical importance of the Russian role in the end of the war. For Hasegawa, the Russian declaration of war on August 8 rather than the use of the atomic bomb was the cause of Japanese surrender. The implication was that had the Americans waited for Russian entry, the bomb would have been unnecessary. He took strong issue with the orthodox view that use of the atomic bomb brought

A NEO-REVISIONIST VIEW

an end to the war. Looking for a way out of the war the Japanese had sought Russian support. The Japanese army, the emperor, and civilian peace advocates were seeking Russian peace mediation and would have pressed on despite the atomic bombs. "Soviet entry into the war shocked the Japanese even more than the atomic bombs because it meant the end of any hope of achieving a settlement short of unconditional surrender."[46] The Russian declaration of war dashed Japanese hopes of Soviet support or mediation of a negotiated peace and was decisive in causing their surrender. Many historians, however, have doubted whether it is possible to separate the impact of the Russian declaration of war from the atomic bombings and even some Japanese leaders at the time were not sure which was more influential.

A third provocative theme was Hasegawa's harsh characterization of Truman (Figure 4.1). He attributed hidden motivations to the president. Truman was bent on avenging the humiliation of Pearl Harbor and "felt a strong need to bring Japan to its knees or, to put it more bluntly, to exact revenge." Critics argued that Hasegawa offered little evidence that vengeance was a motive for the bomb.[47] He further described Truman as calculating and dissembling in the way he justified the use of the bomb and sought to keep the Soviets out of the war. Drawing on newly opened Soviet archives as well as the work of Russian historians, he provided evidence

---

[46] Tsuyoshi Hasegawa, *Racing the Enemy: Stalin, Truman and the Surrender of Japan* (Cambridge: Harvard Belknap Press, 2005), p. 3.
[47] See for example Marc S. Gallicchio in *Journal of Cold War Studies* 9, no. 4 (Fall 2007): 168–170.

Figure 4.1 Churchill, Truman, and Stalin, meeting in Potsdam, Germany, July 1945.
Source: Keystone-France/Gamma-Rapho/Getty Images

that Stalin had expected to sign the Potsdam Declaration, even brought his own draft, but Truman deliberately ignored Stalin's expectation. Hasegawa argued that had Stalin's signature been on the Potsdam Declaration, the Japanese would have recognized the futility of their resistance and surrendered. Stalin, for his part, was looking for a pretext to break the Soviet–Japanese neutrality pact and join the war and share in the spoils of victory. Driven by ulterior motives, Truman "concocted" excuses to justify the use of the bomb.[48] Hasegawa argued that Truman deliberately chose to make

---

[48] Hasegawa, *Racing the Enemy,* pp. 152, 183.

the Potsdam Declaration unacceptable to Japan by refusing to include any modification of peace terms knowing that when it was rejected he could justify the use of the atomic bomb.[49] "Truman was in a hurry. He was aware that the race was on between the atomic bomb and the Soviet entry into the war. That was why he concocted the story of Japan's 'prompt rejection' of the Potsdam Proclamation as the justification for the atomic bomb."[50]

Several friendly critics were dubious of his claim that Truman had been dissembling and manipulative.[51] Barton Bernstein found the characterization "unduly cynical" and questioned the need to find new motives for what was always the intention, which was to use the bomb when it was ready. He found the evidence "flimsy" that Truman deliberately devised the Potsdam Declaration to be unacceptable to Japan so as to have cause for using the bomb or that he was driven by revenge for Pearl Harbor. More importantly, Bernstein faulted the limited time frame. Focusing his analysis on the spring and summer of 1945, Hasegawa missed the fact the "the basic decision on using the bomb flowed from overwhelming, long-held assumptions" that Truman inherited. For this reason, Bernstein wrote, "there is no need to seek the hidden motives of Truman."[52]

---

[49] See *H-Diplo Roundtable Reviews* VII, No.2 (2006): Roundtable on Hasegawa, *Racing the Enemy*, p. 10

[50] Hasegawa, *Racing the Enemy*, p. 183.

[51] See for example Robert Jervis in *Political Science Quarterly* 120, no.4 (2005–06): 675–676; J. Samuel Walker in *Pacific Historical Review* 75, no.3 (August 2006): 535–536.

[52] *H-Diplo Roundtable* on Hasegawa, *Racing the Enemy*, pp.9–17.

Concluding his book, Hasegawa boldly offered a balance sheet of responsibility for the tragedy. Japan's policymakers "must bear the responsibility for the war's destructive end more than the American president and the Soviet dictator." The emperor was especially culpable. "His delay in accepting the Allied terms ensured the use of the bomb and Soviet entry into the war." The Russians had pretended to offer the possibility of mediating but ultimately "betrayed Japan when it desperately needed their help in ending the war." Finally and pointedly, Hasegawa challenged Americans to deal honestly with their moral responsibility for the use of the bomb rather than excusing it in the way that the orthodox interpretation did as necessary to end the war and save American and Japanese lives. "The myth serves to justify Truman's decision and ease the collective American conscience." America's citing of Japanese "moral lapses," such as the Nanjing massacre and the Bataan death march and other atrocities, "does not excuse" the use of the bomb. There were alternatives to the bomb and "our self-image as Americans is tested by how we can come to terms with the decision to drop the bomb."[53]

Reflecting in 2019 on how his binational background formed his views, Hasegawa told interviewers:

> Since I am both Japanese and American, I would like to make it clear which voice I use to make the following points. Although as an American citizen, I believe that the use of the atomic bomb should be recognized as a war crime, as a Japanese I would like to stress that when we talk

---

[53] Hasegawa, *Racing the Enemy*, pp. 298–302.

about Japan as a victim, we also have to think that Japan was also a perpetrator of war ... [and] that Japan must also take responsibility for war crimes.[54]

Predictably, Hasegawa's themes drew the ire of anti-revisionist historians. They were critical of many aspects of his work, but especially agitated by his characterization of Truman. The Japanese historian Asada Sadao, who had studied in the United States before returning to teach at Doshisha University in Kyoto, was Hasegawa's most bitter critic, characterizing his book as "a rehash of an old revisionism."[55] Asada, who was the premiere historian of the prewar Japanese–American naval rivalry, had written articles[56] on the Hiroshima decisions which were widely cited by American historians as authoritative and trustworthy. Asada's views, which were informed by his use of Japanese sources, were in line with the orthodox view in emphasizing the role of the bomb in causing surrender. He was dismissive of Hasegawa's framework of a race between Stalin and Truman and critical of his use of Japanese sources. More than anything else, it was the tone of Hasegawa's critique

---

[54] Yamaguchi, Yoshida, & Compel, "Can the Atomic Bombs on Japan Be Justified?"

[55] For an autobiographical account, see Sadao Asada, *Culture Shock and Japanese–American Relations: Historical Essays* (Columbia, MO: University of Missouri Press, 2007). For the quotation, see p. 204.

[56] Asada Sadao, "The Mushroom Cloud and National Psyches: Japanese and American Perceptions of the A-Bomb Decision, 1945-1995," *The Journal of American-East Asian Relations* 4, no.2, (Summer 1995): 95–116. Also Asada Sadao, "The Shock of the Atomic Bomb and Japan's Decision to Surrender – A Reconsideration," *Pacific Historical Review* 67, no.4, (November 1998): 478–511. The essays are reprinted in Asada, *Culture Shock*.

and especially his characterization of Truman which, he wrote, "comes close to placing Harry S. Truman, a plain-speaking 'man from Missouri,' on the same 'moral' plane as Generalissimo Joseph Stalin (and Japanese warlords), and I for one find it difficult to identify with such a moral equation."[57]

Hasegawa's achievement of providing the first international history of the Hiroshima decision and new documentation from Russian and Japanese sources won the acclaim of many historians. No other historian had been able to work in the Russian, Japanese, and American archives. It gave him the opportunity to frame new issues in the debate over the Hiroshima decision. But his provocative themes were also met with doubts. His interpretative foundation of a race between Stalin and Truman left many historians unconvinced. Hasegawa's contention that Truman deliberately made the Potsdam Declaration unacceptable to the Japanese so as to justify the use of the atomic bomb left many unpersuaded. Above all, his assertion that it was the Russian entry into the war rather than the atomic bomb that brought about surrender drew the criticism of many reviewers who believed that the influence of the two events on Japanese leaders could not be disentangled.[58] When asked which event was more important, Robert Butow would clasp his hands together and respond, "I cannot separate them and I don't believe anyone can."[59]

---

[57] *The Journal of Strategic Studies* 29, no. 1 (February 2006): 171.
[58] See Kort, *Columbia Guide to Hiroshima*, pp. 107–109.
[59] See the Oregon Public Broadcasting documentary video "Rain of Ruin: The Bombing of Nagasaki."

The Revisionist Challenge

The worst fears of Stimson, Conant, and the others who formulated the orthodox defense came to pass. The "teachers of our next generation" mounted a full-scale challenge to the orthodox defense of the Hiroshima decision as part of a broader reinterpretation of the origins of the Cold War and of the prevailing views of the American past. The revisionists' sweeping challenge to orthodoxy was met with anger, outrage, and something akin to what we would today call cancel culture by the older generation. The debate was "vituperative and ill-tempered," as one close observer wrote. "What made the controversy so highly charged were the implicit questions it raised, which had to do with nothing less than the United States' moral standing in the world."[60] More than any other issue that angered the World War II generation, it was the revisionists' moral critique and the challenge it posed to telling the American story in a way that upheld Americans' sense of themselves.

The revisionists brought the moral issue to the forefront of the controversy. It was the issue that the participants in the decision had sought to surmount. The World War II generation was comfortably complacent that the United States occupied moral high ground in its foreign policy. Few issues have ever provoked the profession so much as the Hiroshima decision and the origins of the Cold War. In so doing, the revisionists polarized the historians' community and shattered its comity. The debate became not only one of

---

[60] Novick, *That Noble Dream*, p. 447.

the most controversial in recent American history but also one of the most acrimonious and was at odds with the announced professional standards of their discipline. The American Historical Association emphasizes in its Statement of Professional Standards that it prizes "civility" and "mutual respect" as norms of the profession. Historians will disagree and debate, sometimes "vehemently," but their "preeminent value" is a commitment to "tolerance and openness to new ideas."[61]

In retrospect, however, we can see that the debate was healthy. Although the revisionists' challenge disrupted the customary civility of the historical profession, the controversy proved useful. It helped to frame the debate into a broad controversy over what factors other than purely military ones had shaped the decision to use the bomb and whether viable alternatives had been available to decision-makers. As such, the works by Alperowitz, Hasegawa, and other revisionists became important markers in the anatomy of the debate.

---

[61] Statement on Standards of Professional Conduct of the American Historical Association, adopted in 1987 and periodically updated.

5

Historians and Moral Judgments

The epicenter of the Hiroshima controversy was the moral issue of using the horrific new weapon that killed a quarter of a million people, mostly civilians. In the days after the bombing, the editors of *Newsweek*, stunned by what science had made possible, wrote that "there was a special horror in the split second that returned so many thousand humans to the primeval dust from which they sprang."[1] The historian Jill Lepore observes that "Hiroshima marked the beginning of a new and differently unstable political era, in which technological change wildly outpaced the human capacity for moral reckoning."[2]

As much as any other event in American history, the Hiroshima decision forced historians to reckon with moral issues. Making moral judgments, however, was something many historians had long opposed, believing that their role was to explain while remaining detached and dispassionate. The use of the bomb awakened an old argument in their profession. It is one of the great debates involving the methods and purposes of their craft.[3] Is it part of the historian's role to make moral judgments? Or should they confine

---

[1] Lepore, *These Truths*, p. 522. [2] Lepore, *These Truths*, p. 522.
[3] Donald Bloxham, *History and Morality* (New York: Oxford University Press, 2020) explores the long-standing controversy over whether historians should engage in moral evaluation of the past.

their work to explaining events and leave judgments to their readers? If it is the ideal of the historian's craft to remain detached and objective as a social scientist might do, then abstaining from reaching verdicts on the past may be proper. If it is a purpose of history to evaluate, to teach, and to socialize the young, then it may be appropriate for historians to take a moral stance. If they do pass judgments, by what standard? It was this last question that became a focal point of the historians' controversy over the Hiroshima decision.

The Case for Moral Neutrality

During most of the nineteenth century, moralizing, teaching ethics by historical example, was still common. History was taught as the handmaid of moral philosophy.[4] But, with the professionalization of history and the adoption of a scientific ideal, by the end of the century the discipline no longer approved of making moral judgments. Rather, it was the purpose of historians to explain the past. They would readily agree with Benedetto Croce, the Italian historian, that it is not their place to "bustle about as judges, condemning here and giving absolution there." It is not their role to moralize and presume to express opinions about the good or bad ways of their subjects. Historians ought not to act as "a judge, still less a hanging judge." Historians must maintain a detached and dispassionate approach and avoid moral judgment on individuals and their misdeeds.[5]

---

[4] Felix Gilbert, *History: Choice and Commitment* (Cambridge, MA: Belknap Press of Harvard University Press, 1977), p. 451.
[5] Quoted in Carr, *What Is History?* p. 77.

THE CASE FOR MORAL NEUTRALITY

The noted English historian Herbert Butterfield, despite his own personal Christian belief, argued that making moral judgments and asserting them as the verdict of history was not the role of the historian.

> The historian, whose art is a descriptive one, does not move in this world of moral ideas. His materials and his processes, and all his apparatus exist to enable him to show how a given event came to take place. Who is he to jump out of his true office and merely announce to all of us that it ought never have happened at all?[6]

Butterfield's belief was that only God can truly judge.[7] Historians must not arrogate to themselves "the voice of god." They must not regard themselves as the judge when by their methods and equipment they are "fitted only to be the detective."[8] Rather, the historian "is neither judge nor jury; he is in the position of a man called upon to give evidence."[9]

Another strong opponent of moral judgments was the English historian E. H. Carr, one of the most widely

---

[6] Butterfield's opinion was asserted in his famous tract *The Whig Interpretation of History* (New York: Scribner's, 1951), in which he chastised historians for reading their values back into history and traced the triumph of liberal causes. See p. 120.

[7] See Bailyn, *Sometimes an Art*, p. 27.

[8] Butterfield, *Whig Interpretation*, p. 107.

[9] Butterfield, *Whig Interpretation*, p. 131. Once the impartial history was already written, the historian could then independently choose to interpret it, which Butterfield certainly did, but that was not permitted in the writing of what he called "technical history." He insisted that writing history and making moral judgments must be done on separate tracks. See Michael Bentley, "Herbert Butterfield and the Ethics of Historiography," *History and Theory* 44, no. 1 (February 2005): 55–71.

read commentators on the historian's craft. Historians ought not to judge individual leaders, because they are part of a society and a reflection of it. Historians should reserve their moral judgments for "events, institutions, or policies of the past."[10] It was wrong, he wrote, to condemn the slave owner but appropriate to explain the slave-owning society and how it came about and was surmounted. A sympathetic supporter of the Bolshevik revolution despite its brutal suppression of the opposition to its planned society, Carr was inclined to overlook the human toll that was involved. Inevitably, he argued, progress in human society comes at the expense of some people and what is important is that it brings progress and the greater good for more people.

> Suffering is indigenous in history. Every great period of history has its casualties as well as its victories. This is an exceedingly complicated question, because we have no measure which enables us to balance the greater good of some against the sacrifices of others: yet some such balance must be struck.... The thesis that the good of some justifies the sufferings of others is implicit in all government.[11]

Many historians have, in fact, relied on the utilitarian principle that the greatest good for the greatest number should suffice as a standard of moral judgment.

Marc Bloch was one of the most respected writers on the historian's craft who lived in the worst of times and was brought down by its evil when, as a member of the French

---

[10] Carr, *What Is History?* p. 78.   [11] Carr, *What Is History?* p. 79.

resistance, he was executed by the Gestapo. It is noteworthy that in his unfinished work *The Historian's Craft*, he was insistent on resisting moral judgments: "Are we so sure of ourselves and our age as to divide the company of our forefathers into the just and the damned?"[12] Passing judgment on historical figures is a serious responsibility and not to be taken lightly. Because moral standards change over time, it is wrong to apply those standards to a different age.

The greatest of all historical mistakes, as the historian of science Stephen Jay Gould observed, is "arrogantly judging our forebears in the light of modern knowledge perforce unavailable to them."[13] Moral values can change through time and are therefore relative. Historians should not judge individuals or societies of a different time in the past.

The Case for Moral Engagement

Other historians, however, argue that the ethical dimension is an inescapable part of their work. Their discipline comes out of a great humanistic tradition and historians should not ignore this dimension. The erudite historian Lord Acton was famous for staking out a position at odds with many historians then and since, holding that the historian cannot be indifferent to moral considerations. In his 1895 Inaugural Lecture at Cambridge, he exhorted historians "never to debase the moral currency or lower the standard of rectitude but try others by the final maxim that governs your own lives,

---

[12] Marc Bloch, *The Historian's Craft* (New York: Vintage, 1953), p. 140.
[13] Gaddis, *Landscape of History*, p. 140.

and to suffer no man and no cause to escape the undying penalty which history has the power to inflict on wrong."[14]

The eminent historian and philosopher Isaiah Berlin took issue with Carr's view that history was determined by vast impersonal forces and that passing moral judgment on individual leaders was wrong. Berlin asserted that individuals had free will to make choices and therefore must be held responsible for the consequences of their decisions. Historians should not excuse individuals as simply reflections of their times or their societies. Genghis Khan and Hitler and Stalin should of course be denounced for their massacres.[15] In a famous essay, he took aim at historians who emphasize the role of great impersonal forces that determine the course of history and who therefore do not subject individual leaders to moral judgments. Those historians who give credence to the power of vast irresistible forces, deterministic theories of historical development, deprive humans of choice and action and thereby make moral judgment an empty notion. If free will is ruled out, humans are puppets. To Berlin such theories fly in the face of common sense and the way we ourselves live our lives making decisions and choices. When we do this, we don't believe that we are controlled, nor should we believe that individuals in the past were controlled by vast impersonal forces. Humans are capable of voluntary action and must

---

[14] Gertrude Himmelfarb, *The Moral Imagination from Adam Smith to Lionel Trilling* (Lanham, MD: Rowman & Littlefield, 2006, 2nd ed.), p. 100.

[15] Isaiah Berlin, *Historical Inevitability* (New York: Oxford University Press, 1954), p.76.

accept human responsibility for their actions because there is a "limited but nevertheless real area of human freedom."[16]

Many historians see their purpose as an educative one, to teach their students, the reading public, and future generations. They see danger in a detached and neutral stance. When historians choose to be value-free in their writings, they leave a moral vacuum. The historian of modern France Gordon Wright, in a presidential address to the America Historical Association, argued that it should be possible to find a middle way for liberals between aloof neutrality and a preachy judgmentalism so as to offer their readers, and especially their students, the model of a coherent value system.[17] Historians should not be neutral when they encounter misdeeds and cruelty. They should make explicit what their values are but also allow their readers space to reach their own conclusions. The historian Melvyn Leffler writes, for example, that "the test of one's scholarly credentials and ethical values is ... whether one is committed to history as a way of learning about how to preserve a more decent and humane world."[18]

Historians and the Social Sciences

Political scientists sometimes say that making moral judgments marks a distinction between their discipline and the

---

[16] Berlin, *Historical Inevitability*, p. 78.
[17] Gordon Wright, "History as a Moral Science," *American Historical Review* 81, no. 1 (February 1976): 1–11.
[18] Melvin Leffler quoted in *Bridges and Boundaries: Historians, Political Scientists, and the Study of International Relations*, edited by Colin Elman and Miriam Fendius Elman (Cambridge, MA: MIT Press 2001), p. 400.

HISTORIANS AND MORAL JUDGMENTS

historians' craft. A leading political theorist, Robert Jervis, argued that "many political scientists want to be scientific and believe that evaluations of the actors, especially on moral dimensions, have no place in such an enterprise."[19] He saw the proclivity of some historians to make moral judgments as a fundamental difference with political scientists "who see their task as explaining behavior not judging it."[20] Addressing the Hiroshima controversy, Jervis drew a sharp distinction in the approach of the two disciplines. Rather than debating why Truman dropped the bomb and whether it should be condemned, political scientists would see it as confirming generalizations or patterns that they find in international political behavior. In a surprisingly blunt observation Jervis in effect asked: What is all this historiographical fuss over moral issues about? Political scientists, for their part, insist on the comparative method in reaching their theories and generalizations and they fault historians who mostly ignore this critical method. Armed with a realist principle derived from comparative analysis, Jervis wrote that while historians argue fiercely about why Truman dropped the bomb,

> I would start with the generalization that unless there are pressing considerations to the contrary, states involved in total war will use all the weapons at their disposal. . . . Do we find cases in which a country had a new weapon of

---

[19] Robert Jervis quoted in *Bridges and Boundaries*, p. 399.
[20] Robert Jervis, "International Politics and Diplomatic History: Fruitful Differences" *H-Diplo | ISSF Essays, Number 1, p. 9.* Originally Published by H-Diplo/ISSF on 12 March 2010.

enormous power that might terminate the conflict on favorable terms and declined to use it? I cannot think of any. The basic methodological point is that, assuming there aren't any or at least aren't many such cases, at one level I would not see any reason to go any further because the explanation for Truman's behavior is nothing peculiar to Truman, to the U.S., or to the specific situation. Rather it is just another instance of the prevailing ugly pattern of international politics.

To pass moral judgment on Truman when he has acted as any other leader under like circumstances, Jervis concluded, would be regarded as "naïve" by political scientists who are concerned with reality and understanding human beings as they are, not as they should be.[21]

The historian Paul Schroeder, however, responded to Jervis by explaining the importance of history as a moral undertaking. The study of history, he said, is like a mirror. It tells us who we are as humans. It is about self-knowledge. It is about our identity. The goal of history is "to expand the range and increase the depth of our understanding of what it means to be a human being."[22] And that is a matter that requires moral judgments not scientific detachment and generalizations.

This exchange between Jervis and Schroeder raises an interesting and debatable issue about the historical discipline and its relation to the social sciences (sociology, psychology, anthropology, economics, and political science). Sarah Maza

[21] Robert Jervis, "International Politics and Diplomatic History: Fruitful Differences," in *H-Diplo | ISSF Essays, Number 1*. Originally Published by H-Diplo/ISSF on 12 March 2010.
[22] Robert Jervis quoted in *Bridges and Boundaries*, p. 415.

clarifies the distinction this way: "[Historians'] project is to order, and make sense of, a complicated set of events at a particular point in the past. Their purpose is not to extract from one historical situation a generalization that can be applied to another."[23] However, historians frequently borrow concepts from the social sciences and history is often considered a social science as well as one of the humanities. Historians often debate among themselves whether their discipline is an art or a science. University administrators sometimes puzzle over whether to place history departments in the humanities or the social sciences. As John Tosh wisely observes, "history cannot be defined as either a humanity or a social science without denying a large part of its nature.... History is a hybrid discipline which owes its endless fascination and its complexity to the fact that it straddles the two."[24]

Hiroshima and the Historians' Moral Perplexity

Despite the traditional resistance of many historians to engage in moral judgments, those who write on the end of the war in the Pacific find it almost impossible to avoid confronting the moral issues posed by the decision to use nuclear weapons on Hiroshima and Nagasaki. The horror and suffering at ground zero which John Hersey and others described made it hard for historians to adhere to the view that they should hold to a detached and dispassionate

[23] Maza, *Thinking about History*, p. 164.
[24] Tosh, *Pursuit of History*, p. 45.

approach to their studies (Figure 5.1). Too many observers raised moral issues to allow historians to ignore the question and to remain morally neutral and detached. The advent of the nuclear age and its implications for human survival seemed simply too profound to treat dispassionately. Participants in the decision fearing moral judgment hoped to resolve or even to suppress the issue. In his *Harper's* article, Stimson wrote that there was no other choice, that it had ended the war, and that it had saved lives. For a time, that understanding carried the day. Americans were reassured. But the revisionist generation, galvanized by the events and the radical politics of the 1960s, rose as *enfants terribles*,

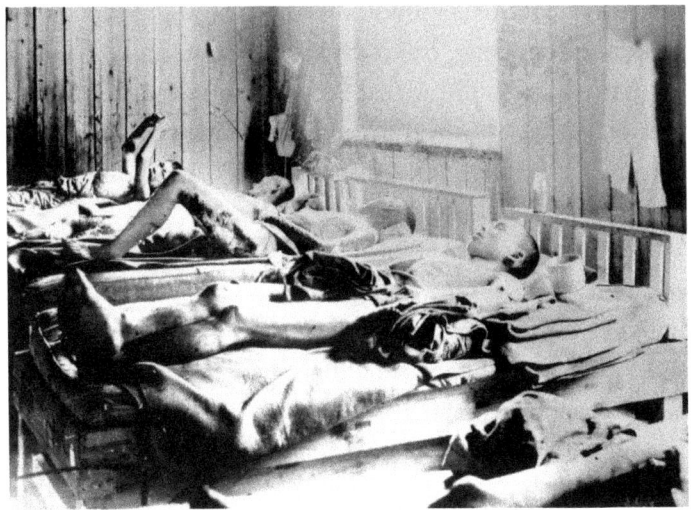

Figure 5.1 Atomic bomb survivors in Hiroshima, suffering the effects of radiation.
Source: Ann Ronan Pictures/Hulton Archive/Getty Images

insisting that there *were* choices. They raised the issue that the orthodox interpretation had hoped to preempt. For them, history was a tool for radical change. They self-consciously proclaimed a committed history. The study of the past had a moral purpose in that it could demonstrate the need for change in the present and future. They dismissed the idea of a neutral, nonjudgmental role for the historian. By refusing to accept the inevitability of an invasion they raised the morality issue in a direct way. Abandoning any pretense of detached or dispassionate approach to their subject, they argued that if an invasion could have been avoided, then the utilitarian interpretation, that is, that use of the bomb saved lives, could not stand. They expressed moral outrage at the use of the atomic bomb against innocent civilians. Their insistence provoked a persistent controversy over how to reckon with moral judgment of the bombing. The controversy revealed a deep moral perplexity among historians. By what standard should the decision-makers be held morally accountable? Unable to adhere to the ideal of a dispassionate stance, historians' responses took a variety of approaches.

There were long-held and widely shared ethics for legitimate warfare. One of the oldest guidelines for how war should be fought was the principle of proportionality, which held that the harm done should not be out of proportion to the good accomplished. The principle had its origins in the Enlightenment and even earlier in the philosophy of Thomas Aquinas. Wars must be fought with only enough force to achieve victory and directed at legitimate targets. Civilians should be protected. Proportionality required tempering the extent and violence of warfare. Robert McNamara will be remembered for wrestling with his guilt for the Vietnam debacle which occurred while he was secretary of defense. But he also felt deep remorse for his role during the last year of the war against Japan when he served under General LeMay and was charged with measuring the effectiveness of the B-29 carpet bombing campaign which devastated over sixty cities. "Proportionality," McNamara said,

> should be the guideline in war. Killing 50% to 90% of the people of 67 Japanese cities and then bombing them with two nuclear bombs is not proportional to the objectives we were trying to achieve. . . . LeMay said, "If we'd lost the war, we'd all have been prosecuted as war criminals." And I think he's right. He, and I'd say I, were behaving as war criminals. LeMay recognized that what he was doing would be thought immoral if his side had lost. But what makes it immoral if you lose and not immoral if you win?[25]

International law, as set forth in Geneva protocols, had outlawed the killing of noncombatants and the use of poisonous gas and other bacteriological materials in the conduct of war. When Japan began bombing Chinese cities in 1937 and when civilian populations were bombed in other parts of the world, Americans were shocked.[26] After the outbreak of fighting in Europe, Franklin Roosevelt had urged belligerents to refrain

---

[25] Transcript of the documentary film "The Fog of War: Eleven Lessons from the Life of Robert S. McNamara," directed by Errol Morris (2003). See also Thomas Hurka, "Proportionality in the Morality of War," *Philosophy and Public Affairs* 33, no. 1 (Winter 2005): 34–66.

[26] John W. Dower, *War without Mercy: Race & Power in the Pacific War* (New York: Pantheon, 1986), pp.38–39.

from the killing of civilians. On September 1, 1939, Roosevelt made an "urgent appeal to every Government which may be engaged in hostilities publicly to affirm its determination that its armed forces shall in no event, and under no circumstances, undertake the bombardment from the air of civilian populations or of unfortified cities."[27] Roosevelt said: "Ruthless bombing from the air ... which has resulted in the maiming and in the death of thousands of defenseless men, women, and children, has sickened the hearts of every civilized man and woman, and has profoundly shocked the conscience of humanity."[28] But once the United States entered into what became total war, the old norms crumbled, and Americans became accustomed to targeting whole cities and their civilians. Revisionists expressed moral outrage, but historians of the orthodox persuasion found reasons to defend the bombing.

Moral Philosophy

Moral philosophers attempted to provide a standard by which historians might make their moral judgment of Hiroshima. Theorists of just war (*ius in bello*) found the Hiroshima decision and the carpet bombing of German and Japanese cities a focus for their thinking of how wars should be fought and what was permissible in the conduct of war. They pondered how the just war tradition, which reached back centuries, should be updated in its application to the new atomic era.

---

[27] Dower, *War without Mercy*, pp. 38–39. See also Bundy, *Danger and Survival*, p. 63.
[28] Dower, *Cultures of War*, 220.

MORAL PHILOSOPHY

Let us consider two well-known moral philosophers who offered clear answers to the issues raised by the Hiroshima decision. Both emphasized the killing of noncombatants as unjust and the importance of tempering the degree of violence in proportion to the desired objective.

Michael Walzer writing in his classic *Just and Unjust Wars* (1977) argued that Japanese civilians should not have been targeted in the firebombing and in the use of atomic weapons.

> The destruction of the innocent, whatever its purposes, is a kind of blasphemy against our deepest moral commitments. . . . How did the people of Hiroshima forfeit their rights? Perhaps their taxes paid for some of the ships and planes used in the attack on Pearl Harbor; perhaps they sent their sons into the navy and air force with prayers for their success; or perhaps they celebrated the actual event, after being told that their country had won a great victory in the face of an imminent American threat. Surely there is nothing here that makes these people liable to direct attack.[29]

Walzer concluded that if killing hundreds of thousands of innocent noncombatants was the cost of achieving unconditional surrender, then that war goal should have been modified.

The Harvard political philosopher John Rawls, best known for his writing on justice, rights, and equality, offered

---

[29] Michael Walzer, *Just and Unjust Wars: A Moral Argument with Historical Illustrations* (New York: Basic Books, 2nd ed.,1977), pp.262–264.

a similar argument. For most of his career, Rawls shunned discussion of contemporary practical politics. He did, however, write a noteworthy article on the Hiroshima decision at the time of its fiftieth anniversary. Rawls had won a Bronze Star serving in the South Pacific, experiencing some of the fiercest fighting during World War II. When Japan surrendered, he was part of the American Occupation force. Seeing the devastation of Hiroshima and the other firebombed cities profoundly affected him.[30] The article that he wrote in 1995 protesting the use of the bomb posited a standard of conduct in war of "democratic peoples ... [who] have different ends of war than the nondemocratic, especially totalitarian, states." The war against Japan failed his test of how a liberal democracy should conduct itself in war because it had attacked civilian populations, violating their human rights. They were not responsible for the war. It was imperative to provide the postwar era with a model of what a just society should be. Rawls held that fighting a just war required a statesman as leader – one who thinks not of the next election, not of revenge or retaliation, but rather of how to achieve a just and lasting peace. Lincoln and Washington were statesmen. "Truman was in many ways a good, at times a very good president. But the way he ended the war showed he failed as a statesman." For Rawls,

> Hiroshima and the fire-bombing of Japanese cities were great evils that the duties of statesmanship require leaders to avoid. ... Another failure of statesmanship was not to

[30] Thomas Pogge, *John Rawls: His Life and Theory of Justice* (New York: Oxford University Press, 2007), p.12.

try to enter negotiations with the Japanese before any drastic steps such as the fire-bombing of cities or the bombing of Hiroshima were taken. A conscientious attempt to do so was morally necessary. As a democratic people, we owed that to the Japanese people.

Rawls was firm in his rejection of utilitarian standards of the greatest good for the greatest number because they ignored the rights of individuals, which he saw as fundamental. It was unacceptable to engage in carpet bombing that took the lives of innocent civilians.[31]

But historians are not moral philosophers, like Rawls or Walzer, who are seeking to establish a set of abstract and transcendent principles to guide or to judge behavior. It was well and good for moral philosophers to formulate their views in the abstract. As Edmund Burke wrote, there is a big difference between a "statesman and a professor in a university." The latter has the leisure to ponder his ideas, whereas a former must deal with circumstances of the moment. If he makes the wrong decision, "he may ruin his country forever."[32] Statesmen like military leaders must make decisions when timing and conditions are uncertain. As General George Marshall put it, "battlefield decisions were taken under conditions of 'chronic obscurity' – that is, under excessive pressure on the basis of incomplete and defective information."[33] Both Walzer and Rawls were fulfilling their roles as moral

---

[31] John Rawls, "50 Years after Hiroshima," *Dissent* (Summer 1995): 323–327.
[32] Kort, *The Columbia Guide to Hiroshima*, p. 114.
[33] Arthur Schlesinger, Jr., "The Historian as Participant," *Daedalus* 100, no. 2 (Spring 1971): 354.

philosophers, but for historians assessing the actions of politicians, decision-makers, and military leaders in the practical everyday world, the issues of moral judgment remained.

The Utilitarian Calculus

The foundation of the orthodox defense of the Hiroshima decision was that America was waging a just war against aggressors who violated the accepted rules of war and were fighting an unjust war. Truman, in his address to the nation on August 12, 1945, explained: "We have used [the bomb] against those who attacked us without warning at Pearl Harbor, against those who have starved and beaten and executed American prisoners of war, against those who have abandoned all pretense of obeying international laws of warfare." And Truman added, in what became the centerpiece of the orthodox defense: "We have used it in order to shorten the agony of war."[34] Participants in the decision acted with good results. The defense is sometimes called "consequentialist" because the consequences of the decision were good. The outcome of the bomb was the end of the killing. It brought an early end to the war.

But a further defense was needed because the consequence was not only the end of the war but also the horrible death of noncombatants and suffering of the civilians that Hersey's *Hiroshima* had described. Consequentialism is closely related to utilitarian theories of ethical conduct. It was utilitarian ethical theory which was made to carry the burden of defense that participants in the decision mounted.

---

[34] Quoted in Walzer, *Just and Unjust*, p. 264.

The entire thrust of Stimson's *Harper's* article was designed to foreclose moral condemnation and instead claim the high ground by asserting the utilitarian judgment that the bombing had served the greatest good for the greatest number, that is, the bomb had avoided the greater loss of life that would have ensued from an invasion or the prolonging of the war. By averting an invasion, the use of the bomb, as awful as it was, had been the only moral choice to make. It had saved American and Japanese lives. The *Harper's* article did not confront the distinction between soldiers and noncombatant lives that theology, moral philosophy, and international law made. With this moral reasoning, Americans who broadly accepted the utilitarian defense became obsessed with estimating casualty numbers which an invasion would cost. The numbers needed to be greater than the lives lost at Hiroshima and Nagasaki. Some estimates have seemed greatly inflated. The danger of such ethical justification was that it smacked of cold calculation of cost–benefit analysis or, as one critic put it, "morality reduced to arithmetic."[35]

Finally, the orthodox view, Stimson's article, and defenders of Truman question the application of absolutist ethical reasoning to the use of the bomb. "As I look back over the five years of my service as Secretary of War," Stimson concluded, "I see too many heartrending decisions to be willing to pretend that war is anything else than what it is. The face of war is the face of death; death is an inevitable part of every order that a wartime leader gives." Historians defending

[35] Jim Holt, "Morality, Reduced to Arithmetic," *New York Times*, August 5, 1995.

Truman argued that leaders, especially in time of war, are forced to make decisions that did not allow for the moral purity that political philosophers described. The Notre Dame University historian (and Catholic priest) Wilson Miscamble defended Truman by citing Machiavelli that the values of a responsible leader in government cannot be the morals of an ordinary individual, for the leader is responsible for the well-being of his state. He "cannot observe all those things for which men are held good, since he is often under a necessity, to maintain his state, of acting against faith, against charity, against humanity, against religion." The prince must "know how to enter into evil, when forced by necessity."[36] Truman as a responsible leader charged with a priority for the interests of his own people had been forced to leave aside his religious beliefs to save American lives and end the war.

Realists like Machiavelli or more recently Hans Morgenthau have always argued that "there was no way to avoid doing evil in the conduct of foreign policy as even the most moral statesman was bound to commit inhumane acts. International relations was not a field for anyone seeking perfection or saintliness."[37] In his essay on Machiavelli, the historian and philosopher Isaiah Berlin summed up Machiavelli's argument:

> He does not seek to correct the Christian conception of a good man. He does not say that saints are not saints, or

---

[36] Wilson D. Miiscamble, *The Most Controversial Decision: Truman, the Atomic Bombs, and the Defeat of Japan* (Cambridge: Cambridge University Press, 2011), p. 121.

[37] Gewen, *The Inevitability of Tragedy*, p. 393.

THE UTILITARIAN CALCULUS

that honourable behaviour is not honourable or to be admired; only that this type of goodness cannot, at least in its traditionally accepted forms, create or maintain a strong, secure and vigorous society, that it is in fact fatal to it. He points out that in our world men who pursue such ideals are bound to be defeated and to lead other people to ruin, since their view of the world is not founded upon the ... truth that is tested by success and experience – which (however cruel) is always, in the end, less destructive than the other (however noble).[38]

Morals and the values of success in governing are separate worlds.

Perhaps that is what President Barack Obama was getting at when he told Japanese reporters in 2016 shortly before he became the first sitting president to visit Hiroshima: "It's important to recognize that in the midst of war, leaders make all kinds of decisions. It's a job of historians to ask questions and examine them. But I know as somebody who has now sat in this position for the last seven-and-a-half years that every leader makes very difficult decisions, particularly during wartime."[39]

The military historian Richard Frank believed that the utilitarian moral defense of the use of nuclear weapons on Hiroshima and Nagasaki could be made even stronger than was usually argued. Obsession with casualty figures of American lives that were prevented by using the bomb and

---

[38] Isaiah Berlin, *Against the Current: Essays in the History of Ideas*, (Princeton: Princeton University Press, Second Edition, 2013), pp. 61–62.
[39] Interview with NHK as reported in *The Guardian* newspaper, May 22, 2016.

averting an invasion hardly begins to deal with the complexity of the situation. Frank argued that when the bomb was used Americans were about to begin bombing the transportation system and this together with the naval blockade prefigured immense loss of Japanese lives if the war had been even more protracted. He also called attention to the numbers of other Asian people who were dying while the war continued. "It might have exceeded one hundred thousand per month in China alone." Thus, the utilitarian calculus should not only weigh the American lives saved by using the bomb to shorten the war but also take account of the lives of Japanese who would have perished in a prolonged war as well as "the vast numbers of Chinese and other Asian noncombatants." In short, the bombs' use saved far more lives than is calculated in the usual orthodox defense. Although hundreds of thousands of Japanese noncombatants had their rights violated dying in the firebombing of the cities and the atomic bombing of Hiroshima and Nagasaki, Frank concluded,

> those Japanese noncombatants, however, held no stronger right not to be slaughtered than did the vast numbers of Chinese and other Asian noncombatants, the Japanese noncombatants in Soviet captivity in Asia, or the Japanese noncombatants (not to mention Allied prisoners of war and civilian internees) who would have perished of starvation and disease in the final agony of the blockade. Thus, alternatives to the atomic bombs carried no guarantee that they would end the war or reduce the amount of human death and suffering.[40]

[40] Frank, *Downfall*, p. 360.

For Frank and other defenders of the decision, the utilitarian calculus provided the necessary moral justification for the use of the bomb.

Racism and the Decision

Pervading the entire controversy over the morality of the Hiroshima decision is the issue of racism and whether it motivated the use of the bomb against Japan. Spoken or unspoken, the issue is always there. When my Waseda University professor asked me if we Americans would have used the bomb on Germany, he was asking what many Japanese suspected – that racism was involved in the decision. Emperor Hirohito in his postwar reflections laid emphasis on racism as a cause of the Japanese–American conflict by the rejection of the racial equality clause in the Versailles treaty, the Japanese exclusion act in 1924, and the treatment of Japanese immigrants in the United States.

Gandhi had written to Franklin Roosevelt in July 1942 that the "declaration that the Allies are fighting to make the world safe for freedom of the individual and democracy sounds hollow, so long as India, and for that matter Africa, are exploited by Great Britain, and America has the Negro problem in her own home." The British historian Matthew Jones traces how the issue dogged American policymakers in the Cold War. "In Asia as a whole, the charge that racism lay behind the use of the bomb against Japan gained much credibility."[41] Cold War

---

[41] Matthew Jones, *After Hiroshima: The United States, Race and Nuclear Weapons in Asia, 1945–1965* (Cambridge: Cambridge University Press, 2010), p. 35.

liberals like the historian Arthur Schlesinger, Jr. wrote that if they were to win the allegiance of peoples in Asia and Africa, Americans must "reform our own racial practices – not only repeal such insulting symbols as the Oriental exclusion laws, but demonstrate a deep and effective concern with racial inequities within the United States."[42] Another Cold War liberal, Norman Cousins, editor of the *Saturday Review*, launched the project known as Hiroshima Maidens to bring disfigured *hibakusha* to the United States for corrective surgery. The novelist James Michener teamed with Richard Rodgers and Oscar Hammerstein in musicals to highlight mixed racial romance. *South Pacific, The King and I, Sayonara,* and *Teahouse of the August Moon* deliberately romanticized the ideal of racial tolerance. Despite such efforts, racism in America was always a continuing problem. At the time my Waseda professor questioned me, the civil rights movement was erupting in racial riots and conflict in American cities.

From top to bottom, American society was pervaded by a strong sense of racial hierarchy. The young Franklin Roosevelt, to cite a particularly important example, held strong racist views. In 1925, while visiting Warm Springs, Georgia, for treatment of his legs, which had been paralyzed by polio, he wrote a column in the (Macon, Georgia) *Telegraph* newspaper justifying resistance to Japanese immigration on the West Coast and passage of the Japanese exclusion act as a step in preventing "the undesirability of mixing the blood of the two peoples." He wrote that

---

[42] Arthur M. Schlesinger, Jr., *The Vital Center: The Politics of Freedom* (Boston: Houghton Mifflin, 1949), p.235.

Californians have properly objected on the sound basic ground that Japanese immigrants are not capable of assimilation into the American population. ... Anyone who has traveled in the Far East knows that the mingling of Asiatic blood with European or American blood produces, in nine cases out of ten, the most unfortunate results. There are, throughout the East, many thousands of so-called Eurasians – men and women and children partly of Asiatic blood and partly of European or American blood. These Eurasians are, as a common thing, looked down on and despised, both by the European and American who resides there, and by the pure Asiatic who lives there.[43]

Many Black leaders expressed feelings that racism had played a part in the willingness to use the bomb on the Japanese.[44] By the fiftieth anniversary of the bombing of Hiroshima and Nagasaki only 31 percent of Blacks approved, while 64 percent of whites approved.[45] Interestingly, we now know that it was a Black war correspondent in Japan after the war, Charles Loeb, who challenged the American military's insistence that radiation had not caused the sickening and

---

[43] See Donald Scott Carmichael, ed., *F. D. R. Columnist: The Uncollected Columns of Franklin D. Roosevelt* (Chicago: Pellegrini & Cudahy, 1947), pp. 56–60. The column was dated April 30, 1925

[44] Vincent J. Intondi, *African Americans against the Bomb: Nuclear Weapons, Colonialism, and the Black Freedom Movement* (Stanford: Stanford University Press, 2020), pp, 9–29 studies the intertwining of African-American leaders' movement for racial justice with the anti-nuclear movement.

[45] Barton J. Bernstein, "Truman and the A-Bomb: Targeting Noncombatants, Using the Bomb, and His Defending the 'Decision'," *Journal of Military History*, 62 (July 1998): 569.

death of Hiroshima residents. Loeb's exposure of this cover-up appeared in articles distributed by the National Negro Publishers Association and were not more widely reported. It appears that Loeb's reporting contributed to the Black leaders' feelings that racism was involved in the Hiroshima decision.[46]

There can be no doubt that anti-Japanese racism was rampant in wartime America. "Probably in all our history," the distinguished American historian Allan Nevins wrote, "no foe has been so detested as were the Japanese."[47] The United States had interned over 110,000 Japanese-Americans living along the Pacific Coast by Executive Order 9066, which Roosevelt signed on February 19, 1942, authorizing the Army to remove them to remote camps in the western United States. Most Americans could see no distinction between Japanese and Japanese-Americans. Internment represented a continuation of, actually an intensification of, pervasive racist sentiment in the prewar attitudes of Americans toward Japan and Japanese immigrants. Neither German-Americans nor Italian-Americans were subject to internment.

Did racist hate play a direct role in the decision? If it could be shown that the use of the bomb was motivated by anti-Japanese racism, then historians would have to render a strong moral condemnation. Yet archival materials relating to the decision reveal limited evidence that racist attitudes *directly* influenced the decision to use the bomb and most

---

[46] William J. Broad, "The Black Reporter Who Exposed a Lie About the Atom Bomb," *New York Times*, August 9, 2021.

[47] Quoted Dower, *War without Mercy*, p. 33.

RACISM AND THE DECISION

historians of the decision therefore give the issue no sustained attention. Gar Alperovitz, for example, concluded that "it is all but impossible to find specific evidence that racism was an important factor in the decision to attack Hiroshima and decision."[48] Similarly, Barton Bernstein after his considerable research concluded that there may have been

> some subtle strains of racism endorsing the decision to use the bombs. Probably policy-makers found it easier to use the bomb against yellow people (the Japanese) than against whites (the Germans), but racism did not dictate the decision to drop the bombs on Japan. US leaders would undoubtedly have used the bombs against Germany if they had been developed in time to speed a surrender in Europe.[49]

The pioneer of Asian-American studies Ronald Takaki made the most sustained examination of available evidence of racist influence. He explored the pervasive racial stereotypes that were part of Truman's upbringing and were implanted in his instinctive attitudes which easily led him to succumb to "the raging hate rooted in a long history of animosity against the Japanese, as well as the fierce memory of Pearl Harbor."[50] While underscoring inherent racist attitudes Takaki concluded that the influence could not be found more specifically in policymaking documents. John Dower,

---

[48] Quoted in Gordin and Ikenberry, eds., *The Age of Hiroshima*, p. 58.
[49] Barton Bernstein, "Shatterer of Worlds: Hiroshima and Nagasaki," *Bulletin of Atomic Scientists*, 31 (December 1975): 18.
[50] Ronald Takaki, *Hiroshima: Why America Dropped the Atomic Bomb* (Boston: Little, Brown, 1995), p.146.

author of the pathbreaking study *War without Mercy*, concluded that "vengeance and racism were powerful sentiments that shaped the conduct of the war on both sides, and to pretend otherwise is dishonest."[51] Race hate led to the dehumanization of the enemy and the psychological distancing that facilitated the targeting of civilians in carpet bombing and then with nuclear weapons.[52] Historians have tended to leave the issue in those general terms. The historian Sean Malloy has proposed that the role of racism ought to be understood in the broader perspective of Western imperialism in Asia and the American pursuit of hegemony "in a region long seen as peopled by racial inferiors in need of Western guidance."[53]

The Challenge

The American students enrolled in the course that I taught on the Hiroshima decision always came to it with the same question: "How was it that our country was the one to use the bomb?" Japanese exchange students tended to come to the course with a sense of victimization, wondering: "Was it necessary to use the bomb when we were already beaten?" At the heart of these questions were the moral issues which made the Hiroshima decision so controversial.

---

[51] John W. Dower, "Three Narratives of Our Humanity," in *History Wars: The Enola Gay and Other Battles for the American Past*, edited by Edward T. Linenthal and Tom Engelhardt (New York: Henry Holt, 1996), p. 86.
[52] Dower, *War without Mercy*, p. 11.   [53] Dower, *War without Mercy*, p. 69.

In all of the conflicting interpretations we consider, historians deal centrally with the morality of the decision. The moral issues were too stark to be sidestepped. The deliberate targeting of Japanese civilians in the firebombing of sixty cities and in the use of the bomb to break morale and compel unconditional surrender fits what today might be defined as state-sponsored terrorism and would elicit harsh judgment. But should historians read today's values back to the Asia Pacific War? Barton Bernstein threads the needle carefully. On the one hand, "historians must make the effort to understand the moral-political context in 1945 for American policymakers." Historians must explain that "abstaining from using it on Japan would have made no moral or political sense for [Truman]. . . . Not using the bomb might prolong the war, cost US and Allied lives." No one who could conceivably have been president, Bernstein writes, would have decided differently. On the other hand, explaining the moral–political context in 1945 does not mean approving it or "refusing to make moral judgments – about the atomic bombing, and about the lack of a serious quest for likely alternatives."[54]

Historians are always challenged to find a delicate balance. They must reserve their moral judgments until they have fulfilled their obligation to be a dispassionate analyst of the past. The basis of any moral judgment should always be clear to the readers, leaving them the possibility of making

---

[54] *H-Diplo Roundtable Reviews*, Volume VII, No. 2 (2006), p. 16. Roundtable on Tsuyoshi Hasegawa, *Racing the Enemy: Stalin, Truman, and the Surrender of Japan*. Commentary by Barton J. Bernstein. accessed March 2, 2011, www.h-net.org/~diplo/index.html.

their own judgment. All historians possess moral values which it will be difficult to keep from affecting their interpretations, regardless of how they may strive for neutrality. Historians are always shaped by their particular age and inevitably their presuppositions are intertwined with the basic assumptions of their age. They should strive for self-awareness by reflecting on their own times and upbringing, which are likely to be the source of their values. From such reflection they can endeavor to keep their own moral preferences from distorting the context of the past they are studying. As the historian David Hackett Fisher writes: "Every historian possesses a complex structure of value assumptions, which he cannot adjust to his empirical projects, and cannot keep out of his work." To "neutralize or control his moral preferences" the historian must "make his values as fully explicit, to himself and others, as possible."[55] There is no need to refrain from moral judgments – indeed it may be impossible, but historians should suspend their present commitments sufficiently to enter the past they are studying, understanding the circumstances of people at that time, while still retaining the capacity for moral judgments that do not warp the narrative.[56] These are the deepest obligations of the historian's craft.

[55] David Hackett Fischer, *Historians' Fallacies: Toward a Logic of Historical Thought* (New York: Harper & Row, 1970), p. 79.
[56] I am paraphrasing Bailyn, *Sometimes an Art*, p. 51.

6

Military Historians

A notable change in the historical profession during the second half of the twentieth century was the growth in the number of academic historians in America and the increasing diversity of their interests. Topics of historians' research, observes Lynn Hunt, now include "just about everything from rubbish in ancient Mesopotamia to surfing in modern-day Sydney."[1] Together with the vast expansion of the profession came specialization and the emergence of multiple fields of history. So great was the expansion and diversity of their profession that some historians feared "the loss of any sense of participating in a common venture."[2] Historians might be found studying the same topic and using the same sources but asking different questions. Like every other discipline, history has been subject to trends. In recent decades the trend of topics has been toward groups in society estranged from power or long understudied. Between 1975 and 2015 the most favored fields were cultural history and women's and gender history. Diplomatic history, which had traditionally been strong, was in sharp decline.

Military history was not so much understudied by academic historians as it was largely ignored. In spite of such neglect by academics, there was a great demand from the reading public. In the aftermath of World War II, the return

---

[1] Hunt, *History*, pp. 78–79.   [2] Novick, *That Noble Dream*, p. 584.

home of veterans fed the appetite for military history. In bookstores, it was usually the military history shelves that were the most extensive. Historian Margaret MacMillan writes that the public has "a fascination with great military heroes and their battles of the past; we admire stories of courage and daring exploits in war; the shelves of bookshops and libraries are packed with military histories; and movie and television producers know that war is always a popular subject."[3]

Wars have been so many, the historian Marilyn Young wrote in 2012, that they seem to be "the substance of American history."[4] But paradoxically, military history has been a subfield of the profession that academics slighted. Although war has been central to American life in the twentieth century, the historical profession has been deplorably inattentive to its study.[5] Professionally trained military historians are found in military academies or in government positions, but not so often in history departments at research universities where military history is regarded as largely a popular genre of history done by amateurs for an unsophisticated readership.

---

[3] Margaret MacMillan, *War: How Conflict Shaped Us* (New York: Random House 2020), p. xiii.

[4] Marilyn B. Young, "'I Was Thinking, as I Often Do These Days, of War': The United States in the Twenty-First Century," *Diplomatic History* 36, no.1 (January 2012): 1.

[5] Peter Paret in the *Journal of Military History* symposium on war. (October, 1993), p. 10. See also Robert M. Citino, "Military Histories Old and New: A Reintroduction," *American Historical Review* 112, no. 4 (October 2007): 1070–1090.

Academic historians would be well advised to withhold their ready disdain for amateurs who often fill a public need for storytellers, as my teacher C. Vann Woodward wrote.

> Professionals do well to apply the term "amateur" with caution to the historian outside their ranks. The word does have deprecatory and patronizing connotations that occasionally backfire. This is especially true of narrative history, which nonprofessionals have all but taken over. The gradual withering of the narrative impulse in favor of the analytical urge among professional academic historians has resulted in a virtual abdication of the oldest and most honored role of the historian, that of storyteller. Having abdicated ... the professional is in a poor position to patronize amateurs who fulfill the needed function he has abandoned.[6]

For decades historians' continuing disinterest in military history was noted. The military historian Peter Paret, whose work did gain the respect of academics, wrote in 1971 that "American history is still suffering from the longstanding indifference of American scholars to military history, and their ignorance of it. At the same time, too much of the military history that is being written is the work of conventional and unenterprising minds."[7] He complained that "with few exceptions, the character of the work produced is

---

[6] C. Vann Woodward, "The Great American Butchery," *New York Review of Books*, March 6, 1975.

[7] Peter Paret, "The History of War," *Daedalus* 100, no. 2 (Spring 1971): 385–386.

extremely conventional – descriptive history, centering on leading figures, campaigns, and climactic battles."[8] The historian William McNeil wrote in 1980 that "the study of military history in universities remains seriously underdeveloped. Indeed, lack of interest and disdain for military history probably constitute one of the strangest prejudices of the profession."[9] A 1997 survey showed that the mainstream American history journals paid relatively little attention to military history. The author of that survey, a military historian himself clearly frustrated by the *American Historical Review*'s inattention to World War II, concluded with heavy sarcasm: "The death of at least sixty million people, the Holocaust, and the reshaping of the world by warfare from 1937 to 1945 fall short of deserving a single article in nearly two decades because apparently more important matters had to be discussed."[10] One prominent historian-turned political scientist observed in 2013 that "it's in fact very hard to get a decent academic job if you do military history of any sort."[11] Another observed in 2018 that "war constituted modern American history as much as race, class, gender, religion, capitalism –

---

[8] Paret, "The History of War," p. 381. See also John Shy, "History and the History of War," *Journal of Military History* 72, no. 4 (October 2008): 1032–1046.

[9] William H. McNeill, "Modern European History" in Michael Kammen, ed., *The Past Before Us: Contemporary Historical Writing in the United States* (Ithaca: Cornell University Press, 1980), pp. 99–100.

[10] See John A. Lynn, "The Embattled Future of Academic Military History," *The Journal of Military History* 61, no.4 (October 1997): 780–781.

[11] Marc Trachtenberg, "The State of International History," posted on E-International Relations www.e-ir.info/2013/09/03/the-state-of-international-history/.

you name it – [but] ... too few historians fully engage that fact."[12] In short, as Margaret McMillan writes: "It is a curious neglect, because we live in a world shaped by war, even if we do not always realize it."[13]

Military Historians and the Hiroshima Decision

Although they were neglected in the profession, there were military historians who made critically important contributions to the study of the Hiroshima decision. They provided impressive evidence to push back against the revisionist claim that the Hiroshima decision was basically a political one. They found important military reasons justifying the use of the bomb. Drawing on newly available material, military historians argued that rather than anti-Soviet motivation, American decision-makers were influenced by facts on the ground. Alperowitz's contention that the Japanese were on the verge of surrender when the bomb was used was mistaken. Military historians showed that the Imperial Army in the summer of 1945 was instead engaged in a massive buildup, far greater than had been known, to defend the homeland against an American invasion.

On April 8 the emperor had approved the strategy known as *ketsugō* ("decisive operation") for defense of the homeland. The entire nation would be mobilized for this final

---

[12] Michael Sherry, "War as a Way of Life," *Modern American History*, published online by Cambridge University Press (2018), I, 93–96.
[13] MacMillan, *War*, p. 10.

stand. Troops from Manchuria would be brought back in massive numbers. The aggregate strength of the homeland armies would be close to three million men. Civilians, including women, would be trained. Kamikaze would be prepared. *Ketsugō* would make the invasion so costly in casualties as to force the Americans to abandon unconditional surrender policy and negotiate a peace that would preserve the Japanese state.

The army leaders knew what the Prussian military strategist Carl von Clausewitz (1780–1831) had theorized in his classic work *On War*. In the situation where the invader is intent on destroying the sovereignty of the enemy, the defense can be superior to the offense even though the invader is far stronger. Clausewitz had written:

> In a war in which the objective of the attacker is the destruction of the defender's sovereignty, the difficulties for the attacker are increased by the inherently greater strength of the defender's political/policy motive. This is because the moral stakes for the defender are about existence, which is essential, whereas the attacker is concerned simply with gain which is discretionary. Moreover ... the regular forces of the defender can be augmented by the actions of an aroused citizenry – that is, guerilla war. ... A defender that is too weak to launch an offensive can still obtain favorable terms by discouraging the attacker through protraction of hostilities.[14]

Two military historians in particular who worked outside of research universities made major contributions to

---

[14] Jon Tetsuro Suzuki, *Decoding Clausewitz: A New Approach to On War* (Lawrence, KA: University Press of Kansas, 2008), pp.179–180.

demonstrating that it was facts on the ground that prompted the decision to use the atomic bomb. One was Edward Drea, a researcher at the US Army Center of Military History in Washington, DC, who did his MA degree at Sophia University, a Jesuit institution in Tokyo, before returning for his doctoral work at the University of Kansas. Drea, with academic training and fluency in Japanese, spent his entire career as a researcher in the government. For his first book, *MacArthur's Ultra: Codebreaking and the War against Japan, 1942–1945*, he mined mountains of archival materials in the United States and Japan to produce a rigorous study of Allied code breaking in the Pacific and its influence on decision-making.[15] Prior to American entry into World War II, cryptologists had broken the Japanese diplomatic code. Known as MAGIC (because the code breakers were called "magicians"), it provided important insights on Japanese government and Foreign Ministry diplomatic traffic. Not until September 1943 did cryptologists break the military code, but within months they were intercepting large amounts of Japanese military traffic. Given the name ULTRA (short for ultrasecret), Drea showed its impact on MacArthur's military operations and more importantly its impact on the last months of the war.

Alperowitz, who had read declassified MAGIC intercepts of Foreign Ministry and diplomatic traffic that became available to scholars in the 1950s, argued that Japan was looking for a way to surrender. That claim did not hold up as new sources and materials became available. In the mid

[15] Edward J. Drea, *MacArthur's Ultra: Codebreaking and the War against Japan, 1942–1945* (Lawrence, KS: University of Kansas Press, 1992).

1970s, ULTRA began to be declassified and its intercepts of military traffic told a very different story of the Imperial Army's all-out determination to smash the invasion. ULTRA showed that beginning in the spring of 1945 the Japanese army began rushing troops home from Korea, North China, and Manchuria and preparing a massive buildup in anticipation of an all-out battle on Kyushu. "By accurately tracking the swelling flood of reinforcements that poured into Kyushu through the end of June and into July 1945, ULTRA made OLYMPIC [American plans for invading Japan] seem very costly indeed."[16] Drea concluded that contrary to Alperowitz's conclusions, which had been based only on MAGIC intercepts, ULTRA showed that Japanese military leaders were not prepared to surrender. Drea concluded that ULTRA's findings "surely influenced the American decision to use atomic weapons against Japan."[17] He used Japanese-language sources, consulted prominent scholars in Japan, and wrote in a restrained, judicious, nonpolemical style. He was a professional historian whose groundbreaking study represented a rebuttal to the revisionist position, but working as a military historian in a government

---

[16] Drea, *MacArthur's Ultra*, p. 211.

[17] "The gap between ULTRA data and that of other intelligence sources on the extent of the Japanese defense of the home islands was enormous. ULTRA accurately portrayed a Japanese military determined to fight to the death on the sacred shores of its homeland, while MAGIC told of the Japanese government and Foreign Ministry's search for ways to end the war. In this cruel paradox, ULTRA's domination of MAGIC surely influenced the American decision to use atomic weapons against Japan." Drea, *MacArthur's Ultra*, p. 201.

research position his important work typically received little attention and was ignored by mainstream history journals.

Drea's subsequent work *In the Service of the Emperor* explored the culture of the Japanese army and included a persuasive analysis of Hirohito's character and motivation, which we will discuss in the next chapter.[18] Historians in postwar Japan gave much greater attention to military history since they were deeply engaged in understanding and explaining the rise of militarism, which had brought such disaster to their country. Consequently, there is a rich bibliography of Japanese historical research on its military. Drea notably was able to use this research in his work relating to the Hiroshima decision in a way that few other American historians could. Drea's next book, *Japan's Imperial Army, Its Rise and Fall, 1853–1945*, made extensive use of new Japanese sources, provided a synthesis of available scholarship, and reflected the value of working with leading Japanese scholars of military history.[19] Like his other works, however, it did not receive the attention that a topic so central to modern Japanese history deserved.

The most influential contribution of a military historian to the ongoing debates about the Hiroshima decision

---

[18] Edward J. Drea, *In the Service of the Emperor: Essays on the Imperial Japanese Army* (Lincoln: University of Nebraska Press, 1998). This book included an exceptionally useful bibliographic essay. Barton Bernstein wrote that Drea's *In the Service of the Emperor* was a "thoughtful work" but "attracted little attention," sold few copies, and received "only a handful of reviews." *The End of the Pacific War*, p. 54.

[19] Edward J. Drea, *Japan's Imperial Army, Its Rise and Fall* (Lawrence, KS: University of Kansas, 2009).

was made by Richard Frank, who had two academic strikes against him: He was a military historian, and he was not credentialed, that is, he lacked the doctorate, "the historian's indispensable badge of competence."[20] A Vietnam War veteran, working as an independent scholar without academic training in history, he had authored a book on the battle of Guadalcanal before undertaking a deeply researched study on the end of the Asia Pacific War. Frank's *Downfall: The End of the Imperial Japanese Empire* was published in 1999, and like Drea's book was largely ignored by academic historians and mainstream journals. It was, however, reviewed in the *New York Times*, which brought it to my attention.[21] I found it valuable in its new findings and conclusions regarding the Hiroshima decision and assigned it to my students. One enterprising graduate student who was writing his paper for my course telephoned Frank to ask him questions. Frank expressed surprise to my student that his book was actually being assigned at a research university!

    Frank was sympathetic with the orthodox view that the bomb was used to end the war quickly by breaking a deadlock in the Japanese government and averting the need for an invasion. Unlike Drea, Frank was not fluent in the Japanese language but depended on translators for use of selected documentary evidence. Building on Drea's work, Frank painstakingly ferreted out more details of the MAGIC and ULTRA intercepts. More of these were declassified in the 1990s, which he discovered had been held back because they showed that the

---

[20] Cohen, *Making History*, p. 253.
[21] Reviewed by J. Samuel Walker, *New York Times*, December 12, 1999

United States had been intercepting the traffic of many governments, including those of its allies. The intercepts showed that, with the emperor's approval, the army planned a last stand in the homeland to force the Allies to negotiate a peace that would save some semblance of Japanese honor. Frank provided a new picture of the Japanese army's *ketsugō* strategy and he also showed that the army had not just one demand of preserving the imperial institution as *sine qua non* for negotiation, but three more: no Allied occupation of Japan, self-disarmament, and self-conducted war crimes trials. By laying out the army's strategy, a detailed picture of the size of the swelling buildup, and the four (instead of one) conditions, he succeeded in undercutting the argument that Japan had been on the verge of surrender. Dismissing the revisionist contention, he wrote: "It is fantasy, not history, to believe that the end of the war was at hand before the use of the atomic bomb."[22]

Frank showed that by mid summer of 1945 the buildup had to be alarming to the American policymakers and strategists. "Ultra demonstrated that the Japanese defense of Kyushu exceeded the original estimates by more than three times in combat divisions and two to four times in aircraft."[23] His new findings convinced him that the massive Japanese buildup influenced American policymakers and strategists to the extent that they might have to forego an invasion. "The Japanese were correct to believe that – in a nonnuclear arena – they could secure bargaining leverage to force a negotiated peace. But once American leaders learned of the odds facing Olympic [code name for the invasion], there is no prospect that

---

[22] Frank, *Downfall*, p. 239. [23] Frank, *Downfall*, p. 340.

any other consideration could have stayed the use of atomic weapons."[24] The atomic bomb when it became available cut the Gordian knot. With knowledge of the massive buildup and its prospect of unacceptable casualties, Allied invasion plans made the use of the bomb inevitable. "Given the abrupt change in the military calculus and the sterile prospects for diplomacy, the chance that atomic weapons would not have been employed is nil."[25] The Japanese army's *ketsugō* strategy forced America's choice. "The fundamental political reality is that it was Japanese, not American, leaders who controlled when and how the Pacific War would end." Frank held that diplomacy would have made no difference. There was no credible evidence, he wrote, that modifying unconditional surrender or "a different Allied policy might have brought about an earlier surrender."[26] Moreover, he gave little credence or even attention to the revisionist claim of anti-Soviet motivation as a deciding factor. It was at best a "reinforcing reason, not an underlying one."[27] The Hiroshima decision was, in short, a military decision not a political one as revisionists claimed.

The Nagasaki Bombing

Frank like most other historians gave little attention to the bombing of Nagasaki. The issue was a very minor part of the debate among historians. It was regarded as following from and linked to the Hiroshima decision. As the historian Martin Sherwin wrote, "the destruction of Hiroshima and Nagasaki

---

[24] Frank, *Downfall*, p. 343. [25] Frank, *Downfall*, p. 359.
[26] Frank, *Downfall*, p. 343. [27] Frank, *Downfall*, p. 250.

was the result of a *single* decision."[28] In General Groves' thinking, it was assumed that more than one would be used. Once the Hiroshima decision was made, Truman left the further use to the military to determine. The military had a target list of cities and when Kyoto was struck from the initial target list at Stimson's insistence, Nagasaki was added. Kokura was to be the second city hit by the bomb, but when the crew on *Bockscar*, the plane carrying the bomb, found it under the clouds they proceeded on to the next target. Nagasaki might well have been avoided, but weather, human decision, and misfortune befell it.

Frank's brief commentary supported the orthodox defense. In his *Harper's* article, Stimson had described the use of the second bomb as a psychological weapon to shock the Japanese leadership. He quoted Karl Compton's recently published article in which a swift use of a second bomb created the "dread of many more." Frank defended the use of the bomb on Nagasaki as necessary to convince the military leaders that the United States had more than one and would not be deterred in using the bomb again.[29] Although many Japanese thought the second bomb gratuitous, the Japanese historian Asada Sadao held that "from the standpoint of its shock effect, the political impact of the Nagasaki bomb cannot be denied. Army Minister Anami's wishful thinking was shattered; if two bombs were available, then maybe there were three or even four."[30] I once invited Iokibe Makoto, Japan's well-known historian of the end of the war, to lecture to my class on the surrender. When

---

[28] Sherwin, *A World Destroyed*, p. 209. Italics in original.
[29] Frank, *Downfall*, p. 348n.
[30] Asada, "The Shock of the Atomic Bomb," p. 492.

a student asked him if the Nagasaki bomb was necessary, he surprised many in the class by responding that "yes" it was necessary to persuade the military hardliners. On the other hand, there were many historians like Barton Bernstein who have found reason to believe that it

> was almost certainly unnecessary. It was used because the original order directed the Air Force to drop bombs "as made ready" and, even after the Hiroshima bombing, no one in Washington anticipated an imminent Japanese surrender. Evidence now available about developments in the Japanese government – most notably the emperor's then-secret decision shortly before the Nagasaki bombing to seek peace – makes it clear that the second bomb could undoubtedly have been avoided.[31]

Harvard historians Edwin Reischauer and Akira Iriye expressed much the same belief.[32]

Casualty Projections

Frank was at pains to lay to rest the "obsessive and misplaced American controversy over casualty projections."[33] The orthodox

---

[31] Barton J. Bernstein, "The Atomic Bombings Reconsidered," *Foreign Affairs* 74, no.1 (January–February 1995): 150.

[32] Edwin O. Reischauer, *My Life Between Japan and America* (New York: Harper and Row, 1986), p. 101. Quoted in George R. Packard, *Edwin O. Reischauer and the American Discovery of Japan* (New York: Columbia University Press, 2010), p. 76. Akira Iriye's view is found in the Oregon Public Broadcasting film *Rain of Ruin: The Bombing of Nagasaki*.

[33] Packard, *Edwin O. Reischauer and the American Discovery of Japan*, p. 338.

CASUALTY PROJECTIONS

view always insisted that the use of the bomb by averting massive casualties had saved lives and thus was the moral choice. The revisionists, on the other hand, insisted that Truman, Churchill, Stimson, and their defenders had vastly exaggerated the number of lives saved to salve their guilt and justify their decision. The controversy has been obsessive because if it could be persuasively argued that the Hiroshima decision had prevented the loss of a much larger number of lives than an invasion, then Americans' belief that they had done the right thing could be maintained.

Frank, while finding abundant evidence to support Stimson's postwar assertion of possibly one million casualties, nevertheless found the controversy parochial and ill-defined. Neither side of the polemics could know the answer to this question. No one could know how much fighting remained in order to project losses accurately.[34] At the time of surrender, the naval blockade had already induced mass starvation. Had the war continued the Allies were about to attack the transportation system, which would have greatly increased the starvation of noncombatants. In addition, Frank made the telling observation that the controversy among the Americans rarely took account of the casualties suffered by the Chinese and other Asian peoples who were victims of the Japanese in the continuing war. He believed that "it might have exceeded one hundred thousand per month in China alone."[35]

---

[34] Packard, *Edwin O. Reischauer and the American Discovery of Japan*, p. 342.
[35] Packard, *Edwin O. Reischauer and the American Discovery of Japan*, p. 359.

Many essays in military journals argued for high casualty projections as justifying, even requiring, the use of the bomb. They took issue with critics like Barton Bernstein who thought such projections were exaggerated. Bernstein, while admitting that he had made mistakes in earlier essays in which he insisted on estimates of low levels of casualties, was at the same time critical of the use of evidence, reasoning, and scholarly standards of "military journalism," which was his reference to the work of many military historians.[36] He was particularly critical of the work of D. M. Giangreco, whose many articles culminated in his book *Hell to Pay*, which was widely praised in military journals. Bernstein wondered whether popular military history could ever adhere to the same standards for evidence and the use of sources as academic history.

Stung by the criticism, Giangreco, who was an editor of *Military Review* at the US Army Command and General Staff College, responded that academic historians did not understand the methodologies and procedures of how the US Army's casualty projections were formed. Lacking such knowledge, they failed to dig deeply enough in the archives for the details and thus simply regarded postwar claims of

---

[36] See Barton J. Bernstein, "Reconsidering 'Invasion Most Costly': Popular-History Scholarship, Publishing Standards, and the Claim of High U.S. Casualty Estimates to Help Legitimize the Atomic Bombings," *Peace & Change* 24, no. 2 (April 1999): 220–248. See especially p. 244 n23. See also for Bernstein's self-criticism his essay in *Judgment at the Smithsonian*, especially pp. 178–185.

CASUALTY PROJECTIONS

Truman and Stimson as "fraudulent."[37] Giangreco in his comprehensive study of fatality estimates drew on US operational plans, Japanese plans for defense, the nature of the terrain, the weather, US estimates of how much blood would be needed for the wounded in the invasion, and official orders for Purple Heart medals – all to argue for massive casualty projections by way of justifying the use of the bomb.[38] Giangreco also called attention to various estimates of high-level casualties that Truman received while he was weighing invasion plans. A memo from former president Herbert Hoover to Stimson and Truman warning that without a negotiated settlement it might cost "the lives of 500,000 to a million boys" disturbed Truman and Stimson. An even higher estimate was made by an independent study done for Stimson's staff by William B. Shockley, a scientist who later won a Nobel Prize, who concluded that "we shall probably have to kill at least 5 to 10 million Japanese. This might cost us between 1.7 million and 4 million casualties, including 400,000–800,000 killed."[39] Marshaling such arguments and evidence, Giangreco tartly responded to his critics.

The contretemps between Barton Bernstein and military historians over casualty projections laid bare the divisions between academic and military historians. From what

[37] D. M. Giangreco, "'A Score of Bloody Okinawas and Iwo Jimas': President Truman and Casualty Estimates for the Invasion of Japan," *Pacific Historical Review*, 72, no.1 (February 2003): 93–132.
[38] D. M. Giangreco, *Hell to Pay: Operation Downfall and the Invasion of Japan, 1945–1947* (Annapolis: Naval Institute Press, 2009 and expanded edition 2017).
[39] Kort, *Columbia Guide*, p. 102.

we have discussed in this chapter about academic historians' ignoring of military history, one useful corrective would be for academic historians to make more room in their journals and conferences for military history. Both could gain from greater interchange.

Assessing Frank's *Downfall*

More than fifty years after Stimson and other participants in the decision defended the use of the bomb, Frank's book gave new justification for the orthodox view of the American use of the bomb. It was many years before it got the recognition it deserved from other historians working on the Hiroshima decision. In the meantime, his book's appeal was primarily with a large reading public, and he has been a favored speaker to audiences drawn to military history who by and large support the orthodox interpretation of the Hiroshima decision.

While recognizing the importance of Frank's contribution to the debate, a reader might take issue with or find problematic aspects of his interpretation. First is the short time frame. His focus is on the last year – especially the last months – of the war, which does not allow sufficient attention to how Roosevelt's unconditional surrender policy influenced the way America chose to fight the war. Ruling out any role for diplomatic negotiations from the very outset of the war gave priority to military strategy and the maximum use of force to win the war. Moreover, by insisting on sweeping but very vague surrender terms – the intention to occupy and remake Japanese political structure, permanently disarm Japan, and carry out war crimes trials – it left the Japanese in the dark as to what surrender would mean and it provoked all-out resistance from the Japanese Imperial Army. To achieve total victory America had to plan invasion of Japan, which set the stage for the dilemma that the use of the bomb would solve. Problems with a short time frame will be further discussed in Chapter 8.

A second issue is Frank's conclusion, which may seem problematic to the reader. The deaths suffered in the way the war ended, he concluded his book, "were not gratuitous. American goals were not simply victory but peace. Had American leaders in 1945 been assured that Japan and the United States would pass two generations in tranquility and still look forward with no prospect of future conflict, they would have believed their hard choices had been vindicated – and so should we."[40] In this somewhat facile conclusion, he emphasized that the Japanese have caused the world no trouble since surrender and that should further satisfy anyone who had doubts about the Hiroshima decision. Frank's implication seemed to be that the use of the bomb to gain unconditional surrender was necessary so that America could occupy and democratize Japan. Belief that American intervention was required to reform Japan became a common American assumption and encouraged many subsequent American interventions to democratize other countries. A historian of modern Japan might contend that history had demonstrated that Japan was capable of reforming itself. The Meiji Restoration, the Meiji constitution, and the democratization movement during the Taisho period (1912–26)

---

[40] Kort, *Columbia Guide*, p. 360.

demonstrated Japan's ability to adapt to new realities. The reforms made in the Meiji period have been called by the British historian John Keegan "one of the most radical changes of national policy in history."[41] Others have made the same observation. The Princeton historian R. R. Palmer once wrote that "the Westernization of Japan" in the Meiji period "still stands as the most remarkable transformation ever undergone by any people is so short a time."[42]

Military History in a Cultural Context

One of the reasons academic historians tended to ignore the work of military historians was their perceived failure to situate their studies in a wider social and cultural context. The eminent British military historian Michael Howard midway through his distinguished career came to conceive his discipline in a broadened way. "The history of war, I came to realize, was more than the operational history of armed forces. It was the study of entire societies. Only by studying their cultures could one come to understand what it was that they fought about and why they fought in the way that they did."[43] Military history is increasingly incorporating cultural and social history, recognizing that, as the British military historian John Keegan wrote, "[w]ar embraces much more than politics ... it is always an

---

[41] John Keegan, *The Second World War* (New York: Penguin, 1989), p. 241.
[42] See R. R. Palmer and Joel Colton, *A History of the Modern World* (New York: Knopf, 1995, 8th ed.), p. 582.
[43] Michael Howard, *Captain Professor: A Life in War and Peace* (London: Continuum Press, 2006), p. 145.

expression of culture. Often a determinant of cultural forms, in some societies the culture itself."[44]

One historian whose approach to military history and to the Hiroshima decision drew academic praise for the breadth of its treatment was Michael Sherry, a professor at Northwestern University, whose 1987 book *The Rise of American Air Power: The Creation of Armageddon* traced the way in which Americans came to rely on technology as a substitute for a clear military strategy for winning World War II. He places his military history in a broad context of social and intellectual history that helped him win the prestigious Bancroft Prize in history. Instead of the emphasis on the Hiroshima decision as a revolutionary event, Sherry described it as the result of a long evolution of American thinking about strategic air power.

He traced the conception of the airplane as a new weapon of war from World War I. Air power enthusiasts like Billy Mitchell touted its economy, efficiency, and technological innovation in contrast to the expense of a naval fleet. They saw it as better suited to American self-reliance and isolationist sentiment, defending America without venturing abroad.[45] Well before Pearl Harbor, strategists were already thinking of aerial bombardment as a winning card in any future war. Rather than trench warfare, land armies, and sea warfare, which characterized World War I, here was a new

[44] Quoted in Wayne E. Lee, "Mind and Matter–Cultural Analysis in American Military History," *The Journal of American History* 93, no. 4 (March 2007): 117.

[45] Michael S. Sherry, *The Rise of American Air Power: The Creation of Armageddon* (New Haven, CT: Yale University Press, 1987), p. 39.

technology that promised swift success by its ability to strike behind the lines and be a psychological menace to the enemy.

Franklin Roosevelt, although known for the deep influence that naval affairs had on his thinking, was attracted to air power. In May 1940, as Hitler swept over Europe, Roosevelt called for a production capacity of "at least 50,000 planes a year."[46] The following June came the creation of the Army Air Force and its leaders soon began focusing their sights on a more autonomous position. They were determined to demonstrate their branch's capabilities, enhance their budget, and gain independence from the other services. In his cultural history and links to social influences, Sherry shows how writers, advertisers, and Hollywood celebrated American air power. John Steinbeck, to take one good example, wrote *Bombs Away: The Story of a Bomber Team* for the Army Air Force.

Writing on "the sociology of air war," Sherry described how the premium on sophisticated technology in air warfare forged a close alliance among the Air Force, industry, and science.[47] The point was to harness civilian science to military power, to plan development and employment of new weapons. Air power "required a vast apparatus of technology, production, logistics, and economic and political analysis."[48] The sudden growth of the human infrastructure during the war was eye-popping. "The air force alone employed some 500,000 civilians by war's end. ... In the

---

[46] Sherry, *The Rise of American Air Power*, p. 91.
[47] Sherry, *The Rise of American Air Power*, p. 188.
[48] Sherry, *The Rise of American Air Power*, p. 187.

eyes of the technocrats the 'dehumanized rhetoric of technique reduced the enemy to quantifiable abstractions' and led Japan to be viewed as little more than 'a vast laboratory in destruction.'"[49] The unconditional surrender policy that promoted the use of maximum force gave priority to perfecting the ability of new technology to destroy urban targets. For the crewmen in the bombers "the enemy was rarely met face to face. His death and destruction were either unnoticed or observed at an impersonal distance." Japanese atrocities and revenge for Pearl Harbor helped brush aside moral qualms. "Racist attitudes enhanced the attraction of air power, above all by minimizing the claims of conscience."[50]

In the air war against Japan, Sherry's fundamental purpose in showing the evolution of air power was to argue that the incremental advances in firebombing urban populations made use of the atomic bomb almost reflexive. Early in World War II, models of Japanese towns with wooden houses and tatami floors were constructed in Utah to experiment with how best to burn civilian neighborhoods in bombing campaigns.[51] The B-29, an extraordinary technological feat, was designed particularly for a mission of attacking urban areas to paralyze the industrial economy. Sherry showed how American fascination with the use of technology in war, which he labels "technological fanaticism," took the place of a rational pursuit of war goals. The emphasis on the

---

[49] Quoted in Dower, *Cultures of War*, p. 263.
[50] Sherry, *Rise of American Air Power*, p. 115.
[51] Dylan Plung, "The Japanese Village at Dugway Proving Ground: An Unexamined Context to the Firebombing of Japan," *The Asia-Pacific Journal* 16, no. 3 (2018), online.

maximum destructive power from the air led to the transition from precision bombing to area bombing. When bombs were blown off course by wind currents the new head of strategic bombing Curtis LeMay ordered nighttime bombing at low altitude and using a primitive form of napalm to incinerate Japanese cities, starting with Tokyo. On March 9–10, 1945, 334 B-29s carried out a nighttime bombing that destroyed sixteen square miles of the heart of Tokyo and caused upward of 100,000 deaths of the city inhabitants (Figure 6.1). That raid was followed with similar attacks that laid waste to large parts of sixty Japanese cities.

In the last year of the war, the Air Force was given little oversight. Nor was it guided by any clear strategy. "After September 1944, no one outside the air force carefully examined its methods of bombing. Whether it chose to blast factories, mine sea-lanes, or level cities was largely for [Air Force chief] Arnold and his subordinates to decide."[52] Employing air power was pursued without an integrated strategy for defeating Japan. Means were increasingly divorced from ends. Destruction was pursued "without a clear notion of its relationship to victory."[53] When would the war end? LeMay told Arnold in June 1945 that he was running out of targets. "The air force approach to war," Sherry concluded, "[was] rich with the emptiness of strategic reasoning about how to win the war and of the desire to even formulate it. Destruction would win the war, and the war would have to end when the destruction was complete." In

---

[52] Sherry, American Air Power, p. 221.
[53] Sherry, American Air Power, p. 234.

Figure 6.1 Tokyo was repeatedly fire-bombed in 1945 along with sixty other cities.
Source: Keystone-France/Gamma-Keystone/Getty Images

his memoirs LeMay summed up the strategy in stark terms: "Bomb and burn them until they quit."[54]

Ultimately, Sherry argued, the Armageddon of Hiroshima and Nagasaki should be seen as the outcome of a steady accumulation of decisions until the use of the atomic bomb became inevitable (Figure 6.2). He argues against focusing on "the decision" to use the atomic bomb and against telescoping years of action into one choice. Truman's "decision" was one of noninterference. "The sin of atomic bombing" was the result of "a slow accretion of large fears, thoughtless

---

[54] Sherry, American Air Power, p. 300.

MILITARY HISTORIANS

Figure 6.2 Days after the Hiroshima bombing, an Allied correspondent stands in the rubble, looking toward the ruins of the Prefectural Industrial Promotion Hall, now preserved as the centerpiece of the Hiroshima Peace Memorial Park.
Source: Los Angeles Examiner/USC Libraries/Corbis/ Getty Images

assumptions, and incremental decisions."[55] By August 1945 a powerful momentum had built up over decades favoring the use of technology and air power that made use of the bomb almost inevitable. Sherry's book wove together "all the relevant strands: the policy-makers, the cultural factors, bureaucratic pressures, sociological dimensions, technological

[55] Sherry, American Air Power, p. 363.

influences and much more, in addition to the fighting men and their battles."⁵⁶

Sherry spent a substantial part of his career in the study of war in American history. But he pondered in 2018, shortly after his retirement, why had "the study of war drifted toward the sidelines since the 1970s?" He preferred to see the study of war as much broader than the subfield of military history, because it pervaded and influenced all aspects of society and made it more difficult to "get a fix on." While noting the recent appearance of important new relevant works, he concluded with a plea for more historians to recognize and engage "the centrality of war to modern American history."⁵⁷

Recentering Military History

It is a virtue of the historian's craft that through debate and controversy it can be self-correcting. Over much of the postwar period, the discipline turned its attention to long overlooked fields and the study of individuals and groups in society estranged from power and influence. New questions of subalternity drew historians' attention. All this was overdue, but as its focus turned in that direction, the discipline tended for a generation to marginalize political, diplomatic, and especially military history. This trend was reflected in the underappreciation of the important work of Edward Drea and

---

⁵⁶ Review by Ken Booth, *International Affairs (Royal Institute of International Affairs)* 64, no.1 (Winter 1987–1988): 113–114.
⁵⁷ Sherry, "War as a Way of Life," pp. 93–96.

Richard Frank, whose contributions to the debate on the Hiroshima decision and support for the orthodox interpretation should have had an important place. Nevertheless, as Marilyn Young wrote, attention to war could not be avoided because it was woven into the substance of American history.[58] More recently, ferment within the historical community has begun to correct this neglect.[59] Surveys indicate that while the military still struggles to find a place in academia largely because of its association with popular military history, many important works are being published by academic historians.[60] For example, Margaret MacMillan's 2020 book *War: How Conflict Shaped Us* drew on aspects of war throughout the past to show how war had over and over influenced our institutions and values. As military historians find more ways to integrate their work with social and cultural history, the prospect of attention to military history will brighten.

---

[58] Young, "I was thinking, as I often do these days, of war," pp. 1–15

[59] See for example Daniel Bessner and Frederik Logevall, "Recentering the United States in the Historiography of American Foreign Relations," *Texas National Security Review* 3, no. 2/ Spring 2020; Niall Ferguson, "The Decline and Fall of History" (2016) www.niallferguson.com; Hal Brands and Francis J. Gavin, "The Historical Profession is Committing Slow-Motion Suicide," *Texas National Security Review* (December 10, 2018).

[60] See Lynn, "The Embattled Future," pp. 777–789; and also Ronald H. Spector, "Teetering on the Brink of Respectability," *The Journal of American History*, 93, no. 4 (March 2007), pp. 1158–1160.

7

Gauging Japanese Responsibility

Never had the United States fought against a country that it knew so little about. In her postwar classic analyzing Japanese culture, the anthropologist Ruth Benedict wrote that Japan was "the most alien enemy the United States had ever fought in an all-out struggle."[1] Japanese studies in the West was in its infancy. Benedict was one of several social scientists called to Washington during the war to try to figure out what made Japan tick. Her book *The Chrysanthemum and the Sword* (1946) grew out of the discussions among these social scientists. She brought a formidable intellect to her task. She had been instrumental in moving the field of anthropology away from its existing view of behavior as racially determined. Rather, behavior was the expression of customs, institutions, and ways of thinking inherited from the distinctive histories of different people. Benedict described the Japanese as a people of contradictions: "Both aggressive and unaggressive, both militaristic and aesthetic, both insolent and polite."[2] But her book was inevitably flawed since she did not know the language and had never been to Japan. Later, the book was harshly criticized for being ethnocentric and for her failure to transcend her own cultural dispositions.

---

[1] Ruth Benedict, *The Chrysanthemum and the Sword* (Cambridge, MA: Houghton Mifflin, 1946), p. 1.
[2] Benedict, *The Chrysanthemum and the Sword*, p. 2.

In the early postwar years most history departments in the West were still remarkably Eurocentric – meaning that they taught only the history of the Western world. Only a handful of universities gave any attention to the language, culture, and history of Japan and other parts of the non-Western world. At Oxford, Hugh Trevor-Roper, Professor of Modern History, wrote in 1965 that Africa had no history, but only "the unrewarding gyrations of barbarous tribes in picturesque but irrelevant corners of the globe." The English historian John Russell Vincent as late as the 1990s wrote: "[W]e do not understand Asia and will not need to."[3] In America, too, the history profession remained stubbornly parochial in the postwar period. "Eurocentric tendencies," writes Sarah Maza in her study of historiography, "are deeply embedded in historical writing, in the West and beyond, because professional historical scholarship – departments, journals, professional association – took shape in the later nineteenth century in Europe and America when those regions did indeed dominate most of the world's peoples."[4] In Japan, the modern historical profession was founded at the University of Tokyo with the appointment in 1887 of one of Ranke's disciples to introduce Western methods of historiography into the university curriculum.

In the postwar period, when study of the non-Western world was in its infancy in America, it was labeled "foreign area studies," which carried the connotation of being something a bit peculiar but strategically important for the

[3] Evans, *In Defense of History*, p. 153.
[4] Maza, *Thinking About History*, p. 77.

United States in the Cold War. When the United States first became entangled in Vietnam in the 1960s, no American had studied the history of that country through native sources. While there were by the 1960s a respectable number of specialists studying Russia, China, and Japan, their works were still at early stages.

Serious study of Korea, for example, in the United States or, in fact, anywhere outside of South Korea was only beginning in the 1970s. Even at the University of Tokyo there was no appointment in Korean history. As one of that university's professors later told me, "[i]t is our shame." In my department of history at the University of Washington, where I taught Japanese history, when I sought to persuade my colleagues in the late 1960s to accept appointment of a historian of Korea, the idea was greeted with skepticism. "Do Asian historians read Herodotus and Thucydides?" asked the professor of Renaissance and Reformation history. The professor of French history proposed that all of us Asian historians form our own department of history, presumably because what we did was fundamentally different. After a vote on that proposal failed, the department with misgivings voted to appoint James Palais as an assistant professor of Korean history. In subsequent years, my longtime friend went on to write major works that defined the history of Korea, to train a generation of Korean historians who held positions in many departments in North America and Japan, and to win over my formerly skeptical colleagues to the value of his historical writing.

Since the 1980s, the geographical horizons of the historical profession in the West have greatly widened.

Teaching in the fields of Asian history in America has grown exponentially, thanks in part to national security concerns and the resulting government and foundation support. Japan studies was also the beneficiary of large-scale Japan Foundation support in the 1970s and the 1980s. By the end of the twentieth century most American universities had at least one historian specializing on Japan. With their linguistic capability they had access to Japanese materials and scholars in Japan. This expansion provided studies of individual leaders, of nationalism, of the nature of Japanese fascism, and of many other topics significant to broadening and deepening the background from which to understand the various causes of the Hiroshima decision.

With these developments, it became possible to understand and explain the decision in a broader context and to gauge Japanese responsibility for the tragic end to the war. Especially, the critical question could be asked what responsibility the emperor had? If he could exercise his power to end the war after the atomic bombs had been dropped, why not before? Hirohito was an elusive and enigmatic personality. He was viewed by some as a pacifist, by others as an activist in military planning, by others as a constitutional monarch, or as a reactionary adherent to imperial myths. Historians have yet to reach a consensus.

Writing Contemporary History

The demonization of Hirohito in wartime propaganda ensured that there would be sensational and popular treatments of his responsibility for the war and its conduct. In the first postwar decades, there were several biographies of Hirohito, but there was only one scholarly treatment of his role which had a long shelf life, and it became a widely respected and quoted source in historians' writings on the Hiroshima decision.

Robert Butow in his 1954 study *Japan's Decision to Surrender*, almost universally regarded as a "classic,"[5] described how the worsening war situation divided Japanese leadership into two factions: The hardliners ready to fight until the allies agreed to abandon their unconditional surrender policy and the peace party that was prepared to seek an early end to the conflict. The atomic bombings and the Soviet entry into the war caused the emperor to intervene in the deadlock of the two factions to bring about surrender. Butow described Hirohito as a constitutional monarch who had been an onlooker in politics, who reigned but did not rule. He was not permitted "to direct the affairs of state or to meddle with the machinery of government. ... His role was that of a bystander watching with interest the turmoil of political activity taking place around him but never interfering no

---

[5] For example, Richard Frank wrote in 1999: "In a special category is the classic work of Robert Butow, *Japan's Decision to Surrender*, published in 1954 but still invaluable as a guide to sources and as an exemplar of scholarly analysis and supple prose." *Downfall*, p. 447. Michael Kort writing in his *Columbia Guide to Hiroshima and the Bomb* (2006): "In his classic account of Japan's surrender, Robert Butow credits both factors [the bomb and Russian entry] with creating the conditions that led to Hirohito's crucial intervention." Sadao Asada likewise writes that "Robert J.C. Butow's classic monography (1954), has largely stood the test of time." *Culture Shock and Japanese-American Relations*, pp. 175–176.

matter how personally concerned for the outcome he might be."⁶

That Butow's book endured for half a century as the most highly respected treatment of the end of the war in the Pacific was a remarkable achievement. Historians' writings on contemporary history rarely stand the test of time. Writing contemporary history is sometimes suspect by historians who generally feel that a substantial amount of time must pass before one can have the necessary sources, perspective, and dispassion to interpret events. Yet, it is probably true that the writing of history began with the writing about one's own time. Writing contemporary history began as far back as Thucydides, who said that his narrative depended "partly on what I saw myself, partly on what others saw for me."⁷ The acceleration of history in the mid twentieth century and the crisis-ridden times gave greater acceptance to the writing of contemporary history.

As his close friend and colleague for many years at the University of Washington, I had opportunity to assess Butow's approach to the historian's craft. In our pastime of hiking in the Cascades he would often talk about his research and the painstaking way in which he went about his work. His achievement owed much to his scrupulous scholarship. (It was this meticulousness that led him to discover in the Roosevelt Library at Hyde Park a hitherto unknown recording

---

⁶ Robert J. C. Butow, *Japan's Decision to Surrender* (Stanford: Stanford University Press, 1954) p. 229.

⁷ Quoted in Arthur M. Schlesinger, Jr., "On the Writing of Contemporary History," *The Atlantic*, March 1967.

of FDR's Oval Office discussions on the eve of the war with Japan.[8])

After intensive wartime language study in the United States, Butow had arrived in Japan in the days after surrender as an intelligence officer in the Occupation. Fascinated by the events that had just transpired, he returned to the United States and wrote his doctoral dissertation at Stanford, which was published in 1954. Butow recognized that writing contemporary history carried with it dangers and was wise enough to hedge his conclusions with the caveat that his arguments were tentative. He was careful in his judgments not to go beyond what his sources revealed. Time might simply pass by such accounts. "The writing of 'recent history' is difficult at best," he acknowledged; "at worst, it degenerates into a form of disguised fiction with little or no claim upon the *historical.* The years ahead may reveal new sources of untapped information or may seal into oblivion a part, at least, of what is presented here." Despite this limitation, Butow found justification for writing contemporary history. "Had it not been for those who wrote of events close to themselves, who recorded the history of their own times, our present record of the past would be far less rich, far less intimate, than is generally admitted."[9] Because of his impeccable scholarship, based as

---

[8] Robert J. C. Butow, "The Story Behind the FDR Tapes," *American Heritage* (February/March 1982) vol. 33, no. 2, p. 10.

[9] Butow, *Japan's Decision*, p. vii. Italics in original. He cautiously speculated that modifying unconditional surrender policy to allow retention of the imperial system might have averted use of the atomic bomb. "What complex of factors" prevented seizing this opportunity "is not yet known." p. 135.

it was on painstaking use of Japanese materials, including diaries, letters, and interviews with Japanese, Butow's book remained for decades the most influential treatment of both the emperor's wartime role and the Japanese decision to surrender.

In the meantime, other Western historians, lacking not only Japanese language competence but also deep understanding of Japanese culture, gave limited attention to Japanese responsibility for the use of the bomb. In Japan, the prevailing Marxist influence on historians ensured that translation in 1951 of Alperowitz's British mentor P. M. S. Blackett's revisionist treatise became "the bible for Japan's left-wing historians, peace activists, and even textbook writers."[10] For decades postwar Japan with its strong sense of victimization took readily to believing that the bomb was used needlessly – and even worse as an experiment to test the new scientific achievement. As one Japanese historian described it, the residents of Hiroshima and Nagasaki were "killed as human guinea pigs for the sake of [America's] anti-Communist, hegemonic policy." Or as the well-known *Taiheiyō sensō e no michi* (The Road to the Pacific War) put it, "500,000 citizens [of Hiroshima and Nagasaki] were utterly meaninglessly sacrificed for America's cruel political purposes."[11] Japan's postwar disposition to see itself as victimized by the bomb together with a reluctance to criticize the imperial institution tended to dampen assessment of Japan's own responsibility for the tragedy.

[10] Asada, "The Mushroom Cloud," pp. 97, 108–110.
[11] Asada, "The Mushroom Cloud," pp. 108–109.

Nevertheless, there were historians in Japan who began to make such an assessment. The writings of the Japanese historian Yoshimi Yoshiaki were especially valuable. He represented a school of people's history (*minshūshi*) or "history from below" approach, which turned its attention away from simply focusing on the elites. Yoshimi's 1987 book *Grassroots Fascism* [12] grapples with the extent to which ordinary Japanese people bear responsibility for the war. In my lectures on wartime Japan the topic I found hardest to explain was the brutality and cruelty of the rape of Nanjing in 1938 when Imperial Army soldiers went on a rampage of pillage, looting, and rape, leading to the slaughter of many tens of thousands – estimates vary widely – in the wartime capital. Drawing on a remarkable range of letters and diaries, Yoshimi presents a sobering picture of Japanese soldiers' brutality and racist treatment of other Asians during their wartime service abroad. Yoshimi found a mix of enthusiasm for the "holy war" with remorse for its cruelty. To take an example, he records the thoughts expressed in one soldier's diary of massacring civilians in a Chinese village:

> Following orders, one after another, even though they were decent folk, we bayonet even women and children to death. It's the epitome of cruelty. Fifty or sixty people in one go, sweet young girls, innocent children they cry and beg for mercy putting their hands together. It's the first time in my life I do something so cold-blooded. Oh how I hate war.

Reading letters and diaries of Japanese soldiers serving in China, Yoshimi found evidence of brutalization "so overwhelming that

---

[12] *Kusa no ne no fashizumu: Nihon minshū no sensō taiken* (1987).

it becomes impossible to see such phenomena as the Rape of Nanjing, for example, as an isolated 'incident.'"[13]

For decades before World War II the government had used education, the media, and a variety of grassroots organizations to mobilize nationalist sentiment among the populace. By the 1930s, in the crisis days of the Great Depression, nationalism became a runaway force, gripping every part of society. Yoshimi ultimately concludes that ordinary Japanese were both victims of imperial consciousness and victimizers perpetrating it; they were not only agents but also conduits of fascism. It was only as the war dragged on and the deaths and bombing took their toll on the civilians that popular support began to wane, causing leaders increasing worry over the domestic situation.[14] *Grass Roots Fascism* not only made an important contribution to the study of the popular mentality and mood in the war, it was also a pioneering work for its approach to methodology in historical writing.

The Death of Hirohito

After the death of Emperor Hirohito in 1989 the taboo in Japan on discussion of his role and responsibility receded (Figure 7.1). New memoirs and records came to light and many Japanese historians began to raise issues of his responsibility. Until the time of his death, the emperor was often

---

[13] Yoshimi, *Grassroots Fascism*, p. 32.
[14] The translator Ethan Mark provides a useful introduction to Yoshimi's pathbreaking work. *Grassroots Fascism: The War Experience of the Japanese People* (New York: Columbia University Press, 2015).

Figure 7.1 Emperor Hirohito is the subject of much debate for his wartime role. He is shown here on June 28, 1930.
Source: Imagno/Getty Images

portrayed by Japanese historians as a peace-loving man, dominated by the military, a constitutional monarch who could not interfere with politics and therefore was not responsible for the course of the war.

During the American Occupation of Japan an understanding of the emperor's wartime role was deliberately obscured by MacArthur's decision to use him to legitimate Occupation reforms. In a momentous initiative, MacArthur decided to retain the imperial institution and to absolve the emperor of any war responsibility. During the war he had often been the face of the enemy along with Hitler and Mussolini and at the time of surrender a substantial portion of Americans favored his trial as a war criminal. In the face of this opinion, MacArthur took a direct hand in protecting the emperor and in shielding him from any responsibility for the war. MacArthur's strategy was to lay the blame for the war on the military leadership for misleading the people. By absolving Hirohito of war responsibility, MacArthur wanted to use the emperor's traditional sacred role to legitimate the Occupation's reforms in the eyes of the public. He was referred to as a man of peace who had opposed the war. In the new constitution drafted under MacArthur's direction, the emperor was retained as a constitutional monarch and defined as "the symbol of the State and of the unity of the people with whom resides sovereign power."

Despite MacArthur's maneuver, it was inevitable that eventually left-wing historians would assess Japan's own responsibility for the tragedy of Hiroshima and Nagasaki. Shouldn't Japanese leaders – especially the emperor – have acted earlier to end a war that was clearly lost? After the fall of Saipan in July 1944 when Japan came within range of B-29s and the Tōjō government resigned, leaders in Tokyo knew that Japan was headed for defeat. Yet the war continued for another year, during which more than half a million Japanese civilians perished. Did Japan's failure to surrender when it was clear that it had lost the war not give it major responsibility for the tragedy of Hiroshima and Nagasaki? If the emperor could bring about surrender in August 1945, why not many months earlier when Japanese leaders recognized the cause was lost? Why did Japanese leaders insist on holding out to preserve the imperial system?

In time, it was not only left-leaning historians who began to raise the issue of the emperor's responsibility. In 1988, as the emperor lay dying, the mayor of Nagasaki, Motoshima Hitoshi, a man of remarkable personal courage, responding to questions put to him in the city assembly and afterward by the media, asserted that the emperor bore partial responsibility for the war and its calamitous termination. "It is clear," he said, "from historical records that if the Emperor, in response to the reports of his senior statesmen, had resolved to end the war earlier, there would have been no battle of Okinawa, no nuclear attacks on Hiroshima and Nagasaki."[15] His statement ignited an immense media uproar in Japan and many demanded that the mayor, a Christian, retract his statement, apologize, and resign. He stood his ground, however, and eventually he was shot by a right-wing nationalist. He recovered, though, and was even reelected.

The issue of Japanese responsibility received relatively little careful scholarship until the emperor's death in 1989, by which time not only did new and important materials become available but also the historical profession in the West overcame its provincial nature. As historians in the West began to get language competence and gain access to the work of historians in Japan, serious attention to the role of

---

[15] Quoted in Norma Field, *In the Realm of a Dying Emperor* (New York: Vintage Books, 1993), p. 178.

the emperor became a major consideration in the debates about the Hiroshima decision.

The emperor was an enigmatic figure – and remains so today. He kept a diary that would surely be revealing but it remains locked away in the Imperial Household records, like so many other relevant imperial documents that are unlikely to be opened for the foreseeable future. In addition, great amounts of government documents were deliberately destroyed at the time of surrender before Occupation forces arrived. All ministries destroyed their records, as did the local governments. The military historian Edward Drea tells us that "a week-long bonfire consumed the war ministry's and general staff's most sensitive, and likely most incriminating documents."[16]

From a young age, Hirohito was indoctrinated in imperial myths, beliefs, and customs of his own divinity. Even though he did receive a scientific education, which gave him his lifelong interest in marine biology, he came to accept the sacred nature of his role, its origins, and the burden he must bear of preserving the imperial system. We know, for example, that as the likelihood of an allied invasion of Japan loomed, he worried for fear that the imperial regalia might fall into enemy hands. The regalia of sword, jewel, and bronze mirror were said to be handed down from the sun goddess, Amaterasu Omikami, and were the symbols of his legitimacy.

By the time he ascended the throne in 1926, generations of Japanese were being indoctrinated in the unique nature of Japan, the Japanese, and the Japanese state – all

---

[16] Drea, *The Imperial Japanese Army*, p. 260.

were bound up in the mystical concept of *kokutai*, which referred to Japan's unique national polity or its sacred imperial system (*tennōsei*). Nationalism was shaped by official ideologues to embrace the idea of Japan as a family state, the emperor as the father of the nation and the subjects as his children. At the heart of the *kokutai* ideology were the Shinto beliefs in Japan's origins in the imperial family's descent from the sun goddess. The emperor cult was woven together with the native folk religion of Shinto to indoctrinate a nation of true believers in the ideology. Its success in mobilizing the populace was achieved through relentless indoctrination. Also, living in an island nation that had not known immigration for nearly two millennia, Japanese could well find their identity in ethnic community. National shrines such as the one dedicated to the sun goddess at Ise, the Yasukuni shrine in Tokyo, which enshrined all those who died in Japan's modern wars, as well as local shrines underwrote the imperial cult. Hirohito thus became the Japanese version of the charismatic leaders of fascism in the West. But, at the same time, he was more deeply rooted in the culture, more invulnerable because of his sanctity, and more compelling because of his mysterious remoteness.

Seen only rarely by his subjects, closely overseen in his behavior by a powerfully conservative Imperial Household Ministry, and not heard by his subjects until the surrender broadcast in 1945, Hirohito and his personal beliefs and influence remained controversial. It was only with his death in 1989, as new memoirs and records came to light, that a number of historians – both Japanese and non-Japanese historians – raised new issues about his responsibility.

Western historians of Japan who gained advanced language training, who did primary research as well as drawing on the secondary works of Japanese scholars, were now fully involved in the controversies surrounding Hirohito and his role.

Herbert Bix's Hirohito

Left-leaning historians in Japan first made extensive use of the new materials. With the taboo on discussion of his responsibility lifted, they began to argue that the emperor was involved in political and military decision-making, that he knowingly gave legitimacy to the nationalist cause, and that he was an enthusiastic advocate of military campaigns. They saw him as supportive of the army and resistant to ending the war in early 1945 when civilian political leaders came to him privately and urged him to take immediate steps to end the futile war effort lest growing social unrest lead to a socialist upheaval and the overthrow of the imperial system from within.

Drawing on the new sources and the interpretations of these Japanese historians, the American historian Herbert Bix won the Pulitzer Prize for his book *Hirohito and the Making of Modern Japan*, published in 2000.[17] He dismissed Robert Butow's characterization of Hirohito as "the myth of the emperor as a standard European-style monarch, constitutionally bound to obey the decisions of his advisers and

---

[17] Herbert P. Bix, *Hirohito and the Making of Modern Japan* (New York: Harper Collins, 2000).

unable to declare his own will except when his ministers deadlocked."[18] Quite to the contrary, Bix portrayed the emperor as a "fighting generalissimo," involved in political and military decisions, who bears responsibility for failing to exercise the leadership needed to end the war. The result was that "surrender was delayed, Tokyo was firebombed, the battle of Okinawa was fought, and atomic bombs were dropped on Hiroshima and Nagasaki mainly because the emperor would not exercise the leadership needed to end the war."[19] In short, Hirohito was responsible for "prosecuting the war of aggression"[20] and "deeply involved in supervising the actual conduct of military operations."[21]

Perhaps the strongest evidence Bix found for the emperor's activist role was ironically provided by the emperor himself. In 1990, a lengthy document came to light that Hirohito himself had dictated shortly after surrender perhaps in anticipation that he might be charged in the war crimes trials or that he might decide to abdicate. Known as the *Monologue* (*dokuhakuron*), Hirohito described himself as an active participant in political and military strategy but as an advocate of peace. Bix found this self-serving and

[18] Herbert P. Bix, "Japan's Delayed Surrender: A Reinterpretation," in Michael J. Hogan, ed., *Hiroshima in History and Memory* (Cambridge: Cambridge University Press, 1996), p. 85.
[19] Herbert P. Bix, "The Showa Emperor's 'Monologue' and the Problem of War Responsibility," *Journal of Japanese Studies* 18, no.2 (Summer 1992): 352.
[20] Bix, "The Showa Emperor's 'Monologue' and the Problem of War Responsibility," p. 356.
[21] Bix, "The Showa Emperor's 'Monologue' and the Problem of War Responsibility," p. 354.

unpersuasive and instead saw it as proof that the emperor trusted in the military to win a decisive battle that would force the Americans to negotiate a peace treaty which would preserve the *kokutai* and the imperial system.[22] The works of many Japanese progressive historians like Yoshida Yutaka and Yamada Akira, who were longtime critics of Hirohito's wartime role, strongly influenced Bix's study.

Bix belonged to the revisionist generation. In his graduate school days at Harvard he participated in anti-Vietnam War demonstrations and was a founding member of the Committee for Concerned Asian Scholars (CCAS), known for its critique of American imperialism. But Bix parted company with Alperowitz and those revisionists who placed the blame for the use of the bomb on anti-Soviet motivations of Truman and his advisors. For Bix, while the "truculence" of Truman was an important factor, it was primarily the "unrealistic and incompetent actions of Japan's highest leaders" and especially the "stubborn personality" of Hirohito, who failed to "look reality in the face" and sue for peace.[23]

A full assessment of Hirohito's role as head of the military required an understanding of the "emperor system" (*tennōsei*) in modern Japan. A strength of Bix's prize-winning book was that it provided an impressive study of the emperor's education, showing how he was bred on the mythic, theocratic implications of his position and absorbed "the idea enshrined in the Meiji constitution, that he embodied a timeless, genealogical line of sovereign emperors,

---

[22] Bix, *Hirohito*, pp. 589–592.   [23] Bix, *Hirohito*, pp. 520–521.

descended through the male line, and 'unbroken' from the age of the gods."[24]

Many historians believed that Bix "puts to final rest the belief that the emperor was an uninformed, helpless puppet in the hands of the military."[25] Some historians, however, find Bix's view of the emperor as "fighting generalissimo" overdrawn. The emperor was certainly a believer in Japan's imperial destiny, but he was a procrastinator, often misinformed, and inclined to adhere to the traditional role of the emperor as not involving himself in politics, reigning but not ruling. It seems clear that because of his upbringing and education he was consistently motivated by an obligation to preserve and protect the sovereignty of the throne. When he did intervene in politics it was usually to safeguard the imperial system. His training was inescapably influenced by the elaboration of the imperial cult in modern times. Even its mythical symbols, the regalia, were essential to imperial legitimacy. After the war, in his *Monologue*, he explained his "sacred decision" (*seidan*) to surrender in self-serving terms:

> The main motive behind my decision at that time was that if we let matters stand and did not act, the Japanese race would perish and I would be unable to protect my subjects [*sekishi*, literally, infants, children]. Second, [the Privy Seal] Kido agreed with me on the matter of defending the *kokutai*. If the enemy landed near Ise Bay, both Ise and Atsuta shrines would immediately come under their

---

[24] Bix, *Hirohito*, p. 121.
[25] Ben-Ami Shillony book review of Bix, *Hirohito* in *Journal of Japanese Studies* 28, no. 1 (Winter 2002): 142.

control. There would be no time to transfer the sacred treasures [regalia] of the imperial family and no hope of protecting them. Under these circumstances, protection of the *kokutai* would be difficult. For these reasons, I thought at the time that I must make peace even at the sacrifice of myself.[26]

The military historian Edward Drea in his well-researched but underappreciated book *In the Service of the Emperor* argued that Hirohito shared the assumptions of Japan's nationalist ideology and imperial destiny, but he had been averse to going to war with the West, because such a conflict could risk the imperial system. In the end, however, he acquiesced in the decisions for war in the fall of 1941. The emperor placed a great deal of trust in Tōjō and his army faction to control the more fanatical elements of the military and he supported the *ketsugō* strategy as the way to preserve the imperial system in the face of the unconditional surrender demand. Above all, through most of the war Hirohito clung to the belief that one decisive military victory would compel the United States to negotiate surrender terms and thus save if not the empire, at least the imperial system, the *kokutai*. Under the influence of the Imperial Court Ministry, Drea wrote, the emperor was cautious and procrastinating, reluctant to inject the throne into politics and allowing opportunities to end the war to pass, expecting that the *ketsugō* strategy would prevail.

Domestic unrest as an additional threat to the imperial system weighed too on the Court and the political elite. The civilian elite came to fear the growing popular disaffection from the war effort. This growing nervousness about

[26] Bix, "Japan's Delayed Surrender: A Reinterpretation," p. 110.

domestic unrest was demonstrated most notably by the Yoshida anti-war group (Yohansen), which petitioned the emperor in February 1945 to seek surrender, even unconditional surrender, lest a social uprising destroy the *kokutai*. The emperor, however, chose to adhere to the *ketsugō* strategy. The Japanese historian Hatano Sumio argues that the paralyzing dilemma, created, on the one hand, by fear of army revolt if peace were pursued and, on the other hand, by fear of popular upheaval if the war continued, was only solved by the bomb and Soviet entry.[27] To the end, the emperor often seemed to value preservation of the imperial institution more than the well-being of his people.[28] Or perhaps he believed the two could not be separated. Too late, he finally acted only when the fate of the imperial system was imperiled by impending invasion and the atomic bombs.[29]

It is a strength of Drea's book, which drew relatively little attention from other historians who as we have discussed

---

[27] Jeremy Yellen's important article, an early draft of which he wrote in my seminar, agrees with Hatano. See Jeremy A. Yellen, "The Specter of Revolution: Reconsidering Japan's Decision to Surrender," *International History Review* 35, no. 1 (February 2013): 205–226.

[28] See the thoughtful essay by Edward J. Drea, "Chasing a Decisive Victory," in Drea, *In the Service of the Emperor*, pp. 169–215.

[29] The emperor also wanted to avoid a battle in the homeland and believed that "the conditions" in the Potsdam Declaration together with the subsequent clarifying exchange of notes with Truman ensured the chances of the Imperial institution surviving the "unconditional surrender." See Suzuki Tamon, *"Shūsen" no seijishi, 1943-1945* (Tokyo: Tokyo daigaku shuppankai, 2011), pp. 175–186. See also Hatano Sumio, *Nihon gaikō no 150nen: Bakumatsu/Ishin kara Heisei made* (Tokyo: Nihon gaikō kyōkai, 2019), p. 245.

tended to marginalize military history, that he provided an insightful analysis of the character of the Japanese military, its leaders as well as its ordinary fighting men, their beliefs and cultural mores. Obliquely countering Bix's indictment of the emperor as a "fighting generalissimo," Drea wrote that "while the emperor alone cannot be said to have been more responsible than anyone else for delaying Japan's surrender, the unrealistic and incompetent actions of Japan's military and civilian leaders prolonged the war."[30] They misled and misinformed the emperor. After all, in trying to determine what responsibility Japan may have had for the Hiroshima decision, it would not be fair to lay the entire blame on the emperor. Japan's military must surely also be scrutinized for its role in prolonging the war.

Drea, in another important and underappreciated book, *Japan's Imperial Army*, drew on "the new military history" written by historians in Japan, to explain the mistakes and shortcomings of the army that contributed to the disastrous outcome. In contrast to historians in America, historians in Japan focused attention on the military, which had been so central to their national disaster. As Drea put it, throughout the war, "instead of the army serving the interests of the state, the state came to serve the army."[31] Army leadership, personified by the war minister Anami Korechika, believed that a decisive victory could be achieved by will and esprit in combat (Figure 7.2). Anami, along with most other military leaders, lacked capacity for strategic thought and "the intellectual framework to think beyond the present engagement."[32] The brutality that characterized the

[30] Drea, *In the Service*, p. 210. [31] Drea, *Japan's Imperial Army*, p. 256.
[32] Drea, *In the Service*, p. 74.

Figure 7.2 General Anami Korechika, war minister, committed suicide following Japanese surrender on August 15, 1945.
Source: Bettmann/Getty Images

harsh treatment involved in training recruits carried over into atrocities against the enemy soldiers and civilians. Along with Yoshimi's *Grassroots Fascism*, Yoshida Yutaka's study of the grim battlefield experience of ordinary army soldiers[33] adds another dimension to the *minshūshi* (people's history) approach, which supports Drea's argument that "officers at all levels condoned or connived at murder, rape, arson, and looting."[34]

The emperor's fear of the army's reaction, Drea wrote, was a determinant of his procrastination: "How would the army react to attempts by the court to end the conflict? Could or would Anami control the military? Would hotheaded officers rebel, insisting Japan must fight to the death? These uncertainties

---

[33] Yoshida Yutaka, *Nihnongun heishi: Ajia-Taiheiyō sensō no genjitsu* (Tokyo: Chūō Kōron Shinsha, 2017).

[34] Drea, *Japan's Imperial Army*, p. 259.

and the specter of a military coup d'etat haunted Hirohito to the end."[35] Drea leaned toward blaming the military leaders more than the emperor; they misled him and insisted on fighting to the bitter end.[36] The constitution gave the military substantial autonomy and ability to influence policy. The political role of the Japanese military and its ideology are central to the post–World War I period, during which time six army generals served as prime ministers, all of whom, even Tōjō, had trouble controlling subordinates. In his classic work on civil–military relations *The Soldier and the State*, Samuel Huntington writes that "Japan had 'the most political army' in the world."[37] The major obstacles to the peace process in Japan were the ideology and the demands of the army. By the 1930s the doctrine that prohibited surrender and insistence on fighting to the death were fixed in the army's creed.

In 2019, records of Tajima Michiji, the Grand Steward of the Imperial Household Agency from 1949 to 1953, were made public. The documents were based on his conversations with the emperor and revealed Hirohito's reflections on his own responsibility for the war, his wish to abdicate and to make a public apology for the catastrophe of the war at the time the Occupation came to an end in 1952. Prime Minister Yoshida Shigeru, however, stopped him from making a public expression of remorse for the war because it would tend to suggest the emperor's culpability. His readiness to abdicate was also blocked by Yoshida. Among the topics revealed in the Tajima papers were

---

[35] Drea, *In the Service*, p. 209. [36] Drea, *In the Service*, p. 210.
[37] Samuel P. Huntington, *The Soldier and the State: The Theory and Politics of Civil-Military Relations* (Cambridge: Harvard Belknap Press, 1957), p. 126.

Hirohito's remarks on the difficulty of controlling the army, its disorder, and insubordination (gekokujō). As a result of the Tajima documents, writes the historian Carol Gluck, "when they are fitted into the frame of other materials that have appeared since his death in 1989, the emperor becomes a fuller historical figure."[38]

Japanese leaders bear heavy responsibility for the tragedy that befell their people. They embarked on a war against a power with no less than eight times their material strength without a clear endgame. "Sometimes people have to shut their eyes and take the plunge," said General Tōjō, the new prime minister, in 1941.[39] With blind faith and desperation, Japan's leaders led their country into a war that could not be won. "It is a common mistake in going to war," Thucydides observed, "to begin at the wrong end, to act first, and wait for a disaster to discuss the matter."[40] The hope of the *ketsugō* strategy that by winning a decisive battle they might compel the enemy to negotiate a peace that would save the empire proved reckless. With their cities burning and hundreds of thousands of their people perishing, the military and the emperor, infused with a narrow nationalist ideology, allowed successive opportunities to end the hostilities go by until it was too late.

---

[38] Carol Gluck, "New Hirohito Documents Show Emperor's Thoughts on the War," *Nikkei Asia* (September 13, 2019).

[39] Quoted in Kenneth B. Pyle, *Japan Rising: The Resurgence of Japanese Power and Purpose* (New York: PublicAffairs Press, 2007), pp. 203–204.

[40] Quoted in Robert Gilpin, *War and Change in World Politics* (Cambridge: Cambridge University Press, 1981), p. 202.

8

A Wider Perspective

One of the important choices historians must make is to decide the time frame to apply to the event they are interpreting. They can narrow the lens through which they approach the subject and study factors in the immediate realm of the particular event. The advantage of a narrow focus or microhistory is that it allows the exploration of the event in great depth. One historian, for example, wrote on how the Chinese Revolution affected a village of a few hundred families. "By getting in very close, tightening your focus to a single person or tiny corner of the world, you can operate on a level, the nitty-gritty of social history, invisible to historians who work on a more general register."[1] Historians can widen the lens to see history in a broader time perspective. Choice of a broader time frame can shed light on larger historical developments conducive to explaining the event. It may demonstrate that the event being studied was shaped and influenced by longer-term processes than were first perceived. William McNeil, for example, writes macrohistory on such topics as the history of diseases or the history of the pursuit of power. In such grand topics it becomes possible to see patterns and trends. Most historians work somewhere in between these extremes.

We have seen thus far that historians explaining the Hiroshima decision have tended to focus attention narrowly

[1] Sarah Maza, *Thinking About History*, p. 181.

on the last months of the war. One exception was Michael Sherry's *The Rise of American Air Power*, which we discussed in Chapter 6. Sherry adopted a broader timescale by tracing the decision to accumulated assumptions and attitudes that developed over decades in the evolution of American air power. For the most part, however, historical controversy over the use of the atomic bomb has swirled around the last few months of the war and President Truman's "decision."

Some historians (myself included[2]) believe that concentrating on the summer of 1945 places the issue in too limited a time frame to fully understand the genesis of the Hiroshima decision. The historian Sean Malloy concluded that "one of the weaknesses of much of the literature on the bomb is a narrow focus on Truman and the last months of the war."[3] The events of the summer of 1945 may be the immediate or proximate causes of the decision. The ultimate or root causes may be found earlier.

Historical explanations involve asking "Why?" The study of causes is fundamental to the historian's craft. Choosing a longer time frame for their interpretation compels historians to order their causes. Finding a multiplicity of causes, the historian will need to order them in terms of

---

[2] This chapter draws on several of my writings: Kenneth B. Pyle, "Hiroshima and the Historians: History as Relative Truth," *Asia-Pacific Review* 22, no. 2 (November 2015): 14–27. Also, Kenneth B. Pyle, *Japan in the American Century* (Cambridge, MA: Harvard Belknap Press, 2018), chapters 2 and 3; and Kenneth B. Pyle, "The Making of Postwar Japan: A Speculative Essay," *Journal of Japanese Studies* 46, no. 1 (Winter 2020): 113–144.

[3] Malloy, *Atomic Tragedy*, p. 8.

priority. Which ones are immediate causes? Which are longer term? After first finding immediate causes, they can then look for longer-term ones. Some causes are more important than others. In their analysis historians must construct a hierarchy of causes by sorting out and prioritizing causes. The historian should not leave the reader with an undifferentiated assortment of different causes of a major event. David Hackett Fischer calls this the fallacy of "indiscriminate pluralism."[4] The historian must weigh the different causes to create an integrated and refined interpretation.

After first finding proximate causes in the immediate realm of the event, they can then move back in time to establish a causal chain and find more fundamental or longer-term causes. But how far back to go? How to decide where to stop? Which in the final analysis is the most important cause? The answer to that question, writes the historian Stuart Hughes, is "to locate the factor which, when removed, would make the decisive difference in a given sequence of events – that is, the factor which, if thought away, would render the events in question inconceivable."[5] Similarly, Marc Bloch suggested that historians by "a bold exercise of the mind" revisit the past and try to find "the antecedent which could have been most easily avoided" in causing a certain sequence of results.[6] What antecedent event which

---

[4] Fischer, *Fallacies*, pp. 175–177.
[5] H. Stuart Hughes, "The Historian and the Social Scientist," *The American Historical Review* 66, no. 1 (October 1960): 29.
[6] Marc Bloch, *The Historian's Craft*, pp. 125, 191.

might have been avoided, we may ask, was pivotal in influencing the Hiroshima decision?

A Longer Time Frame

Analyzing the Hiroshima decision in a broader timescale helps to clarify the fundamental causes that impelled the decision. In many of his essays, Barton Bernstein consistently found concentration on the events of the summer of 1945 inadequate to fully explain the decision, pointing out that Truman, coming to the presidency in the way he did, seemed to be swept along by earlier policy decisions. He described Truman's so-called decision as "the implementation of inherited assumptions." Bernstein argued that by the time Truman became president, an "implicit American decision – really a dominant assumption – had long existed: that the bomb would be used against a hated enemy.... Such powerful assumptions about the A-bomb use, and the presence of partial precedents in conventional bombing for such use, prepared the way for Truman. ... The basic decision on using the bomb flowed from overwhelming, long-held assumptions."[7]

Reviewing *Racing the Enemy*, Bernstein wrote that Hasegawa had erred by setting up a too narrow framework for his study. "Because most of Hasegawa's analysis really begins in 1945,

---

[7] H-Diplo Roundtable Reviews, Volume VII, No. 2 (2006), 14–16. Roundtable on Tsuyoshi Hasegawa, *Racing the Enemy: Stalin, Truman, and the Surrender of Japan*. Ccommentary by Barton J. Bernstein. accessed March 2, 2011, www.h-net.org/~diplo/index.html.

there is a serious problem in his not examining in depth earlier policy, not assessing the pre-1945 decisions and implications, and not looking at events in a broader prism than the 'racing' framework."[8] From his extensive research and writings on the decision, Bernstein concluded that "the combat use of the A-bomb was, unfortunately, virtually inevitable. Truman's commitment to its use was, basically, the implementation of the assumption that he had inherited."[9] The bomb was a legitimate weapon to be used. Roosevelt and his advisors never debated *whether* to use it, Bernstein wrote, but *how* to use it.

> Because Truman was following a very prestigious president whom he, like a great many Americans, loved and admired, the new president was not free psychologically or politically to strike out on a clearly new course. Only a bolder man, with more self-confidence, might have tried critically to assess the legacy and to act independently. ... Truman, depending as he did upon Roosevelt's advisors could not easily reassess the prevailing assumption that the bomb was a legitimate weapon to be used in combat with Japan.[10]

Given the immense prestige of his predecessor, the new president was determined to be faithful to Roosevelt's

---

[8] *H-Diplo Roundtable Reviews*, Volume VII, No. 2 (2006), p. 14.

[9] Barton J. Bernstein, "Understanding the Atomic Bomb and the Japanese Surrender: Missed Opportunities, Little-Known Near Disasters, and Modern Memory," *Diplomatic History* 19, no. 2 (Spring 1995): 230.

[10] Barton J. Bernstein, "Roosevelt, Truman, and the Atomic Bomb, 1941-1945: A Reinterpretation," *Political Science Quarterly* 90, no. 1 (Spring 1975): 34–35.

policies. Tellingly, Truman's decision to use the bomb seemed a foregone conclusion to those closest to him. "At no time, from 1941 to 1945," Stimson later recalled, "did I ever hear it suggested by the President, or by any other responsible member of government, that atomic energy should not be used in the war."[11] Churchill likewise recalled "that the decision whether or not to use the atomic bomb to compel the surrender of Japan was never even an issue."[12] General Groves later remarked that Truman's decision was "one of noninterference – basically, a decision not to upset the existing plans."[13] The new president, he added, was "like a little boy on a toboggan."[14] Historians have struggled to find evidence of when Truman at Potsdam, after the successful Trinity test, made the decision and gave his approval of the use of the bomb. In this regard, Bernstein writes: "The reason that careful historians cannot find records of a top-level A-bomb 'decision' is ... because there was no need for an

[11] Stimson, "The Decision to Use the Atomic Bomb." Martin Sherwin writes: "Nowhere in Stimson's meticulous diary ... is there any suggestion of doubt or questioning of the assumption that the bomb should be used against Germany or Japan if the weapon was ready before the end of the war. From the time of the first organizational meeting for the atomic energy project held at the White House on October 9, 1941, members of the Top Policy Group conceived of the development of the weapon as an essential part of the total war effort. They asked whether it would be ready in time, not whether it should be used if it was; what were the diplomatic consequences of its development, not the moral implications of its military use." *A World Destroyed*, pp. 194–195.

[12] Winston Churchill, *Triumph and Tragedy* (Boston: Houghton Mifflin, 1953), p. 639.

[13] McGeorge Bundy, *Danger and Survival*, p. 60.

[14] Malloy, *Atomic Tragedy*, p. 98.

actual 'decision' meeting. Such a question would have been required if there had been a serious question about whether or not to use the bomb on Japan."[15] Most historians agree with Wilson Miscamble, for example, who in his book *From Roosevelt to Truman* concluded that "Truman had to make no profound and wrenching decision to use the atomic weapon.... There is little evidence for the president's agonizing over the matter.... Truman possessed neither the capacity nor the desire to question the logic of the bomb's use."[16]

Unconditional Surrender Policy

A more important assumption that Truman inherited in setting the stage for the use of the bomb was Roosevelt's distinctively personal decision to wage the war to unconditional surrender. As Roosevelt pondered American entry into war, he arranged a secret shipboard meeting with Churchill in August 1941 off the coast of Newfoundland. He wanted, he told the prime minister, a joint declaration of war aims "relating to the civilization of the world." He was beginning to think of the creation of a new liberal international order as a war goal. The Atlantic Charter, issued at the end of their meeting, committed the two leaders to work for self-determination, disarmament of aggressors, free trade, freedom of the seas, and "establishment of a wider and permanent system of

---

[15] *H-Diplo Roundtable Reviews*, Volume VII, No. 2, p. 15.
[16] Wilson D. Miscamble, *From Roosevelt to Truman: Potsdam, Hiroshima, and the Cold War* (Cambridge: Cambridge University Press, 2007), pp. 177–178. See also Miscamble, *Most Controversial Decision*, pp. 45–46.

general security."[17] The principles espoused in the Charter, Roosevelt said in a message to Congress, were so "clear-cut" that "a willingness to accept compromise" was out of the question.[18] He was thinking of a new liberal international order and total victory as a war goal to achieve it. Weeks after Pearl Harbor, in his Annual Message to Congress, he said the nation's purpose must be "to cleanse the world of ancient evils, ancient ills. ... No compromise can end that conflict. There never has been – there never can be – successful compromise between good and evil."[19] His unwillingness to compromise war goals was again apparent a year later when he told Canadian Prime Minister Mackenzie King in a telling remark of later significance, "If the Japanese did not accept unconditional surrender then they should be bombed till they were brought to their knees."[20]

Then, on January 24, 1943, as Roosevelt met with Churchill at their Casablanca conference, the president with prime minister seated beside him met with the press (Figure 8.1). Speaking from notes, Roosevelt made what his biographer called "one of the most momentous and debatable

---

[17] Robert Dallek, *Franklin D. Roosevelt and American Foreign Policy, 1932-1945* (New York: Oxford University Press, 1979), 284; Ruhl J. Bartlett, ed., *The Record of American Diplomacy*, 3rd ed. (New York: Knopf, 1954), pp. 623–625.
[18] Bartlett, ed., *The Record of American Diplomacy*, pp. 623–625.
[19] Samuel I. Rosenman, ed., *The Public Papers and Addresses of Franklin D. Roosevelt, 1942: Humanity on the Defensive* (New York: Harper & Brothers, 1950), pp. 41–42.
[20] Nigel Hamilton, *Commander in Chief: FDR's Battle with Churchill, 1943* (Boston: Houghton Mifflin Harcourt, 2016), p. 29.

Figure 8.1 Roosevelt meeting with Prime Minister Winston Churchill in Casablanca, Morocco, announcing to the press the unconditional surrender policy, January 24, 1943.
Source: Bettmann/Getty Images

pronouncements of the war."[21] It was a public assertion of the far-reaching goal of unconditional surrender.

> I think we have all had it in our hearts and heads before, but I don't think that it has ever been put down on paper by the Prime Minister and myself, and that is the determination that peace can come to the world only by the total elimination of German and Japanese war power. . . .

[21] Frank Freidel, *Franklin D. Roosevelt: A Rendezvous with Destiny* (Boston: Little, Brown 1990), p. 463.

> The elimination of German, Japanese and Italian war power means the unconditional surrender of Germany, Italy and Japan.[22]

Churchill was ambivalent about such absolute war aims but chose not to say so publicly. After he returned to Washington, in a press conference, Roosevelt further explained that he and Churchill "formally reemphasized what we had been talking about before, and that is we don't think there should be any kind of negotiated armistice, for obvious reasons. There ought to be unconditional surrender."[23]

Someone in the press should have asked what were "the obvious reasons" because, in point of fact, this wartime goal was wholly without precedent. World War II was the only foreign war in American history waged to unconditional surrender. All others, before and since, have ended with an armistice and a negotiated peace. The American Revolution, the War of 1812, the Mexican War, the Spanish–American War, and World War I ended with negotiated peace treaties. Unconditional surrender was explicitly rejected as a goal when the Cold War began. Both the Korean and Vietnam Wars ended with negotiated peace agreements. More recently, American presidents have negotiated with Taliban leaders to end the Afghanistan War.

---

[22] Dallek, *Roosevelt and American Foreign Policy*, p. 374.
[23] Samuel I. Rosenman, ed., *The Public Papers and Addresses of Franklin D. Roosevelt, 1943: The Tide Turns* (New York: Harper & Brothers, 1950), pp. 59–60

This war would be different. American diplomats were instructed not to discuss conditions for ending the conflict. Compromise and diplomacy were ruled out. There would be no confidential discussion with the fascist powers for ending the conflict. For Roosevelt, the goal was not simply turning back the enemies' expansionism but, instead, occupying the defeated enemy nations, remaking their domestic orders, and reeducating their people in the ways of democratic and peace-loving nations.

Roosevelt's policy demanded surrender of Japanese sovereignty so that its entire domestic system could be reengineered. Japan would be transformed into a permanently disarmed liberal democratic state, its ancient and complex civilization with its historically embedded conservative traditions would be remade from root to branch. This unprecedented war goal, which had not been carefully deliberated, was pronounced primarily with Germany in mind, but it would turn out to have grave and long-lasting consequences for Japan. Unconditional surrender policy provoked unconditional resistance and put the Asia Pacific War on a path to its catastrophic ending in the horrific battle of Okinawa, the firebombing of over sixty Japanese cities, and finally the use of the atomic bomb. In the last year of the war, upward of a half million Japanese civilians perished.

FDR stubbornly held to this sweeping goal even though many of his own advisors thought it misguided. Secretary of State Cordell Hull and others in the State Department opposed it not only because, as Hull later recorded, "it might prolong the war by solidifying Axis resistance into one of desperation" but also because "the principle logically required the victor nations to be ready to take over every phase of the national and local Governments of the conquered countries, and to operate all governmental activities and properties. We and our Allies were in no way prepared to undertake this vast obligation."[24] Secretary of War Stimson opposed the policy as applied to Japan. So did many of Roosevelt's military advisors, who feared it would lengthen the war and require a bloody invasion of Japan. Both Churchill and Stalin had doubts about such totalistic goals, fearing that the policy would prolong the war by strengthening the determination of the Axis leaders to resist. Churchill from time to time privately urged modification of its terms. Stalin, while seeing the total destruction of Japanese power as in the Soviet national interest, cynically suggested that the Allies "agree to milder peace terms but once we get into Japan to give them the works."[25]

Roosevelt's Reasons

Many historians viewing the war in a broad perspective and looking for the pivotal cause for the Hiroshima decision found it in the unconditional surrender policy. What prompted Roosevelt's determination to choose this historically unprecedented war goal? In his third term as president, Roosevelt dominated American foreign policy as no other president ever has. There was no National Security Council

---

[24] *The Memoirs of Cordell Hull*, 2 vols. (New York: MacMillan, 1948), p. 1570.

[25] Gideon Rose, *How Wars End: Why We Always Fight the Last Battle* (New York: Simon and Schuster, 2011), p. 105.

to temper his personalized diplomacy and the State Department was weak and often not consulted even on major foreign policy issues.

There were several reasons for FDR's decision to foreclose all diplomacy and insist on absolutist goals in World War II. First, he wanted to fire the resolve of the American people, who only recently had clung to isolationism. He cast the war as a crusade. Roosevelt had a gift for shaping public sentiment. Marshaling popular emotions, he made unconditional surrender a shibboleth.

Second, FDR wanted to avoid the political weakness that Woodrow Wilson was accused of in World War I when he favored an armistice and a negotiated peace with Germany. Roosevelt had been Under Secretary of the Navy under Wilson and remembered how the president had been criticized as weak by his opponents for failing to demand unconditional surrender. As his biographer Robert Sherwood often observed, Roosevelt was haunted by the ghost of Woodrow Wilson and often during the war reminded the American people of the mistakes made after World War I.[26] This time the United States would not be satisfied to drive the enemy back to its prewar borders or simply to leave it as a defeated and diminished nation with its sovereignty still intact. The historian Ernest May observed that the president's stubborn adherence to unconditional surrender policy was based on the kind of "superficial reasoning" that policymakers often make, which is to draw false or simplistic lessons from the recent

---

[26] Robert E. Sherwood, *Roosevelt and Hopkins: An Intimate History*, 2 vols. (New York: Bantam Books, 1948), p. 302.

past. "Like generals preparing for the last war, American statesmen in World War II thought only in terms of the last postwar era."[27] As the war against Germany was ending, Roosevelt emphasized that the lessons drawn from the experience with Germany would be applied also to Japan: "Practically all Germans deny the fact that they surrendered in the last war," he declared, "but this time they are going to know it. And so are the Japs."[28] In a statement hailing the landing of American troops in the Philippines, October 20, 1944, the president reiterated the same uncompromising determination and crusading spirit toward total defeat of Japan:

> We have learned our lesson about Japan. We trusted her and treated her with the decency due a civilized neighbor. We were foully betrayed. The price of the lesson was high. Now we are going to teach Japan her lesson. We have the will and the power to teach her the cost of treachery and deceit, and the cost of stealing from her neighbors. With our steadfast Allies, we shall teach this lesson so that Japan will never again forget it.[29]

A third reason for his unconditional surrender policy was that Roosevelt was intent on holding the alliance with

---

[27] Ernest R. May, *Lessons of the Past: The Use and Misuse of History in American Foreign Relations* (New York: Oxford University Press, 1973), p. 18.

[28] Samuel I. Rosenman, ed., *The Public Papers and Addresses of Franklin D. Roosevelt, 1944–45: Victory and the Threshold of Peace* (New York: Harper & Brothers, 1950), p. 210.

[29] FDR press conference, July 29, 1944. Rosenman, *The Public Papers and Addresses of Franklin D. Roosevelt, 1944–45*, p. 339.

Stalin together by avoiding discussion of specific war goals. The latter was deeply suspicious of British and American intentions and resentful of their failure to establish a second front in Europe to aid the Soviets in their resistance to Hitler's invasion. Deferring debate over peace terms could reassure Stalin that the United States and Britain would not reach a separate peace with Hitler. He did not want to risk disagreement with Stalin by discussion of concrete war aims. Roosevelt believed cooperation with Stalin would be necessary in the postwar order. He envisioned four powers – the United States, Russia, Britain, and China – serving as "policeman" to maintain global security after the war.

FDR's final and most important purpose in demanding unconditional surrender was achieving a free hand to shape an American-led postwar order. Nothing less than total victory would satisfy the goal of achieving a new and permanent democratic and peaceful order. The historian Warren Kimball writes that "once in the war [a] conception of world reform was the assumption that guided Roosevelt's actions."[30] Like Wilson, FDR held to the liberal belief that war was caused by domestic conditions. The domestic sources of militarism and aggression must be rooted out if there was to be peace. It would be necessary to have a free hand to reform the internal workings of the Axis societies. Therefore, defeat of the fascist powers was not sufficient. They must be occupied, and their politics and society democratized. With vestiges of fascism and militarism gone, a revolution in world

---

[30] Warren F. Kimball, *The Juggler: Franklin Roosevelt as Wartime Statesman* (Princeton: Princeton University Press, 1991), p. 17.

politics and an American-led world order would be possible. Peace would be maintained by a new system of collective security and policed by the victor nations. Weeks before his death, returning from Yalta, where he had met with Churchill and Stalin in February 1945, in his last address to Congress he declared that the new international order that he sought would "spell the end of the system of unilateral action, the exclusive alliances, the spheres of influence, the balances of power, and all the other expedients that have been tried for centuries – and have always failed. We propose to substitute for all of these, a universal organization in which all peace-loving nations will finally have a chance to join." In the same address, he reiterated that "the unconditional surrender of Japan is as essential as the defeat of Germany – if our plans for world peace are to succeed."[31] America was fighting not for narrowly defined goals of national interest as Churchill and Stalin were. Americans were seeking an end to all wars, a world safe for democracy, and a fresh start in the relations among nations. In short, the goal was a new American-led international order.

Implications of Unconditional Surrender Policy

Diplomacy is an important tool of statecraft. Back channels to an adversary make it possible to clarify war goals, to convey determination to achieve certain ends, to understand how the adversary views reality, to avoid unwanted or inadvertent

---

[31] Rosenman, ed., *Public Papers, 1944–45*, pp. 586, 584.

collisions, and to gauge the risk tolerance of adversaries. The art of diplomacy requires discernment, prudence, wisdom, and patience. It requires the ability to find possibilities of compromise. It understands the value of the balance of power as a core principle of diplomacy.

Roosevelt's goals of unconditional surrender and establishment of an American-led international order had profound implications for how the war against Japan would be fought and ultimately for the decision to use the atomic bomb. To decide from the outset of the war that there would be no place for diplomacy was not only unprecedented in American history but it also exercised great influence on how this war would be fought. We can see five major implications. First, by disdaining diplomacy and any negotiation, the policy abandoned concrete political goals and demanded total victory. The Prussian military strategist Carl von Clausewitz (1780–1831) in his classic work *On War* wrote that "war is a resort to violence to compel the enemy to accept a political objective that could not be obtained by peaceful means."[32] In Japanese–American negotiations on the eve of Pearl Harbor, the United States sought the Japanese withdrawal from China as the basis for resolving the oil embargo and other issues dividing the two nations. But once war began, the goal became total submission of the enemy. This went far beyond what Clausewitz had argued was the purpose of war – namely, achieving goals that diplomacy had failed to achieve.

---

[32] Anne Armstrong, *Unconditional Surrender: The Impact of the Casablanca Policy upon World War II* (New Brunswick: Rutgers University Press, 1961), p. 229.

A second implication was that by foreclosing the possibility of a limited conflict with specific goals it gave priority to military strategy – the militarization of foreign policy. America would depend on hard power to win this war. With diplomatic engagement ruled out, exerting "maximum force with maximum speed" became the strategy.[33] Escalating military pressure was accepted as the way to end the war early and each branch of the American military was motivated to use its power to compel Japanese surrender. The firebombing of scores of cities and the new willingness to deliberately target civilian populations helped prepare the readiness to use the atomic bomb.

A third implication was that unconditional surrender policy provoked unconditional resistance. Ruling out diplomacy, even back channels, and insisting on total conquest strengthened the hand of the Japanese hardliners. Japanese leaders embarked on war with only a sketchy exit strategy. Their memory of how success in the Russo-Japanese War, which came after a crushing defeat of the Russian navy, persuaded the Russians to negotiate influenced their strategy of seeking a decisive battle victory to force the Americans to negotiate. Japanese leaders were taken back by America's unprecedented war aims. Roosevelt spoke only in vague and sweeping terms of what unconditional surrender would mean: dissolution of the Japanese empire, occupation of the country, permanent disarmament, war crimes trials, reconstruction of the political and economic systems, and reeducation of the people. Japanese leaders found it hard to

---

[33] Stimson and Bundy, *On Active Service in Peace and War*, p. 629.

fathom the meaning of such sweeping war goals. What exactly did this policy entail? How long did the Allies intend to occupy Japan? Would the emperor be tried as a war criminal? Might he possibly be executed, and the imperial institution abolished? Would the nation as they knew it come to an end? It was by no means clear what the Americans intended. In his important work on the politics of war termination, Leon Sigal writes: "Unconditional surrender remained open to a variety of interpretations. ... Repeating the vague formula without spelling out its meaning ... left Japan in the dark about the consequences of defeat. Imprecision could reinforce enemy intransigence and confound those in Tokyo trying to sue for peace."[34] The absence of any diplomatic engagement handicapped the peace party in Japan. We know, for example, that in February 1945 a petition signed by an imposing group of conservative civilian elite was presented to the emperor, urging surrender lest continuation of the war lead to a social revolution at home. With only the broadest outline of what the Allies meant by this policy and with no back channels to provide any clarification, the emperor chose to side with the army and hope for a decisive battle that would force the Allies to negotiate.

A fourth implication was that achieving total victory meant that the American military must plan for the likelihood of an invasion of Japan or, if that prospect was to be avoided, the resort to a strangling naval blockade and undertaking the most devastating, even unthinkable, bombings and destruction of civilian life to achieve unconditional surrender and

---

[34] Sigal, *Fighting to a Finish*, p. 93.

complete control of the Japanese homeland. It also meant the urgent need of Soviet entry into the Asia Pacific War to help with the invasion of Japan, which Stalin secretly agreed to do three months after German surrender in return for major territorial concessions in Northeast Asia. While at Yalta Roosevelt also confirmed with Stalin major territorial concessions in return for Russian entry into the war. To the end of his life, Roosevelt remained convinced that he could work amicably with Stalin and bring the Soviet Union into a new postwar order that would keep the peace. David Kennedy, in his magisterial history of the Roosevelt era, concludes that Americans might reflect

> with some discomfort ... on how their leaders' stubborn insistence on unconditional surrender had led to the incineration of hundreds of thousands of already defeated Japanese, first by fire raids, then by nuclear blast; on how poorly Franklin Roosevelt had prepared for the postwar era, on how foolishly he had banked on goodwill and personal charm to compose the conflicting interests of nations.[35]

As American intelligence revealed the growing strength of the Japanese buildup in Kyushu in the summer of 1945, the unconditional surrender policy created a terrible dilemma for Truman and his military advisors. It required either a bloody and costly invasion of the Japanese homeland or a protracted naval blockade to starve the Japanese people and

---

[35] David Kennedy, *Freedom from Fear: The American People in Depression and War, 1929–1945* (New York: Oxford University Press, 1999), pp. 855–856.

continuation of the firebombing of cities. Unconditional surrender policy also required Stalin's entry into the war and a Soviet sharing of the spoils. For the United States the atomic bomb solved the dilemmas created by unconditional surrender policy. With this weapon, invasion was no longer necessary and Russian involvement in the Occupation could be avoided.[36]

A fifth implication was that unconditional surrender became a war slogan and in American public opinion the goal took on a life of its own. By the time Truman became president the policy seemed inviolable. American public opinion by nine to one in the summer of 1945 supported unconditional surrender even if it required an invasion.[37] Brynes advised the president that modifying surrender terms would have terrible "political repercussions"; the president would be "crucified" by public opinion and accused of appeasement.[38]

Taken together all these implications of the unconditional surrender policy set the stage for an Armageddon ending to the war. Only four days after becoming president, in his first address to a joint session of Congress, Truman later recalled: "I was applauded frequently and when I reaffirmed the policy of unconditional surrender, the chamber rose to its feet."[39] Truman inherited this policy as well as the assumption that the nuclear bomb would be used against a hated enemy. Given the immense prestige of his predecessor, the new

---

[36] For the reaction of Japanese leadership, see Suzuki Tamon, *"Shūsen" no seijishi, 1943–1945*, pp. 175–186.

[37] Leon V. Sigal, *Fighting to a Finish*, p. 95.

[38] Miscamble, *The Most Controversial Decision*, p. 101.

[39] Harry S. Truman, *Year of Decisions* (New York: Doubleday, 1955), p. 42.

president was strongly inclined to be faithful to Roosevelt's policies. When the Potsdam Declaration was issued, Truman adhered to the unconditional surrender policy and made no mention of the possibility of keeping the imperial institution. Japan must surrender unconditionally or face "prompt and utter destruction." The Allies would occupy Japan to disarm it and establish a new order in accord with the freely expressed will of the Japanese people. Truman and Byrnes decided that it was politically unacceptable to abandon the policy of unconditional surrender.

Japan's leading authority on its diplomatic history Hatano Sumio suggests that if the Potsdam Declaration had been issued as a diplomatic document through diplomatic channels, it would have helped the Japanese to communicate with the Allies and convey their principal concern with preserving the imperial system. Instead, its issuance as a public proclamation was seen by the Japanese as little more than propaganda and led to Japan's noncommittal (*mokusatsu*) response, which the United States interpreted as rejection.[40]

Truman and the Roosevelt Legacy

One historian who has chosen a narrow time frame so as to dig deep into the American domestic politics of the Hiroshima decision is the US historian Marc Gallicchio, who describes Truman as having an active role in determining the use of the bomb and adhering to unconditional surrender

[40] Hatano Sumio, *Nihon gaikō no 150 nen: bakumatsu kara heisei made* (Tokyo: Nihon gaikō kyōkai, 2019), pp. 232–243.

policy. In a book entitled *Unconditional: Japan's Decision to Surrender in World War II*, he begins his detailed analysis with Truman's presidency in the spring of 1945.[41] For him, Truman pondered a decision while listening to a debate that divided his advisors over modification of unconditional surrender policy. The debate was defined by an ideological divide among Truman's advisors: between progressives who were New Dealers and conservatives who were opposed to the New Deal. For progressives, victory required uprooting Japanese militarism as well as the imperial system, which they saw as a "bastion of reaction that enabled Japan's business and military leaders to oppress the country's workers and peasants."[42] Applying New Deal principles to the occupation would transform Japan into a peaceful and democratic country that would no longer trouble the world. Conservatives, both among Truman's advisors and those outside of government, had no sympathy for extending the New Deal to Japan. They were more worried by a growing clash of interest with the Soviet Union. Stimson, Forrestal, Grew, and others favored modifying surrender terms to permit retention of the emperor. Their view was backed not only by Republicans like Herbert Hoover and Henry Luce and other "Roosevelt haters" but also by business leaders who looked forward to an early conversion to a peacetime economy. They favored a negotiated settlement, modifying unconditional surrender to allow the

---

[41] Marc Gallicchio, *Unconditional: Japan's Decision to Surrender in World War II* (New York: Oxford University Press, 2020), p. 2.

[42] Gallicchiio's response to reviewers in H-Diplo, https://hdiplo.org/to/R T23-18 p. 81.

Japanese to keep the imperial institution and so hope to avoid a costly invasion.

Gallichio argues that Truman kept his own counsel, made his own decision to insist on Japan's unconditional surrender, and emerged as a wise leader whose decision was validated by history. "Unconditional surrender was not an end in itself," Gallichio concludes.

> It was the first step in a process that transformed Japan from a military dictatorship into a more democratic and peaceful nation. This transformation was possible only because Truman rejected the recommendations of his conservative advisors to preserve the monarchy, limit the occupation, and leave Japan in control of portions of its empire. In short, the changes happened because of Truman's resolve that Japan's surrender be nothing less than unconditional.[43]

Gallichio thus joins with Richard Frank in his conclusion that the use of the bomb was validated by the postwar reforms that Americans made in Japan, which made it the peaceful, non-threatening country it is today.

Gallicchio's short time frame and focus on US domestic politics allowed an in-depth study of the debate among Truman's advisors. It, however, did not allow full consideration of the implications of the way in which Roosevelt's policy of ruling out any place for diplomacy influenced how the war would be fought – that is, the five implications already discussed – and how that created the circumstances for the Hiroshima decision.

[43] Marc Gallicchio, *Unconditional: The Japanese Surrender in World War II* (New York: Oxford, 2020), p. 213.

A WIDER PERSPECTIVE

The "Almost Inevitable" Atomic Bomb

Many historians have questioned the unconditional surrender policy. In his classic work on Japanese surrender, Robert Butow observed that "there can be little doubt that the unconditional surrender demand sparked the imagination and perhaps even fired the resolve of many people on the Allied side. What is open to question, however, is the value of the concept as an instrument of policy with respect to the enemy."[44] Butow contended that "an Allied declaration in June–July 1945 allowing a constitutional Japanese monarchy might have produced Japan's surrender before early August, thus obviating the atomic bombings and Soviet entry."[45] The military historian Sir Michael Howard in his study of wartime grand strategy wrote that the announcement of the unconditional surrender policy at the Casablanca conference was made

> without any of the forethought and careful consideration which should have gone to the framing of so major an act of Allied policy.... The question as to whether it would soften the enemy will to resist or to stiffen it does not appear to have been seriously considered at all.... Political warfare specialists might have quoted Sun Tzu's advice, about leaving one's enemy a golden bridge for retreat.... There was no opportunity for such counsels to be heard at Casablanca. Had it been otherwise, the Allied leaders might have reflected a little more deeply on the question

---

[44] Butow, *Japan's Decision to Surrender*, p. 167.
[45] Bernstein writing in *End of Pacific War*, p. 28. See Butow, *Japan's Decision*, pp. 131–135.

whether total victory is necessarily the surest foundation for lasting peace.⁴⁶

With the United States not open to negotiation, the tragedy of Hiroshima and Nagasaki can be seen as inextricably tied to unconditional surrender policy. The eminent French authority on international affairs Raymond Aron wrote that "American diplomacy itself had created a combination of circumstances which made resorting to the atom bombs almost inevitable by its demand for unconditional surrender, by its declaration to 'reform,' 'regenerate,' and democratize Japan, by the timidity of certain leaders not devoid of acumen, and by crusading slogans which precluded negotiations, even of a secret nature."⁴⁷

After the war, the *New York Times* war correspondent Hanson Baldwin described unconditional surrender policy as "perhaps the biggest political mistake of the war. ... Unconditional surrender was an open invitation to unconditional resistance; it ... probably lengthened the war, cost us lives, and helped to lead to the present abortive peace."⁴⁸ The Rand Corporation political scientist Paul Kecskemeti in his study *Strategic Surrender* concluded that the rigidities on both the Japanese and American sides prolonged the war. "Had direct and confidential channels of communication been

---

⁴⁶ Michael Howard, *Grand Strategy, August 1942–September 1943* (British official History of the Second World War) (London: Her Majesty's Stationery Office, 1972), p. 284.

⁴⁷ Raymond Aron, *The Imperial Republic: The United States and the World, 1945–1973* (Englewood Cliffs, NJ: Prentice-Hall, 1974), p. 23.

⁴⁸ Hanson W. Baldwin, *Great Mistakes of the War* (London: Alvin Redman, 1950), p. 13.

established with the Japanese government, it is conceivable that the United States would have been able to clarify the situation and to disabuse the Japanese of their illusions." The Japanese never sent anyone abroad with official instructions to discuss surrender terms with the United States. "On the American side ... confidential conversations with the enemy for the purpose of determining a possible basis for surrender were ruled out on principle." If the United States had made a very determined effort to establish contact, this "would have led to Japan's surrender before the Soviets entered the war, resulting in a far more favorable postwar balance of power in the Far East. But this approach was precluded by the prevailing rules of unconditionality."[49] The refusal to consider compromises abandoned the possibilities of a negotiated peace.

Realist writers have made strong criticism of the unconditional surrender policy, arguing, as the historian John Lewis Gaddis wrote, that "insistence on the total defeat of Germany and Japan had profoundly destabilized the postwar balance of power."[50] In the same vein, Harvard historian Ernest May believed that Roosevelt and his advisors "should have considered alternative shapes which the future might take and at least speculated about a world in which, among other things, Germany and Japan were impotent" and unable to participate in international politics for a long time to come.[51] Hans Morgenthau and George Kennan argued that

---

[49] Paul Kecskemeti, *Strategic Surrender: The Politics of Victory and Defeat* (Stanford: Stanford University Press, 1958), pp. 206–207.

[50] John Lewis Gaddis, *The Long Peace: Inquiries into the History of the Cold War* (New York: Oxford University Press, 1987), p. 236.

[51] May, *"Lessons" of the Past*, p. 18

rather than the doctrine of unconditional surrender, the effective way to maintain peace and achieve international stability was through a balance of power and, as Gaddis wrote, "the wary toleration of adversaries rather than, as a point of principle, their annihilation."[52] Morgenthau, often regarded as the founding father of the discipline of international relations, argued that American policymakers foolishly believed that "crush the enemy; force him into unconditional surrender; reeducate him in the ways of democratic, peace-loving nations; and with democracy established everywhere, peace and good will among nations will be assured."[53] Similarly, the diplomat and historian George Kennan wrote that "of all the failures of United States policy in the wake of World War II, history will rate as the most grievous our failure to approach realistically the responsibilities of power over the defeated nations which we ourselves courted by the policy of unconditional surrender." Kennan maintained that a defeated Japan should have had a role in the regional balance of power and that its total disarmament was a mistaken policy.[54]

These writers believed that an earlier conclusion to the war in the Pacific that left Japan defeated but dependent on American restraint and surrounded by sufficient force to deter future adventurism would have been preferable. Such an outcome, before the bloodletting reached nihilist dimensions,

---

[52] Gaddis, *The Long Peace*, p. 237.
[53] Stanley Hoffmann, "An American Social Science: International Relations," *Daedalus* 16, no. 3 (summer 1977), 44.
[54] George F. Kennan, *The Kennan Diaries*, ed. Frank Castigliola (New York: Norton, 2014), p. 211.

would have changed the course of history. They contend that in its totalist approach of destroying Japanese power, unconditional surrender policy profoundly destabilized the postwar balance of power, allowing Stalin to reestablish his influence in Asia, and contributed to the rise of Chinese communist power and a divided Korea.

Conclusion

Choice of a broader time frame to explain the Hiroshima decision shows how it was shaped and influenced by longer-term processes than were perceived by the narrow focus on the summer of 1945. Broadening the scale of analysis to include FDR's unconditional surrender policy and the underlying goal of a new American world order reveals the dominant long-held assumptions that Truman was implementing in the summer of 1945. The war could have been fought in a different way – in a way that all other wars in American history had been fought and in a way that many of FDR's advisors and Truman's advisors wished. The American historian David Kennedy observed, "America *chose* – I emphasize the word deliberately – to fight a certain kind of war. In doing so, it succeeded to a degree unmatched by virtually all other combatants in that or any other war, in fighting on its own terms."[55] By choosing to fight to unconditional surrender the United States gave priority to military strategy, provoked diehard resistance, and faced the

---

[55] David M. Kennedy, "The Origins of American Hyperpower," in Andrew J. Bacevich, ed., *The Short American Century: A Post Mortem* (Cambridge: Harvard University Press, 2012), pp. 15–16.

CONCLUSION

necessity of a terribly bloody invasion of Japan. The use of the bomb was a solution to the dilemma that America's totalistic goal had created.

Approaching the decision in this broader time frame may raise interesting counterfactual questions for historians to consider. What if the United States had not insisted on Japan's unconditional surrender? What if diplomacy had not been ruled out? Might there have been a negotiated peace as in all other American wars? What if Japan and the United States had reached an armistice in the last year of the war when all belligerents knew Japan had lost? Would a more flexible approach to war termination have brought an earlier end to the war against Japan before killing reached nihilist proportions? Would a negotiated peace that left a defeated Japan with a measure of independence and provided a basis for a balance of power in the region have been preferable? Nothing is predetermined in history. Things could have happened in a different way. Obviously, we cannot know the answers to these counterfactual questions. Nonetheless, posing these counterfactual questions helps historians identify unconditional surrender policy as pivotal to the Hiroshima decision.

We cannot know how a policy different from Roosevelt's would have turned out. Negotiations would have opened the door to Japanese demands for preservation of the emperor system, for qualifications of Allied demands for occupation, disarmament, war crimes trials, and for retention of the Korean colony. Compromising the demand for unconditional surrender policy in 1944 or early 1945 would have left Japan defeated but perhaps still with its sovereignty intact with sanctions to ensure that it would conduct reforms and demilitarization. Sanctions on desperately needed aid, trade, investment, and technology required to rebuild a collapsed economy would have provided powerful and compelling leverage for the Japanese themselves to carry out demilitarization and reform to the satisfaction of the Allies.

Negotiating an armistice and peace agreement would surely have been problematic, but all other foreign wars in American history have ended this way. Hitler and Nazism defied compromise. With Japan, compromises were possible. We know that because almost at once after surrender, the Occupation decided to keep the emperor, retain the conservative bureaucratic establishment, keep in place the large conglomerate concentrations of capital – all of which were pillars of the old regime. Most ironic of all, the United States soon admitted the mistake of permanent disarmament, pressing the Japanese to rearm and become our ally in the Cold War. Considering this postwar retreat from unconditional surrender policy, it might have been better to have had a less absolute set of goals, possibly averting the catastrophic casualties – Americans, Japanese, and other Asians – of the last year of the war, including those first victims of the atomic age.

Historians can speculate but we cannot know how history might have been different if compromise and diplomacy had not been ruled out. They can assert, however, that unconditional surrender policy strongly influenced the way in which the war was fought and paved the path to the Hiroshima decision. It can be seen as the pivotal cause in the hierarchy of causes a historian may construct in taking a broad approach to the issue.

9

Controversy as a Way of Life

The gravity of being the only country to use the atomic bomb posed a lasting challenge for Americans' self-identity. From the early days of their history, Americans had always thought of themselves as a virtuous nation – a nation called to be a model for the world. As the historian Gordon Wood wrote, the American Revolution "gave us our obsessive concern with our own morality and our messianic sense of purpose in the world."[1] In the deeply rooted sentiments of American exceptionalism, America was a force for good, a redeeming nation. It was that sense that Roosevelt evoked during the war by calling Americans to a crusade against the evil of fascism and to a reform of the world. It fell to historians, as custodians of the public memory, trained to carefully and critically reconstruct how things happened in the past, to question and subject to scrutiny the prevailing explanation that the participants in the decision had given to justify the decision. The rise of rebellious revisionist historians in the tumultuous 1960s ignited a protracted debate about the orthodox account of the decision, a contentious debate that continues down to the present day. Historians have interpreted it in more divergent ways than perhaps any other event in recent American history.

---

[1] Gordon Wood, *The Idea of America: Reflections on the Birth of the United States* (London: Penguin, 2011), pp. 320–322.

CONTROVERSY AS A WAY OF LIFE

Tracing the anatomy of the debate, we have seen how disagreements arose in some of the most important interpretations of the Hiroshima decision. What then have historians' discordant views of the decision taught us about their craft? The British military historian John Keegan observed in his book on World War II that "historians are committed to controversy as a way of life, and [the Hiroshima] controversy may never be settled."[2] This is as it should be. Controversy is indeed the way of life for historians because that is the way they have learned to pursue truth, even while knowing that goal is humanly unattainable. The "noble dream" that historians could achieve objective reality or describe how things really happened in the past, as the first professional historians thought, proved untenable. The past is too complicated, the historian's views too personal, the perspective too changeable. The belief that any one person could have the last say on the past as some historians had expected was unsustainable.

It would be hard to find a better example of the essence of the historians' craft – their "way of life" – than the controversy over the use of the atomic bomb. It will probably never be settled. In a limited way, the scientific aspects of the craft may establish agreed-upon facts, which we provided in Chapter 1. But facts do not speak for themselves and with the interpretation of those facts the controversy begins. There will not be definitive histories written of such a momentous event as Hiroshima and Nagasaki. It was not only the end of the world war but also the greatest conflict Asia has ever known. It was the beginning of the nuclear age

---

[2] Keegan, *The Battle for History*, p. 28.

and the realization that the survival of our civilization was imperiled. It was also the beginning of the American world order. It contributed to the Cold War and the arms race.[3] Moreover, it was a human tragedy freighted with moral issues. A turning point in human experience of such proportions is bound to be in permanent contention. Its complexity will raise endless questions that new generations will answer from their perspective, new evidence, new insight.

Argument without End

Of such momentous and controversial developments in the past, the Dutch historian Pieter Geyl, writing about the many divergent ways that French historians had viewed Napoleonic rule, concluded, "No human intelligence could hope to bring together the overwhelming multiplicity of data and of factors, of forces and of movements, and from them establish the true, one might almost say, the divine, balance. ... Truth, though for God it may be One, assumes many shapes to men." In the end, for mere mortals, truth would always be partial and

---

[3] The historian of Russia David Holloway writes that "On August 20, two weeks to the day after Hiroshima, Stalin signed a decree setting up a 'Special Committee of the State Defense Committee' to take charge of all work connected with the use of atomic energy, including first of all the building of the nuclear bomb. ... It was the American success in building the bomb and the American use of the bomb that convinced Stalin of the need for an all-out effort. The decision to set up the special committee marked the beginning of the nuclear arms race that was to dominate world politics for most of the next fifty years." *The End of the Pacific War*, p. 285.

relative. "History," Geyl strikingly concluded, "is indeed an argument without end."[4]

Should multiple competing interpretations and endless controversy discourage us and lead us to question the value of history? Are we bound to be always frustrated in wanting settled truth? Should we agree with Voltaire when he wrote that "History is nothing but a pack of tricks which we play upon the dead"? Or with Thomas Carlyle, who said that history amounted to "a distillation of rumour"? For Oscar Wilde history was "mere gossip" and for Henry Ford "pure bunk."[5] To postmodernists like Michel Foucault history was an "ideological product," a work of fiction in the pursuit of power.[6] Should recognition that in interpreting the Hiroshima decision the achievement of objective truth is beyond the reach of historians then lead us to agree with such harsh views of history's value? If there is no final verdict of history, no immutable truth, should we then question the value of history? By no means!

The Marketplace of Ideas

The realization that objective truth is beyond reach, that history can be at best only partial truth, and that multiple interpretations and controversy among historians are inevitable should not undermine belief in the value of history. On

---

[4] Geyl, *Napoleon*, pp. 15-16.
[5] C. Vann Woodward, *American Attitudes Toward History* (Oxford: Clarendon Press, 1955), p. 3.
[6] Evans, *In Defense of History*, p. 169.

the contrary, disagreement and debate are the way that history advances closer to reality.

In 1919, in a famous dissent in the case of *Abrams v. United States*, a case against government censorship of antiwar leafleting, Supreme Court Justice Oliver Wendell Holmes Jr. wrote that "the best test of truth is the power of the thought to get itself accepted in the competition of the market."[7] Knowledge advances in the free-speech environment that the marketplace of ideas provides. From the clash of ideas and controversy, from argument without end, historians draw closer to truth. In the marketplace of ideas historians strive to persuade readers of their interpretations. Recognizing their fallibility and that they do not get the final say, they seek the approval of fellow historians. "Knowledge is inherently a social process," the writer Jonathan Rauch observed. "It transcends individual effort."[8] Historical knowledge emerges from the clash of ideas. From pluralism and debate historical knowledge can become more objective. Knowledge progresses through a community of historians.

Historical understanding is progressive. It is cumulative. The more controversy, the better. The Hiroshima controversy has taught us a lot about how historical knowledge progresses. We have learned that the clash of ideas and argument without end is the means by which historians pursue truth. Competing interpretations have been argued and

---

[7] Quoted in Jonathan Rauch, *The Constitution of Knowledge: A Defense of Truth* (Washington, DC: Brookings Press, 2021), p. 92.
[8] Jonathan Rauch, *Kindly Inquisitors: The New Attacks on Free Thought* (Chicago: University of Chicago Press, Expanded Edition, 2013), pp. 170–171.

subjected to the scrutiny of the community of historians. The rigors of this process weeded out flawed interpretations and what survived is our corpus of knowledge. We cannot assume that this result is final. As in biological evolution, the great philosopher of science Karl Popper wrote: "[W]e may have to be content with our approximations [of truth] forever." The historian Herbert Butterfield remarked that "it is never safe to forget the truth which really underlies historical research: the truth that all history perpetually requires to be corrected by more history."[9]

We have seen in our examination of the differing approaches of historians to the Hiroshima decision that the clash of ideas, contrary opinions, can be fruitful. More than seventy-five years after the first draft of history was written by the participants, which began the debate about the Hiroshima decision, our knowledge and understanding have come a long way. Some aspects of orthodoxy have been undermined and others have been extended. Revisionist critiques have fueled the debate, but their initial claims have been modified and disputed even by revisionists themselves. Progress in historical knowledge comes when interpretations are validated by other historians. The profession itself has overcome its parochialism as the study of Russian and Japanese materials have contributed substantial new material to internationalize interpretation.

Historians will continue to study and debate the Hiroshima decision. As they do, new evidence and perspectives are inevitable. As Marc Bloch wrote, "The past is, by definition, a datum which nothing in the future will change.

---

[9] Butterfield, *Whig Interpretation*, p. 131.

But the knowledge of the past is something which is progressive which is constantly transforming and perfecting itself."[10] The availability of new materials allows understanding to advance and be cumulative. From new evidence and new perspectives can emerge greater insight. Competing views of a common subject matter generate "new questions, new arguments, and new lines of investigation."[11] As we have traced the development of the controversy in roughly chronological fashion, we can see how contested versions gave us increasing understanding of the different aspects of the Hiroshima decision. From the clash of conflicting interpretations and diverse opinions and contrasting temperaments can come deeper understanding. We have a body of knowledge about how and why the atomic bomb was first used.

The Community of Historians

In the time since the study of history was professionalized under the influence of Leopold von Ranke in the nineteenth century, history became an academic discipline and training for the craft began to be developed. In a century and a half since the American Historical Association was founded with the hope of producing objective history, the profession has progressed in its understanding of what is possible in historical knowledge. Historians recognized that advancing understanding of the past requires a network or a community of scholars that could discuss, debate, and seek validation of their views. It is

---

[10] Bloch, *Historian's Craft*, p. 58.
[11] *American Historical Review, Standards*, p. 6.

a collective enterprise. As the practice of history became more professionalized, historians identified themselves as members of a community engaged collectively in a disciplined study of the past. They shared values and protocols to govern their work. Understanding that no one person alone could be an authority on the past and that multiple, conflicting perspectives were inevitable, they formed and then depended on professional institutions, regulated by norms and values, to serve as a marketplace of ideas. They published journals and held conferences where interpretations are scrutinized and subjected to questioning and criticism, fact and source checking, and peer reviews by other experts. These institutions certified credentials, set agendas, enforced accountability, directed resources, and promoted the training of future generations. Such protocols are designed to maintain a standard for pursuing truth. They are not perfect; they can be subject to fads and blind spots as we saw in the neglect of military history, but with the freedom embedded in the protocols the profession can be self-correcting. The craft itself is still evolving, as we saw it overcome its former parochial concentration on the history of the West.

Historians and the Pursuit of Truth

Historians must be committed to pursuit of objective truth even while acknowledging that it is elusive and that perfect objectivity is impossible. I love the way the writer Johnathan Rauch described the pursuit of truth: "Like north, [truth] is a direction, an orientation, not a destination."[12] As custodians of the public

---

[12] Rauch, *Constitution of Knowledge*, p. 108.

memory, it is the responsibility of the historians to examine the past as they have done with the Hiroshima decision in unrestrained scholarly inquiry. Their role in a free society has never been more important. We live in a time marked by the precariousness of human freedom. Totalitarian regimes seek to extinguish the impulse to liberty and dissent. Control of the past gives them sway over the future. By the same token, just as authoritarian regimes need to control the past, so healthy democracies require open inquiry into the past and the conscientious pursuit of truth. It is the nature of history, as Fritz Stern wrote, that it "records the vast possibilities of the past and suggests to the observer that the same range of possibilities must still prevail, that in some sense history must truly be the story of liberty. Is it not because history can arouse this impulse to liberty and dissent that, as Orwell noted, totalitarian regimes must extinguish it?"[13] Democracies too are subject to challenges that would limit free inquiry. Ours is a time when the foundations of democratic societies are weakened by rampant disinformation and propaganda so that civic life seems in danger of losing its grip on reality. In the face of these current challenges, historians must preserve their profession as a model of integrity in the pursuit of truth. The historical method teaches the complexity of the past, the possibility of interpreting the same facts in different ways, and the importance of debate in the pursuit of truth. To the conflicting interpretations there will be no finality. This is how historical knowledge advances. Controversy and argument without end will take us in the direction of truth.

[13] Stern, *Varieties of History*, p. 31.

SUGGESTIONS FOR FURTHER READING

The two themes of this book, the Hiroshima decision and the historian's craft, have been the subject of voluminous writings. The sheer size of the historical literature requires that we be highly selective in choosing which writings to use in analyzing the anatomy of the debate about the Hiroshima decision among historians. Likewise, we must be limited in our choice of the important reflections by historians on the nature of their profession. Here we will offer some suggestions of significant books and essays for further study of these themes.

Introduction

For writings on the Manhattan Project, readers should consult Richard Rhodes, *The Making of the Atomic Bomb* (New York: Simon & Schuster, 1986) and Cynthia C. Kelly, ed. *The Manhattan Project: The Birth of the Atomic Bomb in the Words of Its Creators, Eyewitnesses, and Historians* (New York: Black Dog & Leventhal, 2007). The exhibition at the Smithsonian's National Air and Space Museum at the time of the fiftieth anniversary of the atomic bombing in 1995 is the subject of Robert P. Newman, *The Enola Gay and the Court of History* (Bern, Switzerland: Peter Lang Group, 2004) and Philip Nobile, ed. *Judgment at the Smithsonian: The Bombing of Hiroshima and Nagasaki* (New York: Marlowe, 1995). A collection of essays on many aspects of Hiroshima and the nuclear age is found in Michael D. Gordin and G. John Ikenberry, ed. *The Age of Hiroshima* (Princeton: Princeton University Press, 2020).

SUGGESTIONS FOR FURTHER READING

Chapter 1

The most widely read book on the historian's craft is E. H. Carr, *What Is History?* (New York: Penguin Press, 1990). A more thorough and recent study is John Tosh, *The Pursuit of History: Aims, Methods and New Directions in the Study of History* (New York: Routledge, 7th ed., 2022). Lynn Hunt, *History: Why It Matters* (Medford, MA: Polity Press, 2018) is another up-to-date treatment of the latest challenges for the historical profession. She has sharpened the views previously included in Joyce Appleby, Lynn Hunt & Margaret Jacob, *Telling the Truth about History* (New York: W. W. Norton, 1994). Sarah Maza, *Thinking about History* (Chicago: Chicago University Press, 2017) is a fulsome discussion of many aspects of history writing. An unfinished but important work by a great historian is Marc Bloch, *The Historian's Craft* (New York: Vintage, 1953). A valuable work by another great historian is Fritz Stern, *The Varieties of History: From Voltaire to the Present* (New York: Meridian Books, 1956). Some of the most thoughtful writings on the historian's craft are found in two books by the eminent historian of early American history Bernard Bailyn: *On the Teaching and Writing of History* (Hanover, NH: University Press of New England, 1991) and *Sometimes an Art: Nine Essays on History* (New York: Knopf, 2015). An important work is Peter Novick, *That Noble Dream: The "Objectivity Question" and the American Historical Profession* (New York: Cambridge University Press, 1988), which traces the changing methods and attitudes of historians regarding objectivity and relativism and the greater diversity of approaches in recent times. Richard Evans, *In Defense of History* (New York: W. W. Norton, 1999) considers the postmodernist challenge and mounts a strong defense of the knowability of the past.

SUGGESTIONS FOR FURTHER READING

Chapter 2

A fundamental source for the Hiroshima decision is Michael Kort, *The Columbia Guide to Hiroshima and the Bomb* (New York: Columbia University Press, 2007). It provides an excellent section on key questions and interpretations of the decision. In addition, it includes a valuable compilation of primary source documents. Barton Bernstein has written several essays on the historiographical controversy, the best of which is "Introducing the Interpretive Problems of Japan's 1945 Surrender: A Historiographical Essay on Recent Literature in the West," in Tsuyoshi Hasegawa, ed., *The End of the Pacific War: Reappraisals* (Stanford: Stanford University Press, 2007) pp. 9–64.

Chapter 3

Stimson's 1947 essay in *Harper's* magazine "The Decision to Use the Atomic Bomb" is readily available online and should be read as the foundation of the orthodox interpretation of the decision. The best study of Stimson's role is Sean L. Malloy, *Atomic Tragedy: Henry L. Stimson and the Decision to Use the Atomic Bomb Against Japan* (Ithaca, NY: Cornell University Press, 2008). An essential work that everyone interested in the controversy must read is John Hersey, *Hiroshima* (New York: Vintage, 1989). Not only was it a journalistic feat but it also stirred participants in the decision to undertake a defense of their role. Not to be missed are the writings on Hiroshima of the leading historian of modern Japan John Dower, both in his *Cultures of War: Pearl Harbor/Hiroshima/9-11/Iraq* (New York: W. W. Norton, 2010) and several insightful essays in his *Ways of Forgetting, Ways of Remembering: Japan in the Modern World* (New York: The New Press, 2012). Two fine works by the historian Wilson D. Miscamble are *From Roosevelt to*

Truman: Potsdam, Hiroshima, and the Cold War (Cambridge: Cambridge University Press, 2007) and *The Most Controversial Decision: Truman, the Atomic Bombs, and the Defeat of Japan* (Cambridge: Cambridge University Press, 2011). The diplomatic role of Joseph Grew in the war is studied in a biography by Waldo H. Heinrichs, Jr., *American Diplomat: Joseph C. Grew and the Development of the United States Diplomatic Tradition* (Boston: Little Brown, 1966). A critical overview of American attitudes is Robert Jay Lifton and Greg Mitchell, *Hiroshima in America: A Half Century of Denial* (New York: Avon Books, 1995). An extensive compendium of documents and excerpts of essays is Kai Bird and Lawrence Lifschultz, eds., *Hiroshima's Shadows* (Stony Creek, CT: (Pamphleteer's Press, 1998).

For the atomic bombing of Nagasaki, the best book is Susan Southard, *Nagasaki: Life After Nuclear War* (New York: Penguin, 2016). An intrepid war correspondent, George Weller, was the first journalist into Nagasaki after its bombing and filed reports that were censored by the Occupation. The reports were later found after his death by his son and were published as *George Weller, First into Nagasaki: The Censored Eyewitness Dispatches on Post-Atomic Japan and Its Prisoners of War* (New York: Crown Publishers, 2006). A comparable book by an Australian journalist whose dispatches were censored by the Occupation is Wilfred Burchett, *Shadows of Hiroshima* (London: Verso Editions and NLB, 1983).

Chapter 4

Revisionists played a big part in the controversy among historians. To understand why revisionism is an inevitable part of the historian's craft one should turn to James M. Banner, Jr., *The Ever-Changing Past: Why All History Is Revisionist History* (New Haven: Yale

University Press, 2021). Gar Alperowitz's *Atomic Diplomacy* (New York: Simon and Schuster, 1965) was at the center of the revisionist controversy. He revised his book in 1985, in a greatly expanded edition with a new title, *The Decision to Use the Atomic Bomb and the Architecture of an American Myth* (New York: Knopf, 1995), although the main thrust of his argument remained unchanged. The Pennsylvania State University historian Robert James Maddox wrote many books and articles critical of the revisionists. Perhaps the best place to start would be his 1995 essay "The Biggest Decision: Why We Had to Drop The Atomic Bomb" in *The American Heritage* (vol. 46. Issue 3), where he succinctly provides his own interpretation. For his critique of the revisionists, see Robert James Maddox, *The New Left and the Origins of the Cold War* (Princeton: Princeton University Press, 1973). Hasegawa's *Racing the Enemy: Stalin, Truman, and the Surrender of Japan* (Cambridge, MA: Belknap Press of Harvard University Press, 2005) has been praised for the author's use of English, Japanese, and Russian sources, but its central thesis that Russian entry into the war was the primary cause of surrender has proved controversial.

Finally, we must stress the irreplaceable contributions to historiography of Barton Bernstein, who has studied the Hiroshima decision more than any other scholar. Robert Newman described Bernstein as "the most knowledgeable student of the decision to use the bomb."[1] Although he began his career as a revisionist, he modified his views over time. He has published dozens of articles on many aspects of the Hiroshima decision but has never gathered his studies in one book. The reader's attention therefore is directed to many of his important essays which are cited in the endnotes of this book.

---

[1] Robert P. Newman, "Hiroshima and the Trashing of Henry Stimson," *New England Quarterly* 7, no.1. (March 1998): 26.

Chapter 5

The philosopher Michael Walzer addresses the Hiroshima decision in his *Just and Unjust Wars: A Moral Argument with Historical Illustrations* (New York: Basic Books, 1977). The Notre Dame historian Wilson D. Miscamble discusses the moral issues from a pragmatic perspective in his important book *The Most Controversial Decision: Truman, the Atomic Bombs, and the Defeat of Japan* (Cambridge: Cambridge University Press, 2011). For the troubled issue of racism and its role in the decision, one must turn first to John W. Dower, *War Without Mercy: Race & Power in the Pacific War* (New York: Pantheon, 1986) before reading Ronald Takaki, *Hiroshima: Why America Dropped the Atomic Bomb* (Boston: Little, Brown, 1995).

Chapter 6

The important works of Edward Drea, especially *In the Service of the Emperor: Essays on the Imperial Japanese Army* (Lincoln, NE: University of Nebraska Press, 1998), and Richard Frank's *Downfall: The End of the Imperial Japanese Empire* (New York: Random House, 1999) have slowly gained the appreciation they deserve for their contributions to understanding the role of military factors in the making of the Hiroshima decision. The analysis of D. M. Giangreco, *Hell to Pay: Operation Downfall and the Invasion of Japan, 1945–1947* (Annapolis, MD: Naval Institute Press, 2009 and expanded edition 2017) is also respected by many historians. The book by the accomplished political historian Margaret MacMillan, *War: How Conflict Shaped Us* (New York: Random House, 2020) served to draw attention to the long-neglected subfield of military history. Putting it in the broader context of social and cultural history in the way in which Michael Sherry has done in *The Rise of American Air Power: The Creation of Armageddon* (New Haven, CT: Yale University Press, 1987) should help generate the respect that this important field surely requires from academic historians.

Chapter 7

To understand the Japanese dimension, one must turn first to the classic Robert J. C. Butow, *Japan's Decision to Surrender* (Stanford, CA: Stanford University Press, 1954). Although some of its conclusions have been modified, it remains a widely cited source of Japanese politics in the months leading up to surrender. The puzzle of the emperor's role and character in the war years has perplexed historians. Butow described the emperor as a constitutional monarch who largely stayed above politics. In contrast, a major work that won the Pulitzer Prize is Herbert P. Bix, *Hirohito and the Making of Modern Japan* (New York: Harper Collins, 2000), which attributes an active, even aggressive, role to Hirohito. Edward Drea's essay "Chasing a Decisive Victory," in Edward J. Drea, *In the Service of the Emperor: Essays on the Imperial Japanese Army* (Lincoln, NE: University of Nebraska Press, 1998), pp. 169–215, adopts a more nuanced view of the emperor. A balanced account is Noriko Kawamura, *Emperor Hirohito and the Pacific War* (Seattle: University of Washington Press, 2015). Yukiko Koshiro, *Imperial Eclipse: Japanese Strategic Thinking about Continental Asia Before August 1945* (Ithaca, NY: Cornell University Press, 2013) offers a new interpretation of the Japanese approach to the Soviet Union at the end of the war. An excellent assessment of the role of popular Japanese support of the war effort is found in the pathbreaking 1987 book of the Japanese historian Yoshimi Yoshiaki, *Grassroots Fascism: The War Experience of the Japanese People* (New York:

Columbia University Press, 2015). The translator from the original Japanese, Ethan Mark, provides a useful introduction to Yoshimi's work.

Chapter 8

An excellent treatment of the problems the unconditional surrender policy created in ending the war is Leon Sigal, *Fighting to a Finish: The Politics of War Termination in the United States and Japan, 1945* (Ithaca, NY: Cornell University Press, 1988). Sigal, a political science professor at Wesleyan University, applied organizational and bureaucratic politics theory to an understanding of the Hiroshima decision. The book is an example of the value of an interdisciplinary approach applying political theory while delving deeply into history to make its point. Kenneth B. Pyle, *Japan in the American Century* (Cambridge: Belknap Press of Harvard University Press, 2018), chapters 2 and 3, discusses the unconditional surrender policy and the Hiroshima decision.

An understanding of the unconditional surrender policy depends on the writings of Roosevelt scholars, of which there are a great many. The long-time authority on his foreign policy is Robert Dallek, *Franklin D. Roosevelt and American Foreign Policy, 1932–1945* (New York: Oxford University Press, 1979). A magisterial study of FDR is David Kennedy, *Freedom from Fear: The American People in Depression and War, 1929–1945* (New York: Oxford University Press, 1999). A splendid essay by the same author is David M. Kennedy, "The Origins of American Hyperpower," in Andrew J. Bacevich, ed., *The Short American Century: A Post Mortem* (Cambridge, MA: Harvard University Press, 2012), pp. 15–37.

Detailed studies of the last year of the war are found in two works: Waldo Heinrichs and Marc Gallicchio, *Implacable Foes: War in the*

Pacific, 1944–1945 (New York: Oxford University Press, 2017) and Marc Gallicchio, *Unconditional: The Japanese Surrender in World War II* (New York: Oxford University Press, 2020).

Chapter 9

For the thoughtful reader Jonathan Rauch's *The Constitution of Knowledge: A Defense of Truth* (Washington, DC: Brookings Press, 2021) offers many insights into the collective way knowledge, including historical knowledge, progresses.

INDEX

Please note: page numbers in *italic type* indicate figures.

1984 (Orwell), 23

9/11 terrorist attack, 8

A Bell for Adano (Hersey), 75
Abrams v. United States, 243
Acheson, Dean, 66
Acton, Lord, 129
airplane, conception of as weapon of war, 175
Alamogordo test
   Groves and Oppenheimer viewing the steel tower, *41*
   Oppenheimer's reaction, 70
   plutonium bomb, 51
Alperovitz, Gar
   Atomic Diplomacy, 100
   Bernstein's critique, 109
   contention that the Japanese were on the verge of surrender, 159, 161
   criticisms, 110–112
   on evidence of racism, 151
   on the origins of the Cold War, 101, 105
   self-criticism, 112
American Historical Association (AHA)
   Beard's presidential address, 28
   founding, 26
   Gordon Wright's presidential address, 131
   Statement of Professional Standards, 124
Anami Korechika, 204, *205*
anti-war leafleting, Supreme Court case against government censorship of, 243
Appleby, Joyce, 19
Aquinas, Thomas, 136
Arendt, Hannah, 22
"argument without end" view of history, 35–36
Aron, Raymond, 233
Asada Sadao, 121, 167
Asian history, growth of American teaching in the fields of, 186
assassinations, of the 1960s, 95–96
Atlantic Charter, 214
atomic bomb survivors in Hiroshima, *135*
atomic bombs
   death toll, 58
   decision to use on Hiroshima and Nagasaki, vii, *see* Hiroshima decision
   deployment and impact, 57–59

INDEX

atomic bombs (cont.)
  potential alternatives to the use of, 83
  public opinion on the use of, 69
  Stimson on the legitimacy of in comparison to any other explosive weapons, 85
  target list of Japanese cities, 15, 50
  wave of second thoughts, 69
authoritarianism, and the manipulation of history, 22–23

B-29 super fortress
  and the firebombing of Japanese cities, 44–45, 177–178
  Enola Gay, 11
"baby boom generation," 94
Bailyn, Bernard, 34, 92, 100
Beard, Charles, 28–29, 33
Becker, Carl, 28–29, 33
Benedict, Ruth, 183
Berlin, Isaiah, 50, 130, 144
Bernstein, Barton
  critique of Alperovitz's work, 109
  on casualty projections, 85, 170–171
  on Eisenhower's postwar claims, 107
  on evidence of racism, 151
  on Hasegawa's theories, 119
  on memoirs and remembrances, 64
  on the inevitability of the Hiroshima decision, 211–213
  on the moral-political context of the Hiroshima decision, 153
  on the necessity of the second bomb, 168
  on the origins of the Cold War, 97, 109
  on the Smithsonian controversy, 13
  review of *Racing the Enemy*, 211
  study of the Hiroshima decision, 108
Bhagavad Gita, 70
Bin Laden, Osama, 8
Blackett, P. M. S., 102, 190
Bloch, Marc, 128, 210, 244
Bockscar, 15, 167
bomb survivors, Hersey's account, 75
Bombs Away: The Story of a Bomber Team (Steinbeck), 176
Brogan, Denis, 96
Brokaw, Tom, 113
Bundy, Harvey, 78
Bundy, McGeorge, 2, 81, 87
Burchett, Wilfred, 74
Burke, Edmund, 141
Bush, George H. W., 9
Bush, George W., 8
Bush, Vannevar, 20, 39–42, 46, 67
Butow, Robert
  approach to the historian's craft, 188–189
  arrival in Japan, 189
  characterization of Hirohito, 187, 198
  Japan's Decision to Surrender, 89, 115, 187
  on Japanese surrender, 232
Butterfield, Herbert, 127, 244

258

INDEX

Byrnes, James, 52, 84
Byrnes, James, Interim Committee role, 46

Camus, Albert, 4
Carlyle, Thomas, 242
carpet bombing of cities,
   see also firebombing of cities, 33, 45, 54, 101, 115, 130, 138–141, 152
Carr, E. H.,
   opposition to moral judgments, 127
Casablanca Conference, 43, 215, 216, 232
casualty projections
   Bernstein on, 85, 170–171
   Churchill and, 169
   controversy, 84–85
     military historians on, 168–172
   Giangreco's work, 170–171
   revisionist view, 169
Chakrabarty, Dipesh, 32
Chiang Kai-shek, 52
China, behavior of Japanese soldiers serving in, 191
Chinese Communist Party, revision of history, 23
Churchill, Winston
   agreement on use of a "bomb," 42
   and casualty projections, 169
   asks Truman about dropping the atomic bombs on Japan, 71
   details of Manhattan Project shared with, 40–42
   in the inevitability of the Hiroshima decision, 213
   meetings with FDR, 43, 214–215, 216
   on his place in history, 64
   Potsdam conference, 50–52, 118
   unconditional surrender policy and, 45, 217–219
civil rights movement, 95–97, 148
civilians
   FDR on the killing of, 137
   targeting of, 44–45
   see also carpet bombing of cities; firebombing of cities
Clausewitz, Carl von, 160, 224
Clinton, Bill, 9
code breaking, 161
cognitive psychology, 30
Cold War
   and Japanese disarmament, 238
   and study of the non-Western world in the United States, 185
   and US attitude toward Japanese disarmament, 238
   generational change and, 93–95
   impact on unconditional surrender policy, 217
   origins, 93
     Alperovitz's contention, 101, 105
     Bernstein's view, 97, 109
     Blackett's argument, 102
     connection to use of the bomb, 101, 102, 105, 108–109
     revisionist challenge to the orthodox interpretation, 123–124

INDEX

Cold War (cont.)
  revisionist observations on, 97–99
  Soviet Union and, 93, 97, 110
  role of the Hiroshima decision, 241
  Vietnam and, 95
Committee for Concerned Asian Scholars (CCAS), 200
Compton, Arthur, 47
  pictured with other leading scientists involved in the Manhattan Project, 67
Compton, Karl, 78, 167
  Interim Committee role, 46
  pictured with other leading scientists involved in the Manhattan Project, 67
Conant, James
  feelings of guilt, 71
  Interim Committee role, 46
  Manhattan Project role, 39, 71
  on historians' potential reactions to use of the bomb, 67
  pictured with other leading scientists involved in the Manhattan Project, 67
  reaction to Hersey's essay, 78, 79
  recommendations on use of the bomb, 48
  role in organizing a defense of the Hiroshima decision, 73
  the Harper's article and, 81–82, 85, 89
Conant, Jennet, 71, 78
conflicting testimonies, "the Rashomon effect," 30
Cousins, Norman, 148

craft, the writing of history as, 15, 24–25
Croce, Benedetto, 126
cultural perspective of military history
  Howard on, 174
  Keegan on, 174
  Sherry's observations, 175–181

democracy
  impact of loss of collective trust in common knowledge, 22
  role of a free press, 20
  Snyder on the role of individual responsibility, 22
Democracy and Truth: A Short History (Rosenfeld), 19
democratic societies, role of historians, 16
Derrida, Jacques, 29
Dower, John, 151
Drea, Edward
  In the Service of the Emperor, 163, 202–204
  Japan's Imperial Army, 163, 204
  on the destruction of Japanese government documents, 196
  on the reasons behind the Hiroshima decision, 161–163
Droysen, Johann, 18

Einstein, Albert, 38, 50, 77
Eisenhower, Dwight, 106–107
Emperor Hirohito, *see* Hirohito
Enola Gay, exhibit at Smithsonian's National Air and Space Museum, 11–13
eurocentrism, 32, 184

260

INDEX

Evans, Richard, 33
Evers, Medgar, 95
Executive Order 9066, 150
eyewitness testimony, unreliability of, 65

"Fat Man" plutonium bomb, death toll, 57
Feis, Herbert, 89
Fermi, Enrico, 47
firebombing of cities, 44–45, 139–141, 146, 153, 177, 218, 225, 228
Fischer, David Hackett, 154, 210
Ford, Henry, 242
"foreign area studies," 184
foreign policy, Morgenthau on the consequences of nuclear weapons for, 4
Foucault, Michel, 29, 242
Franck Report, 50
Frank, Richard
  choice of time frame, 172–173
  on the Hiroshima decision, 164–166, 172–174
  on the revisionist claim of anti-Soviet motivation, 166
  on the utilitarian moral defense, 145
Frankfurter, Felix, 81
free press, role in protecting democracy, 20
From Roosevelt to Truman (Miscamble), 214

Gaddis, John Lewis, 33, 68, 234–235
Gallicchio, Marc, 229, 231
Gandhi, Mahatma, 4, 147
Geneva protocols, 137
Germany
  and unconditional surrender policy, 217–218, 234
  Einstein on the likely use of military applications of nuclear fission by, 38
  surrender of, 47
  the question of whether America would have used the bomb on, 1, 147, 151
  the question of whether Stalin would have used the bomb on, 9
  Woodrow Wilson and, 220
Geyl, Pieter, 35–36, 241–242
Giangreco, D. M., 170–171
Gluck, Carol, 207
Grassroots Fascism (Yoshimi), 191–192, 205
Great Depression, 94, 192
Groves, Leslie, 39, *41*, 58, 167, 213

Hague convention, 86
Hammerstein, Oscar, 148
Harper's Magazine article (Stimson), 82–88, 104, 135, 167
  accepted as orthodox view, 225
  moral perspective, 143
  on the inevitability of the Hiroshima decision, 66
  on the psychological impact of the second bomb, 86
  US discussions of the Soviet Union omitted from, 98
Harwit, Martin, 11–12

INDEX

Hasegawa, Tsuyoshi
  criticisms, 121
  neo-revisionist view of the Hiroshima decision, 114–122
  Racing the Enemy, Bernstein's review, 211
Hatano Sumio, 203, 229
Hell To Pay (Giangreco), 170
Herodotus, 185
Hersey, John, 74–77
hibakusha (atomic bomb survivor), 61, 75, 148
Hirohito, *193*
  belief in the sacred nature of his role, 196
  Bix's analysis, 198–207
  Butow's characterization, 187, 198
  death of, and the examination of Japanese responsibility, 192–198
  Drea's analysis of character and motivation, 163
  fear of the army's reaction, 205
  historians' differing views of, 186
  Japanese critics, 200
  MacArthur's plans for, 193
  Monologue, 199–201
  postwar treatment, 186
  reflections on his own responsibility for the war, 206
Hirohito and the Making of Modern Japan (Bix), 198
Hiroshima
  atomic bomb survivors in, *135*
  days after the bombing, *180*
  uranium bomb dropped on, 57
Hiroshima (Hersey), 74, 78

Hiroshima decision
  the concept, 14
  air power and, 175
  Alperovitz's critical reexamination of, 100
  American and Japanese public opinion on, 6
  Bernstein on the inevitability of, 212–213
  Bernstein's study, 108
  Chinese and Korean views on, 7
  Conant's role in organizing a defense of, 73
  discussions around, 47
  Drea on the reasons behind, 161–163
  Eisenhower's misgivings, 106
  evidence of prior moral objections, 107
  Harper's article as official defense, 82
  Hasegawa's neo-revisionist view, 114–122
  Jervis's realist view, 132
  lessons of the controversy, 243–245
  military historians on, 159–166
  as moral choice, 84
  moral issues as the epicenter of controversy, 125
  participants, 61–62
  awareness of biological effects of radiation, 87
  durability of their version of history, 69–82
  lasting influence of their version of history, 88–90
  wariness of historians, 66–69

262

INDEX

polled as most important event of the twentieth century, 5
public interest in the nature of the debate, 14
racism and, 147–152
Rawls on, 140–141
religious leaders' responses, 73–74
revisionist challenge to the orthodox defense, 123–124
Sherry's approach, 175
Smithsonian controversy, 10–14
Stimson and Churchill on the inevitability of, 213
the apology debate, 9
the utilitarian defense, 142–147
unconditional surrender policy as pivotal to, 237–238
Hiroshima Maidens, 148
Hiroshima Peace Memorial, Barack Obama's visit, 10
historians
 Appleby, Hunt, and Jacob on the role of, 19
 Hunt on topics of research, 155
 importance of independent scholarly inquiry for, 20
 importance of trustworthiness for, 21
 Manhattan Project leaders' efforts to preempt judgment of, 69–82
 participants' wariness of, 66–69
 pursuit of objective truth, 246–247
 responsibility of in a free society, 18–19
 skills required by, 24–25
 the community of, 245
 the professionalization of the craft, 25–27, 245
 value of in a free society, 15
historian's craft, nature of, 15, 24–25
history
 and the marketplace of ideas, 242–245
 and the scientific ideal, 26
 Carr on the influence of historians' background on, 101
 Droysen on, 18
 postmodernists' view of, 29, 242
 postwar emergence of new approaches to study of, 31
 power-wielders' wish to secure their place in, 62–66
 Schroeder on the importance of as a moral undertaking, 133
 Stimson on the recording of, 68
 subfields, 25
 tension between democracy and, 20–21
 the role of controversy, 241–242
history departments in the West, interest in and knowledge of the non-Western world, 184–186
Hitler, Adolf, suicide, 47
Hofstadter, Richard, 95, 103
Holmes, Oliver Wendell, Jr., 243
Holocaust, 21, 158
Hoover, Herbert, 171
Howard, Michael, 174, 232
Hughes, Stuart, 210

INDEX

Hull, Cordell, 218
Hunt, Lynn, 19–21, 32, 38, 155
Huntington, Samuel, 206

In the Service of the Emperor (Drea), 163, 202–204
indoctrination, history as means of in totalitarian regimes, 23
Interim Committee, 46–48, 50, 79
international law, use of the atomic bomb as violation of, 86
internment, of Japanese-Americans, 150
invasion of Japan
    Japanese defense preparations, 159
    potential cost in American and Japanese casualties, 84–85
Iokibe Makoto, 167
Iraq, American invasion, 8
Akira Iriye, 168

Jacob, Margaret, 19
Japan
    ability to adapt and reform, 173–174
    American occupation
        beginning of, 59
        war correspondents' reports, 74
    atrocities against other Asian peoples, 7
    Benedict on, 183
    bombing of Chinese cities, 137
    consideration of Pearl Harbor apology, 9
    expected transformation, 218
    invasion of, casualty projections, 84–85
    kokutai ideology, 197
    Meiji Restoration, 173–174
    neutrality pact with Soviet Union, 52, 55
    postwar national identity, 7, 190
    seizure of Manchuria, 80
    Stalin's neutrality pact, 51
    Supreme War Council, 55
        emergency meeting, 58
    unconditional surrender,
        Churchill's suggestion, 46
        see also unconditional surrender policy
    Western interest in, 184–186
Japan studies, growth of American teaching in, 186
Japanese army
    Drea's exploration of the culture, 163
    Huntington on, 206
    ketsugō strategy ("decisive operation"), 54–56, 159–160, 165–166, 202–203, 207
    massive buildup of troops, 159, 162, 165
Japanese carrier fleet, destruction of, 54
Japanese cities, target list, 15, 50
Japanese culture, Western analysis of, 183–184
Japanese responsibility
    assessment of dampened by Japan's sense of victimization, 190

INDEX

attention paid by Western historians to, 190
death of Hirohito and the examination of, 192–198
death of Hirohito and the examination of, Bix's analysis, 198–207
Japanese historians' writings, 191
left-wing historians' assessment, 194
prewar mobilization of popular nationalist sentiment and, 192
Yoshimi's assessment of, 191–192
Japanese surrender
Alperovitz's contention, 159, 161
Bernstein on the possibility of, 110
Hasegawa's view of the reason for, 116
Hirohito's explanation for, 201
potential path to ignored by Truman, 86, 105
unconditional, *see* unconditional surrender policy
Japan's Decision to Surrender (Butow), 89, 115, 187
Japan's Imperial Army (Drea), 163, 204
Jervis, Robert, 132–133
Jones, Matthew, 147
journalists, as writers of first draft of history, 66, 77
Just and Unjust Wars (Walzer), 139

kamikaze, 160
Kecskemeti, Paul, 233
Keegan, John, 174, 240
Kennan, George, 112, 234–235
Kennedy, David, 227, 236
Kennedy, John F., 95
Kennedy, Robert, 95
Kierkegaard, Soren, 35
Kimball, Warren, 222
King, Mackenzie, 215
King, Martin Luther, Jr., 95
Kissinger, Henry, 63
knowledge, Rauch's observation, 243
Korean history, Western study of, 185
Kurosawa Akira, 30, 65
Kyoto, elimination from list of target cities, 15, 50

Landscape of History (Gaddis), 33
Lasch, Christopher, 97
Lawrence, E. O., 47
pictured with other leading scientists involved in the Manhattan Project, 67
Leahy, William, 106–107
Leffler, Melvyn, 131
legitimate warfare, widely shared ethics for, 136
LeMay, Curtis, 45, 137, 178–179
Lepore, Jill, 63, 96, 125
Leyte Gulf, battle of, 54
literature, relationship of history to, 25, 29
"Little Boy" uranium bomb, death toll, 57
Loeb, Charles, 149–150
Loomis, Alfred, pictured with other leading scientists involved in the Manhattan Project, 67

INDEX

MacArthur, Douglas, 59, 74, 161, 193–194
Machiavelli, Niccolò, 144
MacMillan, Margaret
  on American history's neglect of World War II, 159
  on the public fascination with military history, 156
  War: How Conflict Shaped Us, 182
Maddox, Robert James, 112
Malcolm X, 95
Malloy, Sean
  on awareness of radiation effects, 87
  on the effectiveness of Stimson's essay, 89
  on the narrow focus of bomb literature, 209
  on the role of racism, 152
Manchuria, Russian Red Army's invasion, 57
Manhattan Project, 38–43
  details shared with Churchill, 40–42
  leaders, 39–40, 67
  efforts to preempt judgment of historians, 69–82
  justifications for as first draft of history, 66
  New Yorker essay, 74
  scientists' regrets, 69
  Truman and, 46–50
Marshall, George, 47, 107, 141
May, Ernest, 16, 220, 234
Maza, Sarah, 133, 184
McNamara, Robert, 136–137
McNeill, William, 18, 37, 158, 208
McPherson, James, 92
Meiji Restoration, 173–174
memoirs, historians careful treatment of, 107
memory, unreliability of, 65
Michener, James, 148
military historians
  and the recentering of military history, 181–182
  cultural perspective of military history, 174–181
  on the controversy over casualty projections, 168–172
  on the defense strategy of the Japanese Imperial Army, 159
  on the Hiroshima decision, 159–166
  Frank, 164–166, 172–174
  on the Hiroshima decision, Drea, 161–163
  on the Nagasaki bombing, 166–168
  on the Nagasaki bombing, Japanese historians, 167
military history
  academics' regard of, 156, 174
  Paret's complaint, 157
  popularity of as a genre, 156
  trends in the genre, 155–159
Miscamble, Wilson, 144, 214
Mitchell, Billy, 175
moral perspectives
  as the epicenter of the Hiroshima controversy, 125–126
  ethics for legitimate warfare, 136
  Hiroshima and historians' moral perplexity, 134–138

INDEX

historians and the social sciences, 131–134
Jervis and Schroeder's exchange of views, 132–133
moral philosophy, 138–142
racism and the Hiroshima decision, 147–152
revisionist generation's raising of the morality issue, 135
the case for engagement, 129–131
the case for neutrality, 126–129
the challenge for historians, 152–154
the proportionality principle, 136
the utilitarian defense, 142–147
Morgenthau, Hans, 4, 144, 235
Morrison, Samuel Eliot, 89
Motoshima Hitoshi, 195

Nagasaki
added to list of target cities, 15, 50
military historians on bombing of, 166–168
plutonium bomb dropped on, 57
napalm, 45, 178
Napoleon for and Against (Geyl), 35
National Negro Publishers Association, 150
Niebuhr, Reinhold, 73–74, 85
Novick, Peter, 32
Nuclear Non-proliferation Treaty, Obama on the need to strengthen, 9

Obama, Barack, visit to Hiroshima, 9, 145
objective truth

attainability, 27, 29, 34, 36, 68, 242
historians' pursuit of, 246–247
place of in the historical profession, 26
Stimson on, 68
the move away from as professional goal, 26, 33
see also truth
Okinawa, battle of, 47
On Active Duty in Peace and War (Stimson and Bundy), 68, 81
On War (Clausewitz), 160, 224
Oppenheimer, Robert, 40, 41, 47–48, 70–71, 76
Orwell, George, 23–24, 247
Osama Bin Laden, 8

Palais, James, 185
Palmer, R. R., 174
Paret, Peter, 157
peace in the nuclear age, Yamaguchi Tsutomu's prescription for, 62
Pearl Harbor, 9, 49, 117–119, 139, 142, 151, 177
Peloponnesian War, Thucydides' writing on, 25
Pentagon, building of, 40
Philippines, FDR on the landing of American troops in, 221
politics, potential influence on historical research and writing, 99–100
Popper, Karl, 244
postmodernism, 29–31, 33

267

INDEX

Potsdam conference
   Churchill, Truman, and Stalin pictured at, 118
   Truman's delaying of, 103
Potsdam Declaration, 103, 118–119, 122, 229
   Japanese emperor's acceptance, 58–59
   Japan's reaction, 57
   signatories, 52
   significant omissions, 53
   Truman's prior verbal approval of atomic bomb use, 53
professionalization of history, 25–27, 126, 245
proportionality principle, 136
psychological weapon, Stimson's characterization of the bomb, 86, 167
public opinion polls, American and Japanese views of the Hiroshima decision, 6
Putin, Vladimir, 8

race riots, of the 1960s, 95
Racing the Enemy: Stalin, Truman and the Surrender of Japan (Hasegawa), 116, 211
racism, and the Hiroshima decision, 147–152
radiation sickness
   atomic bomb survivors suffering from, 135
   journalists' reporting, 74
Ranke, Leopold von, 25, 27, 184, 245
Rape of Nanjing, 191–192
Rashomon (Kurosawa), 30, 65

Rauch, Jonathan, 243, 246
Rawls, John, 139–141
Reischauer, Edwin, 168
revisionism
   Alperovitz's *Atomic Diplomacy*, 100
   and the influence of politics, 99–100
   Bailyn's observation, 92
   Bix's place in the revisionist generation, 200
   breadth of revisionist interpretation of Hiroshima decision, 108
   generational change and, 92–96
   McPherson on the importance of, 92
   negative views, 91, 110
   neo-revisionist view, 114–122
   place in the historian's craft, 91
   reaction of mainstream historians, 110–114
   reaction of veterans' groups, 113
   revisionist view of American history, 96–100
   revisionist view of casualty projections, 169
   status of Blackett's treatise, 190
   Stimson's concerns about "the teachers of our next generation," 91
   the challenge to the orthodox defense, 123–124
   the "revisionists," 91
Rodgers, Richard, 148
Roosevelt, Franklin
   attracted to air power, 176

268

INDEX

death, 46
Einstein's letter to, 38
meetings with Churchill, 43, 214–215, *216*
on the killing of civilians, 137
on the landing of American troops in the Philippines, 221
racist views, 148
Stalin's promise to, 51
thoughts about the use of the bomb, 40–43
unconditional surrender policy, *see* unconditional surrender policy
unwillingness to compromise war goals, 215
vision of the postwar order, 222–223
Russian entry into the war, 57
role in Japanese surrender, 116–117, 122
territorial concessions in return for, 227
Russo-Japanese War, 51–52, 225

Satō Naotake, 56
Sayonara (Rodgers and Hammerstein), 148
Schlesinger, Arthur, Jr., 95, 110, 148
Schroeder, Paul, 133
Scott, Joan, 31
Sherry, Michael, 175–181, 209
Sherwin, Martin, 166
Sherwood, Robert, 220
Shillony, Ben Ami, 8

Shinto, 197
Shockley, William B., 84, 171
Sigal, Leon, 226
slavery, controversy surrounding teaching history of in America, 20
Smithsonian controversy, 10–14, 21, 113
Snyder, Timothy, 22
social media
disinformation and, 21
Hunt on the influence of on history, 21
South Pacific (Rodgers and Hammerstein), 148
Soviet Union
and the origins of the Cold War, 93, 97, 110
continues fighting after Japanese surrender, 59
Japan's approach to, 55–56
Stalin, Joseph
knowledge of the Manhattan Project, 51
Potsdam Declaration and, 52, 103, 118
Putin on whether Stalin would have used an atomic bomb against Germany, 8
reaction to news of Hiroshima, 116
Roosevelt and, 222, 227
Truman and, 104, 121–122
Steinbeck, John, 176
Stern, Fritz, 247
Stimson, Henry, *80*

INDEX

Stimson, Henry (cont.)
   claim that use of the bomb had been "carefully considered," 86
   concerns about "the teachers of our next generation," 91
   defense of the Hiroshima decision, 68
   on potential bias of historians, 68
   on the atomic bomb, 3
   on the potential impact of Stalin's signature, 52
   persuaded to write a defense of the Hiroshima decision, 79
   see also Harper's Magazine article (Stimson)
   pictured in the Oval Office with Truman, *80*
   political background, 79–80
   postwar assertion of massive casualties, 169
storytelling, history as, 29
surrender, Japan's willingness if the emperor's position was guaranteed, 105
Suzuki Kantarō, 55, 57
Szilard, Leo, 38

Tajima papers, 206–207
Takaki, Ronald, 151
target list of Japanese cities, 15, 50
Teahouse of the August Moon (Rodgers and Hammerstein), 148
Terkel, Studs, 113
The Chrysanthemum and the Sword (Benedict), 183

The Good War (Terkel), 113
The Historian's Craft (Bloch), 129
The King and I (Rodgers and Hammerstein), 148
"the nuclear revolution," 4
The Origins of Totalitarianism (Arendt), 22
The Rise of American Air Power: The Creation of Armageddon (Sherry), 175
The Soldier and the State (Huntington), 206
The Tragedy of American Diplomacy (Williams), 102
Thucydides, 25, 185, 188, 207
time frames
   benefits of analyzing the Hiroshima decision in a broader scale, 211
   broad versus narrow, 208–209, 236–237
   historians' choices
      Bernstein, 107
      Frank, 145
      Gallicchio, 231
      Hasegawa, 115
      Sherry, 175
Tōgō Shigenori, 56
Tōjō Hideki, 54
Tokyo, fire-bombed, *179*
topics of historical study, trends in, 155
Tosh, John, 16, 33, 134
Toshiko Sasaki, 76
Trevor-Roper, Hugh, 184
Truman, Harry, 10
   address to the nation, 142

270

INDEX

Alperovitz's interpretation of the actions of, 103
and FDR's goal of unconditional surrender, 49, 214
authorisation of Potsdam Declaration, 52
cedes control of the bomb and its use to the military, 54
Hasegawa's positing of a race between Stalin and, 116–119
lack of evidence of an actual A-bomb "decision" by, 213
Manhattan Project, knowledge of, 43, 46
on the successful testing of the plutonium bomb, 51
on the thought of further use of the bomb, 58
pictured in the Oval Office with Stimson, *80*
postwar meeting with Oppenheimer, 70
reliance on advisors, 46
Trump, Donald, 10, 63
trustworthiness of historians, importance for democratic politics, 21
truth
 controversy and historians' pursuit of, 15, 240, 247
 Geyl on history as a search for the, 35–36
 Kierkegaard on, 35
 Oliver Wendell Holmes on the best test of, 243
 Rauch on the pursuit of, 246
 the *Rashomon* effect and, 65
 see also objective truth

unconditional surrender policy, 214–219
and the inevitability of the atomic bombings, 232–235
announced to the press, 43, *216*
consequences for Japan, 218
goal of for FDR, 218
implications of, 223–229
influence on the way America chose to fight the war, 172–173
meaning of for Japan, 225–226
Potsdam Declaration and, 52–53
reasons behind FDR's decision, 219–223
Stimson's opposition, 219
unprecedented nature, 217
United States (US)
 Alperovitz's charge, 101
 and the concept of total war, 138
 entanglement in Vietnam, 185
 government censorship case, 243
 Hiroshima Maidens project, 148
 industrial and technological capacity, 44
 interest in Asian history, 185
 knowledge of Japanese culture, 183
 moral standing in the world, 123
 responsibility for the Cold War, 98
 treatment of Japanese immigrants in, 147
 Williams' assertion, 102
 utilitarian defense of the Hiroshima decision, 142–147

victimization, Japan's sense of, 190
Vietnam Veterans Memorial Wall, 12

INDEX

Vietnam, War in, 93, 95–97, 101, 108, 137, 164, 185
Vincent, John Russell, 184
Voltaire, 242

Walzer, Michael, 139
war
   historians' lack of engagement with, 158
   Keegan on the cultural context of, 174
   popularity of as a subject, 156
   purpose of, 224
   role of in American history, 156, 182
   Sherry on the study of, 181
War: How Conflict Shaped Us (MacMillan), 182
War without Mercy (Dower), 152
What Is History? (Carr), 101
White, Hayden, 29
Wilde, Oscar, 242
Williams, William Appleman, 102
Wilson, Woodrow, political criticisms of, 44, 220
women, lack of involvement in the Hiroshima decision, 61
Women's studies, 31
Wood, Gordon, 94, 99, 239
Woodward, C. Vann, 157

World War I, and criticisms of Woodrow Wilson, 44
World War II
   American Historical Review's inattention to, 158–159
   entry of Russia, 57
   as example of total war, 43
   "good war" narrative, 13, 113
   Japan's *ketsugō* strategy, 54, 56
   as only foreign war in American history waged to unconditional surrender, 217
   postwar appetite for military history, 155
   postwar demographic surge, 94
   Potsdam conference, 50–54
   Russian role in the end of, 116
   unconditional surrender, FDR's policy, 43–46
Wright, Gordon, 131

Yalta conference, 45, 57
Yamada Akira, 200
Yamaguchi Tsutomu, 61–62
Yoshida Shigeru, 206
Yoshida Yutaka, 200, 205
Yoshimi Yoshiaki, 191–192, 205
Young, Marilyn, 156, 182

Zinn, Howard, 98

For EU product safety concerns, contact us at Calle de José Abascal, 56–1°, 28003 Madrid, Spain or eugpsr@cambridge.org.

www.ingramcontent.com/pod-product-compliance
Ingram Content Group UK Ltd.
Pitfield, Milton Keynes, MK11 3LW, UK
UKHW022244220326
469255UK00019B/340